Principles of Conformation Analysis

Volumes I, II & III

EQUUS Reference Guide

Deb Bennett, PhD

EQUINE NETWORK

Boulder, CO

Active Interest Media
DBA Equine Network
2520 55th Street, Suite 210
Boulder, CO 80301
303-625-1600
www.equisearch.com

VP, Group Publishing Director: Tom Winsor
Editorial Director: Cathy Laws
Managing Editor: Amy Herdy
Cover Designers: Abby McDougall and Sandra Jonas

EQUUS *Editor:* Laurie Prinz

EQUUS

www.EQUUSmagazine.com

Order by calling 800-952-5813 or online at www.HorseBooksEtc.com.

Publisher's Cataloging-in-Publication Data
Bennett, Deb.
   Principles of conformation analysis: equus research guide / Deb Bennett. — Boulder, CO : Equine Network, 2012.
   p. : ill. ; cm.
   ISBN: 9781929164608
1. Horses - Conformation.
SF289 .B46 2012 636.1—dc23
2012933007

This book is dedicated
to Faria V. Clark, who sent me
in passionate pursuit of "the ring,"
and to Gail Wood and her students in Kansas,
who set me on the path
of teaching horse anatomy to riders.

Contents

Volume II

Foreword

A construction foreman accosted the builder one morning with a question: "Boss, do you want this house built from the bottom up, or from the top down?" "From the bottom up!" was the exasperated reply. The foreman turned to his crew and shouted, "Tear her down boys; we've got to start all over!"

Most horsemen construct the horse from the outside inward, but Deb Bennett knows and explains how misleading that is. Putting foundations first builds proper awareness and appreciation of equine anatomy and performance. Success and frustration both can be understood better if the structural capacities and limitations of individual horses can be compared. Selection for breeding or use becomes rational when operative mechanisms and principles are known. Dr. Bennett's diverse and scholarly background particularly qualifies her to explain and illustrate her subjects. Horsedom is richer for her contributions.

Read on.

Matthew Mackay-Smith, DVM
Gaithersburg, MD
August 1988

Principles of Conformation Analysis

Volume I

Volume I

Introduction

Sound horse-buying and -breeding decisions require accurate judgment of conformation, based on an understanding of the biological principles of horse construction and action. Those who are about to buy their first horse need to know these principles at least as much as the most experienced horseman: "Let the buyer beware" still prevails in horse trading. In the United States, where government regulation of horse breeding, registration and advertising is unlikely ever to become reality, as it is in many European countries, knowledgeable consumers are the industry's watchdogs. However, you — the consumer — cannot demand good horses if you don't know how they move or how they are built.

I do not teach conformation judging as a series of diagrammatically represented "rules of thumb." A rule of thumb represents a simplification or codification of a biological principle; you can devise your own once you really understand the principles. However, the principles represented in this volume, which tell *why* a horse ought to have certain body structures but not others, are rarely taught. For this reason, Volume I presents structural, biomechanical, genetic, evolutionary and value criteria which can be synthesized to judge equine excellence. A companion text (Volume II) serves as a "practicum" to demonstrate excellent as well as flawed conformation using photographs of real horses. It surveys the horse part by part, from head to toe, and then re-integrates the animal as a balanced, functional whole.

"Conformation" is a term taken from the vocabulary of stock judging; it means "how the body is put together." The biological term "phenotype" takes in more ground; it means "the visible or testable body," which includes many structures (such as intestines and blood cells) and many functions (such as resting heart rate or respiration rate, agility or strength) that are not usually judged in a halter class.

The conformation of an individual horse largely depends upon his bone structure. The remainder depends upon the muscle type he has, the amount of body fat he is carrying and how fit he is. To learn bone structure, you first must memorize the external "points" of a horse (see the "Equine Parts Inventory," illustrated on pages 95 and 96 of this volume). Learning the points of a horse gives you the basic vocabulary to converse with other horsemen. Then you must learn the names and locations of each of the horse's bones. The horseman who does not have a clear idea of the equine skeleton is as helpless in the marketplace as a car buyer who doesn't know a carburetor from a crankshaft. You can get away without learning the skeleton only if you can afford to pay for expert advice when making a purchase.

To make learning the skeleton easier and more meaningful for you, a drawing showing "palpation points" appears in the parts inventory. Palpation points mark places where you can feel bony prominences under the horse's skin. The palpation points help you to "peg out" the skeleton in an individual horse, and you should take every opportunity to practice feeling these points on many different horses. While all horses possess the same bones, the *proportions* of each skeleton are different. It is these proportional differences on the inside which largely determine the different external appearance of each individual horse.

Here and now let me dispel — or at least try to diminish — wishful thinking about horses you plan to ride or to breed. You cannot get blood from a stone. In terms of performance, the most practical as well as the most humane plan is to match a horse's phenotype with the physical work you have in mind for him to do. The principles and criteria for this kind of matching are discussed in the last chapter of this book and in Volume II.

Even if the horse of your dreams has a pedigree as long as your arm, when signing a breeding or purchase contract, you are not buying his breed. Instead, you are buying *the individual horse who stands before you*. This is the animal on which you must bring your judgment to bear. If his structure or movement aren't any good, no amount of "blue blood" will improve them. The chances of an inferior horse with a superior pedigree getting good foals in the breeding shed are no greater than those of a randomly selected individual. Only phenotypically excellent individuals can be counted upon to produce phenotypic excellence. With rare exceptions, what you see is what you get.

This book is about learning how to *see*, and therefore I do not discuss the very important matters of temperament and trainability. For buyers who are also novices in the art and science of horseback riding and training, good temperament is more important than good conformation as a basis for selecting a given horse. If you're a beginner, you will benefit from obtaining one or more of the Fleet Street reference guides, tapes and books listed below that deal with behavior and training. As your experience and expertise increase, you probably will begin to demand greater effort and efficiency from your horses, and it is then that an understanding of the principles of conformation analysis will assume its greatest importance.

RESOURCES

Monographs: "The Touch That Teaches," "Solving Behavioral Problems"
Audio tape: "How To Turn Bad Habits Into Good Behavior"
Book: "An Introduction To The Tellington-Jones Equine Awareness Method"

Figure 1. The intense final moments of a draft halter class in turn-of-the-century America. No glitz here — just excitement over finding a really good horse.

Chapter 1

What Kind Of An Animal Is A Horse?

The principles of conformation analysis reveal it's what's inside that counts

Conformation judging is not a matter of aesthetics. If we as buyers and breeders want sound, long-lived, fertile, athletic horses — horses that represent a sound investment, whose economic value is rooted in their excellence *as horses* — then we must not impose our made-up ideas of what is "beautiful" upon the horse species. Whenever in history this has been tried, the living animals which result have been dysfunctional at best. The results of breeding strictly for fashion almost always are disastrous.

Instead, we must try to take down from before our eyes the anthropomorphic screen which blocks our ability to really see the wonderful "otherness" of horses. Because the horse's body and mind function quite differently from our bodies and minds, we must dedicate ourselves — and open ourselves — to discovering the nature of the equine animal.

The acquisition of this knowledge can be *through* your spiritual or aesthetic sense. It's a thrill and a delight when the sight of the Black Stallion galloping along the beach really "grabs you" but, in an important sense, this "grabbing" is just the opposite of the mistake described above. When you let the horse himself show you what beauty he possesses, you are on the way to becoming qualified to judge equine conformation.

The acquisition of knowledge also should occur through your analytical sense. Far from dulling or mechanizing your ability to discover equine beauty, increasing your analytical skills will empower your aesthetic sense and will justify your judgment. A good judge of conformation knows the names and normal shapes of all the horse's parts and also knows how they ought to work together when the animal moves. At the turn of the century, there were many judges of horse conformation in America whom I would have respected for this kind of expertise. These men were out there in their bowler hats, shirt sleeves rolled up, sweating, with their cutaway coats held over one arm, working county fairs and judging horses *as stock* (Figure 1). Especially after World War II, fashionability became increasingly important, and this type of horse judging became increasingly rare. Nowadays, one rarely sees "stock judging" even at the fairs, except of cattle, sheep, goats and the few draft horses which, like other large domestic mammals, still are widely regarded as farm produce.

Back in 1917, when the American Horse Shows Association (AHSA) was founded, judges recognized three purposes for halter classes. They are:

1. **To identify the horse that is likely to stay soundest longest while doing his daily job.** Most judges accept the idea that this individual will be the one with the best conformation. To accurately assess conformation, the judge should look not just at the horse's silhouette outline but concentrate on the bone structure.

2. **To identify the horse that moves the best.** This is often, but not always, the best-conformed individual. What is "good" in movement is judged relative to the projected use of the class being judged — draft, carriage or saddle horses.

3. **To certify the top winners as bloodstock.** The best-conformed, best-moving individuals are most qualified to breed and thus perpetuate their bloodline.

You will notice that the Hollywood-style auctions and shows, which are the norm today in North America, emphasize flashiness and are unlike this description of how to judge draft, carriage and saddle stock. Show-ring "hype" is designed to fool buyers and inflate prices. Glittered hooves, polished coats and fat-slick, high-headed presentation are appeals to the kind of aesthetic sense that does not come out of the horse but, rather, out of us.

In recent years, European breeders have made large profits in the North American market *because they have a good product*. Their horses are judged "on the triangle" (European-style halter competition which has no trace of glitz) according to strict, biologically based standards of conformation and movement. Young horses are broken to saddle and then systematically tested for performance ability before being certified as breeding stock. Frequently the training of judges, as well as the whole testing and certification process, is government-funded (and sometimes government-regulated). The fact that we are beginning to forget the three purposes of a halter class is especially disturbing in light of the fact that the horse species is now extinct in the wild. We are its only keepers, the only ones who can be responsible for maintaining its innate qualities.

These first two chapters are designed to convey a fairly sophisticated idea of how a riding horse "works." The "rocking-horse model" — an old and inaccurate idea of equine function — is refuted. The all-important inventions and contributions of Federico Caprilli, made about the turn of the century, are set forth in historical pictures and in riding situations that you've probably found yourself in. An accurate understanding of the horse's natural mechanism will certainly help your riding, and it also will enable you to buy or breed a better horse.

To readers of a magazine whose very title identifies the horse genus, "What kind of an animal is a horse?" probably seems the most ridiculous question an author could ask. The abundance of color photography that appears between the pages of EQUUS every month would seem to portray the horse better than thousands of descriptive words ever could.

Yet it has been my experience, in working with thousands of horse owners in clinics across the continent, that there is widespread and serious confusion about just what kind of an animal a horse is. Not that people are at all likely to mistake a horse for a cow, but that most people could not come up with a list of even five traits that uniquely characterize horses.

Let me make this problem a little more clear by recalling a scene from the movie "E.T., The Extraterrestrial." In it, the alien E.T. is examining some of the items in his boy's room. Among the things E.T. picks up and tries to relate to is an oversized, fluorescent orange, plastic circus peanut, which he promptly puts in his mouth and tries to bite. The scene makes everyone in the audience want to say, "No, no! You don't eat that kind of peanut!" Well, why not?

The challenge for horse owners is similar. If you were to be visited for one hour by an alien, how would you describe the horse species so that the visitor would never mistake a horse for any other kind of animal?

"That's easy," you might say. "The horse's neck is fringed with a mane, and it has a tail with hairs growing from very near the top, instead of having a tuft just at the bottom end." Okay, that does differentiate a horse from a cow but not from a sable antelope, a llama, a quagga or a Great Pyrenees.

"All right," you may say. "A horse doesn't have any horns." Well, that takes care of antelopes but not llamas, quaggas or the Great Pyrenees. "Well, horses have hoofs," you would protest in frustration. Yes, but so do llamas and quaggas!

The point is that no one can come up with a way to classify animals — no one can know what kind of an animal a horse is — until he pays attention not only to structures that can be seen from the outside, but also to those that exist on the *inside*. A horse doesn't live or act like a dog or a goat because his physical makeup — bones, muscles, ligaments, physiology, digestive system, brain and nervous system — is unlike that of any other animal.

This solution to the problem of how to classify meaningfully is precisely analogous to the plastic peanut problem. Plastic appears to be a uniform "goop" at the same microscopic level at which a real peanut reveals complex galleries of cell walls. To truly comprehend the way a machine or an animal functions, you must know what it is like on the inside.

This is the philosophy behind my approach to conformation analysis. When I look at a horse, either to assess his conformation or his movement, I look at him from the inside out. This is because 90 percent of

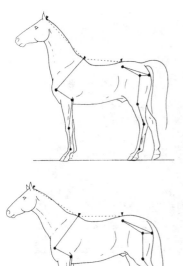

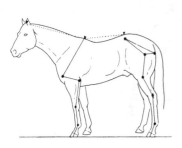

Figure 2. Dissimilar silhouettes of these three American-bred horses derive from differences in their internal skeletal structure, which the marked lines help to delineate. Specifically, their bones differ in *length* and *resting angulation*.

a horse's conformation (the way he looks from the outside) is the product of his bone structure (how he's made on the inside). While every horse belonging to the domestic species possesses the same number and kind of bones, the lengths of the individual bones and the angles at which they join differ from horse to horse. These skeletal differences cause a typical Quarter Horse, for example, to look quite different from a typical American Saddlebred (Figure 2).

At an even finer level, individual members of a given breed also can be characterized on the basis of their bone structure. For example, today's successful halter Quarter Horse is likely to have quite a different appearance from one that has been a champion in cutting or reining. This observation serves to underline the main reason for horse owners and breeders to learn about bone structure: differences in bone structure are absolutely crucial to determining a horse's abilities in performance.

The "Stuffed Toy" Perspective

This leads me to bring up one of my pet peeves in conformation judging. Since horse show halter classes never include cows, sable antelopes, goats or llamas, it is possible for judges to narrow their biological perspective and to forget the lesson of the plastic peanut. Some judges look at the horse not as he really is — a living being supported by an internal girder system called a skeleton — but rather as a kind of stuffed toy.

This makes judging conformation a very simple process: one only has to memorize an outline. Once a judge learns what the "Breed X halter outline" or the "conformation hunter outline" is supposed to be, he pretty consistently can reward that outline by giving it prizes. The aphorism among halter showmen that "fat covers a multitude of sins" merely serves to emphasize that this style of judging is, and has long been, common.

Fashions in the "ideal" halter-horse outline come and go yearly in many breeds, partly because of "stuffed toy" judging. Who stops to ask whether a "small, neat foot" provides enough room for the bones inside to function? Who stops to ask whether the bones inside a "long, elegant neck" can grow normally and stay in alignment? The consequences of

Figure 3. These three views of *Hyracotherium* of 55 million years ago show that the "dawn horse" wasn't too horselike in appearance. In fact, a live *Hyracotherium* probably would not be recognized as a "little horse" — from the outside. Its proportionally short neck, large head, long canine teeth, long back, long hind limbs and lack of definite withers caused *Hyracotherium* to live, act and move unlike a modern horse. *Hyracotherium* and *Equus* are both included in the horse family on the basis of technical details of the bones at the base of the skull and the ankle bones, as well as the shape and position of the cusps of the teeth.

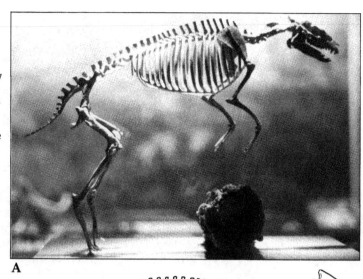

A

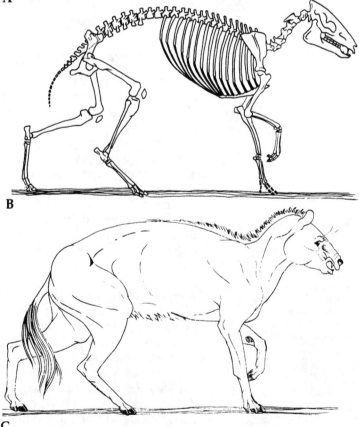

B

C

"stuffed toy" conformation judging for breeding the equine athlete are disastrous.

They're also disastrous for people who just want to buy one good horse that they can ride, maybe show a little and enjoy. Most owners are one-horse owners, and most one-horse owners want a versatile "pleasure horse." But no horse can be a pleasure either to himself or to his owner unless he can stay sound without constant veterinary intervention and unless his particular body structure — his conformation — suits him for the range of activities his owner has in mind.

That is the purpose of this booklet: to help you learn not merely structure but how the particular structure of an individual horse predisposes or "suits" him for certain athletic activities. Since in all the world, and in all of time, no two horses are ever exactly alike, this study is endlessly fascinating. Whether you already own a horse or are just beginning to think about making a purchase, you'll find it helpful to keep in mind the principles that follow. I'm not going to tell you which horse is going to win a model class, nor am I going to advise you to buy a horse because he's from a famous bloodline or is an expensive, fashionable import. Instead, by using real horses as examples, I'm going to teach you the principles of conformation analysis. And the very first principle that must be addressed is: What kind of an animal is a horse?

The functional answer to this question is this: a horse is a kind of animal whose physical and psychological makeup is adapted for running away from his enemies. Over the last 55 million years, the "evolutionary imperative" to do this successfully has profoundly affected the structure of the horse's skeletal, ligamentous and muscular systems. Specifically, a horse's bone structure adapts him for running away:

- in a straight line
- fast
- over moderately firm ground
- over nearly level ground.

One by one, let's focus on the skeletal structures the horse possesses that enable him not just to run away, but to run away *like a horse*.

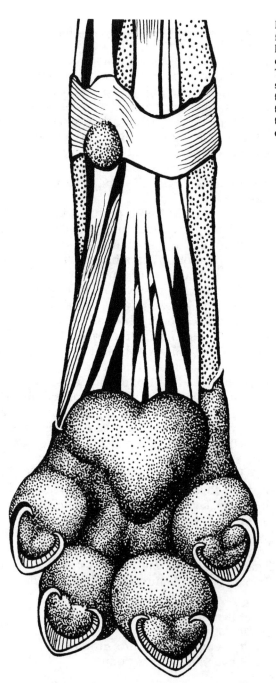

Figure 4. The hoof of *Equus* is familiar to all, but not everyone has a clear idea of what the paw of *Hyracotherium* looked like. This restoration shows the four separate toes of the forefoot of the "dawn horse," each with a toe pad as in a dog's foot. Each toe was capped by a blunt claw or "hoofie."

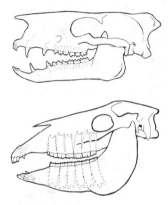

Figure 5. The teeth of *Hyracotherium* (top) are low-crowned and do not project far into the skull or jaw. Its canines are large while its incisors are small. Because its teeth occupy so little of the skull, the eye socket in *Hyracotherium* can be positioned over the row of upper teeth. Fifty-five million years later, the teeth of *Equus* (below) are much taller-crowned and reach far into the skull and jaw, which have deepened as a result. The canines have shrunk, while the incisors have evolved into large, blunt "grass nippers." Because the teeth reach so far up into the skull, the muzzle has lengthened in the modern horse so that the tooth row is pulled forward of the eye socket.

The Straight-Line Feature

Most books that deal with the evolution of the horse tell a story about changes in the teeth and feet that occurred from the earliest member of the horse lineage, *Hyracotherium*, through time to *Equus*. Paleontological research has focused so much upon teeth and feet in studying the history of mammals that a cartoon showing an animal whose total anatomy is a big, toothy mouth and one big foot draws laughs from paleontologists in labs around the world.

In particular, the popular story of the horse's evolution emphasizes how its legs got longer and longer through time and successive generations; this, people are told, is how the horse came to be able to run so fast. Its teeth became taller-crowned and more complex and so were able to withstand a diet of abrasive grasses. This, people are told, is why members of the horse family took to living in the open savanna and prairie rather than in the forest, which was their original habitat.

But what makes a caricature of a mammal that has only a big, toothy mouth and one big foot is that it is missing its backbone — the chain of vertebrae that connect and integrate the functions of the four feet and the movements of the skull and the teeth. By analogy, a car with only a motor and wheels cannot go forward. It also must have a transmission to transfer the power generated by the motor (in a horse, the muscles of the rump) to the wheels (in a horse, the legs and feet).

Understanding how the horse's vertebral column has changed structurally and functionally through time is thus at least as important as understanding the ways its teeth and feet have changed. In *Hyracotherium*, the backbone is much more arched than in the living horse, and the articulations between the individual vertebrae, especially in the lumbar region (between the last rib and the point of the hip), are much looser. This looseness permitted *Hyracotherium* to make movements with its backbone that a modern horse cannot, in particular, twisting movements. Furthermore, the forest horse of 55 million years ago was much more able to bend its spine from side to side than *Equus*. In short, when you envision the way *Hyracotherium* ran, imagine an animal slightly less slinky than a cat but more flexible than most dogs.

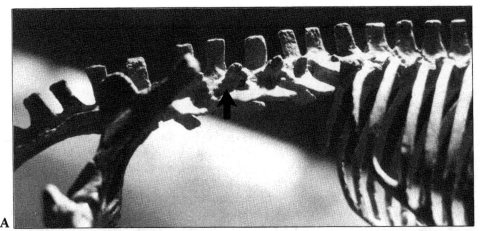

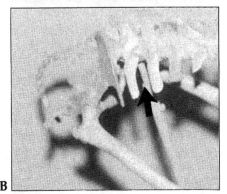
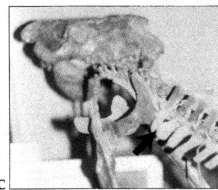

Figure 6. The lumbar span of *Hyracotherium* (top) was much more flexible than that of the modern horse. This close-up shows the obliquely oriented accessory articular processes of its lumbar vertebrae (arrow). The oblique orientation of these processes permitted *Hyracotherium* to make twisting movements with the loin. In contrast, the side "wings" (transverse processes) of the last few lumbar vertebrae of *Parahippus*, the advanced, fast-running horse (above right), touch each other (arrow). This promotes "humping" or "coiling of the loins" — up-and-down flexing of the back. Compare the articulations between the lumbar transverse processes of *Parahippus* with those of a contemporary camel (above left); the camel's lumbar transverse processes don't touch at all (arrow).

When thinking about the evolution of any lineage of animals, it's easy to fall into the trap of thinking that an early ancestor, such as *Hyracotherium*, existed in order to evolve into a descendant with which we are familiar. Of course, this is not true. At any given time, every animal is adapted or is in the process of adapting to the environment in which it lives. In some cases, we even are able to perceive how beautifully detailed and complete is the adaptation of an animal to its environment.

In the case of *Hyracotherium*, we are looking at a skeleton structured to enable its owner to accelerate

L-S joint in front view

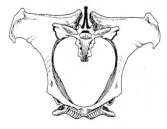

Side view of L-S joint

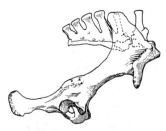

Figure 7. The key modification of the spinal column, which permitted later members of the horse family to become fast-running mammals that flee in a straight line, is the broadening and flattening of the joint between the last lumbar vertebra and the sacrum. This joint, called the lumbosacral (L-S) joint, is the *single* point of articulation in a horse between the whole hindquarter and the freespan of the back.

very rapidly (its hind limbs are longer than its fore-limbs, and it stands high at the croup, making it somewhat similar in posture and proportions to a rabbit [Figure 3c]). Its skeletal structure, combining a flexible backbone with four ground-gripping toes per front foot and three per hind foot, enabled it to change direction rapidly, precisely and fluidly (also like a rabbit or a cat [Figure 4]). A moment's reflection on the nature of the dense Eocene forest environment — where the fossilized remains of *Hyracotherium* are found — will reveal why acceleration and cornering were important. Straight-line flight would have re-sulted in smashups against tree trunks.

In contrast to its Eocene ancestor, the modern horse specializes in straight-line flight. Why did this major change in the style of locomotion occur? Part of the answer is that the nearly universal forest environ-ment of the Eocene gradually gave way to terrains with open spaces — the grass-covered savannas. The lure of the savanna was the nutritious grass which grew lushly upon it, an unexploited resource just waiting for a mammal lineage to adapt its teeth to chewing the abrasive stuff.

But this explanation by itself is not enough, for it treats the history of the horse as if it unfolded in a vacuum. During the period, about 40 million years ago, when open spaces in the forest first started to appear, horses were not magnetically drawn to them. Neither was the horse lineage the first to conquer the problem of chewing and digesting grasses. That feat of dental and gastrointestinal engineering was achieved first by the camel family. In short, camels — not horses — were the first mammals to become adapted to eating and fleeing on open ground. If you had staged a match race between the longest-limbed horse of 40 million years ago (*Mesohippus*) and a con-temporary camel (*Poebrotherium*), the camel would have been the easy winner (Figure 9).

Why? Because members of the camel family were the first to straighten out the strongly arched spine of their more primitive ancestors; the first to limit how much the spine could twist, bend and wobble during running; the first to develop withers to more firmly anchor the neck; and the first to shorten and strengthen the lumbar span to stabilize the coupling between the hind limbs and the back. These are the fundamental adaptations necessary for straight-line

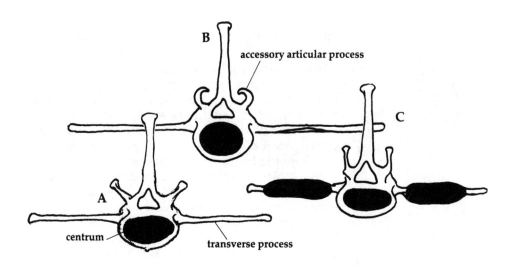

Figure 8. These are front views of the last lumbar vertebra in *Hyracotherium* (A), a cow, camel or antelope (B) and *Equus* (C). In *Hyracotherium*, the accessory articular processes are oblique, and there is only one articulating surface, located on the centrum. In cloven-hoofed mammals (B), the accessory articular processes curl over. This peg-and-socket system permits a cow's back to "lock down" — naturally. In *Equus* (C), the accessory articular processes are vertical. In addition, articulating surfaces form on the transverse processes — an adaptation absolutely unique among mammals in its form and degree of development. In combination, these two features of the equine lumbar vertebrae guarantee that side-to-side and twisting movements of the loin are minimized, while the ability to coil the loin is enhanced.

flight — the kind appropriate to life in the wide-open spaces.

Only about 22 million years ago did one of the two major branches of the horse family finally make a commitment to living in the open and, therefore, to running straight away instead of dodging around bushes and trees. *Equus* is a member of this branch, which, though its members started out with three functional toes on each front foot, eventually stream-lined the leg to one toe — a sort of evolutionary after-thought. Because horses got a late start in adapting for straight-line flight, the horse's back is still more flexible than that of a camel (or of any advanced cloven-hoofed mammal).

Fleet Feet

Once the horse's backbone had lost its primitive arch, had lost most of its ability to twist and flex later-

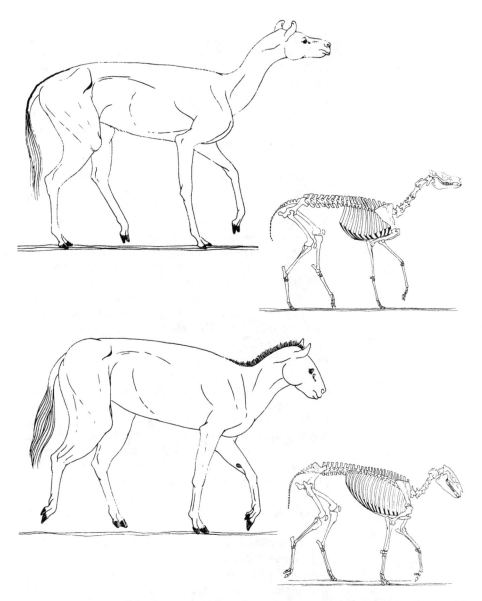

Figure 9. If it were possible to stage a match race between the camelid *Poebrotherium* (top) and the equid *Mesohippus* (below) of 35 million years ago, which one would you bet on? Consider these statistics: at 32 inches and 70 pounds, *Poebrotherium* has a shortened, straight, stiff back. With a long neck and relatively small, light head, this animal has slender forearm bones that are fused together, preventing outward rotation of the hooves during flight. With a level overall body balance, this camelid wastes no energy in straight-line flight. And the challenger: at 26 inches and 70 pounds, *Mesohippus* has a long, arched, flexible back, permitting rotation and lateral bending. With a short neck, relatively large and heavy head and unfused forearm bones which are relatively unstable during flight, this horse's overall body balance causes him to waste energy during straight-line flight as his rump bobs up and down. The winner? *Mesohippus* will get off the starting block first, but at the wire it will be *Poebrotherium* by 20 lengths.

ally in the lumbar region and had gained both withers and a specially strengthened loin coupling (Figures 6, 7, 8), lengthening of its limbs translated directly to increases in speed. Comparing the skeletons of the 55-million-year-old *Hyracotherium* and the 40-million-year-old skeleton of *Mesohippus* shows that over a span of 15 million years, equine body proportions changed very little. Both these animals have large heads, short necks, long torsos and relatively short legs hung from an arching and flexible torso. A marked change in body and limb proportions did not occur in the horse lineage until *Parahippus* of 22 million years ago. It is no coincidence that this genus of horse was also the first to possess the peculiar back anatomy necessary for running straight away (Figure 6a). From *Parahippus* onward, horses became taller and taller, making gains in both absolute height and in the proportional length of the legs.

The elongation of the equine limb is itself a matter of proportion. Whereas the humerus (upper arm) and femur (thigh) bones of the average horse are no longer than the equivalent bones in the average human body, the total length of the equine limbs is much greater. This is because the horse's limbs have "telescoped" in proportion, gaining more length the farther down the limb you look. This increase is most marked in the horse's cannon bones and pasterns, which are the anatomical equivalents of the bones in the palm of your hand and fingers. The "knee" of your horse's front leg is the anatomical equivalent of your wrist. Line up your wrist with your horse's, and you'll see what I mean by telescoping of the equine limb.

This telescoping — and the absolute size of the long-legged beast — is what confers speed upon horses. Yet horses are not the fastest mammals on earth; neither are the much taller and much longer-limbed giraffes. Instead — and to reinforce the point I made before about the importance of the backbone to running — the fastest mammal on earth is the cheetah, a cat that exploits the flexibility of its spine to the maximum, obtaining two periods of suspension per gallop stride (the horse has only one) and thereby doubling the speed it could achieve on long legs alone (a cheetah can gallop about twice as fast as a horse).

On Firm And Level Terrain

The unique structure of the horse's backbone and legs enables us to distinguish his style of locomotion from that of a cheetah, a giraffe, a cow or a camel. But what about the differences between a horse and a goat, a moose, a caribou, a kiang, a donkey or the very similar zebras? All these are long-limbed hoofed mammals just like the horse.

Yet none of these animals is adapted for running over the same *type* of terrain as horses. The mountain goat has proportionally long thighbones that help thrust the goat up cliff faces and short, stout cannon bones that help it to "stay sound" after thousands of jumps down onto rocky ledges. The moose and the caribou both have very big, wide-spreading feet that help adapt them for traversing wet, soft ground (the moose in mountain meadows, the caribou in water-logged parts of the arctic tundra). In short, these mammals are adapted to ground that is grossly "un-level" or "infirm," while the horse seeks the merely hummocky ground of the savannas and plains.

Hard Ground Or Soft?

Even relatively fine differences in adaptation to the types of level ground — hard, medium or soft — are reflected by limb structures of different species within the genus *Equus*. The horse genus includes a range of species adapted to climates and soil types from semidesert at one moisture extreme to fen and marshland at the other. The living equids adapted to the driest conditions and the hardest ground are the donkeys and their wild relatives, members of the species *Equus asinus*. A close second are the so-called "half-asses" — the kiang, the onager, the dziggetai and the kulan. Also adapted to traversing hard, dry ground are the true zebras, members of the species *Equus zebra*. All of these animals possess small, rather upright hooves with thick walls and the overall texture of flint. The frog and the bulbs of the heel project to the rear and occupy a relatively larger proportion of the foot in these species than they do in the riding horse, while the sole is thicker, tougher and more cupped. These adaptations serve to make the hoof a hammer-hard toe-tip that protects the softer structures, which are held higher during running than they are in the riding horse.

In limb structure, and therefore in function and preference for terrain, the riding horse, *Equus caballus*, is very similar to the plains zebra, *E. burchelli*, and the recently extinct quagga, *E. quagga*. All these species possess medium-length, fairly heavy cannon bones with round cross sections and broad, round feet. The sole is not cupped as deeply as in an ass, and the bulbs of heel and frog are smaller. These are features a foot can get away with when it spends a lifetime running on turf.

Within the species *E. caballus*, there is some variation in adaptation to hard or soft ground. The big, feathered foot of the draft horse evolved naturally to fit it for the marshes and fens of northwestern Europe, while the smaller, more upright, harder foot of the Arabian fits it for survival over harder, drier ground. But despite these variations, turf — such as found on the savannas of Africa or the short-grass prairie of Kentucky — is the most ancient, and still the most ideal, footing for riding horses.

Figure 10. Although the setting is informal, this rider has helped her horse to achieve bascule and, as a result, the pair experience improved balance.

Chapter 2

Balance And Bascule

Achieving unity with your horse through the dynamics of bending in two dimensions

Do you remember the last time you fell from a horse? "How can I forget," you may think in reply, as your mind goes back to that slow-motion time, to feel again the frantic grip for the mane, to see again the upside-down picture of hooves passing over your head, looking up at the little glimmer of light reflected from your horse's eye that seemed to say, "I see you, I see you, I will avoid hitting you if I can." Then, the sound rushing back over you like a wave, the jump timbers splintering down, the jarring crash as your shoulder hits pay dirt, the mouthful of dust, the cries of your companions: "Hey! Are you all right?"

As you picked yourself up, dusted yourself off and began trudging after your mount, you were probably thanking your hard hat and your lucky stars that you weren't seriously hurt. Then, if you're like many riders, you began to puzzle out why you fell and what you could do to keep the same scenario from repeating itself.

Perhaps not too surprisingly, riders who are just beginning their equestrian careers are the best folks to ask about what it feels like to take a tumble since most novices are in the process of falling off their horses most of the time. This isn't snide criticism: it's

Figure 11. Balanced and breathing quietly, Olympic equestrian Jessica Ransehousen sits in harmony with her horse Orpheus as he executes a flying change of leads. For the change to be executed correctly, Orpheus first must coil his loins and bascule.

a simple matter of physics. Do you remember your very first riding lesson or your first hour riding "free" upon the back of a horse? For most people, that happy memory is mixed with the memory of stiff, sore legs. A beginner's leg muscles get sore because he or she feels the need to grip the horse in order to stay on. A panicky premonition that you are about to fall off is another version of the same thing; it induces you to grip strongly. As a rider is falling off, he first clutches with his legs, then, in a last-ditch effort, he bends forward at the waist and grabs the horse's mane or neck with his arms.

One of the reasons advanced riders of any discipline don't look like beginners is that they don't feel a need to continuously grip a horse with their legs. Think of how easily the Olympic dressage rider sits through a flying change of leads: her torso is erect, her chest is open, her breathing is slow and regular; her face, hands, arms and back are relaxed, and her legs just caress the horse's sides (Figure 11). A good stock horse and reining trainer show the same degree of "bodily composure" despite the fact that this horse is running flat out for the slide. And competition isn't the only place where such equestrian ease, grace and enjoyment are to be found. How about the little girl down the block — the one who can jump her 12-hand pony over a three-high stack of hay bales — bareback?

What is the secret that keeps these riders so still in the saddle no matter what its style, so "with" their horses — and so far from falling off? *Balance*. The rider who is in balance with his horse doesn't need to grip in order to stay on. The arms, seat and legs of a balanced rider are free to work gently, discreetly and at separate times.

"Well, it's pretty obvious that I fell off because I lost my balance," you may grumble as you rub a sore shoulder or backside, "but if my balance on horseback is off, how can I improve it?" As a first step, a little history may help, for in order to improve balance, it's helpful to understand what it is.

Balance And The Center Of Gravity

The most exciting biomechanical idea current in

Figure 12. The mare's loins and the joints of her hind limbs flex as she "sits down" to a sliding stop. The horse also coils her loins and deeply bends her stifle and hock joints in order to prepare to jump. The space between the rider's bottom and the saddle shows that he has lightened his seat to permit his mount to arch the freespan of her back.

the latter half of the nineteenth century was the discovery of the "center of gravity" (hereafter referred to as the CG). An invisible, infinitely small point, the CG is nevertheless real: it is the point at which a body fundamentally responds to a gravitational field. The CG is the point about which a body spins without wobble and from which it can be suspended without tilting (Figure 13, and see "Finding Your Horse's Center Of Gravity" at the end of this chapter).

Although Newton discovered and described the CG, the idea quickly was applied by others to the ridden horse. Both the rider and the horse possess a CG; part of the trick to "sticking on" is to align and synchronize the separate CGs of rider and horse. Even before Newton's time, sensitive riders, through their "feel," already were aware of the existence of a "balance point" or "axis of movement" in their horses. These riders found that the easiest place to sit is over this axis, for like the axle of a wheel, it is the place in the moving horse which remains most still.

With the naming of this invisible point, riding instructors around the world and in all disciplines immediately began to incorporate the term into riding theory, until today hardly a book or a teacher fails to tell students to "sit over" or "get with" the horse's center of gravity.

This was a grand start in putting the principles of physics to use in the art of riding, but in attempting to explain how to "stick on" — a thing which is, after all, essentially a matter of feel — many instructors have led their students astray. To illustrate to raw cavalry recruits what balance on horseback is like, 19th-century riding instructors reminded their pupils of the wooden rocking horses they'd ridden as children. The rocking horse seemed to make a good model for real horses, because its CG is easy to feel and is located near its middle (Figure 13a).

At the same time, many of the same cavalry instructors taught their students to sit in the "geographical center" of the horse — in the same place that a child sits on a wooden rocking horse. Even today, some instructors believe that sitting far back or pulling the horse's head up or back can lighten its forehand — after all, according to the "wooden horse" model, what goes down on one end must rise up on the other (Figures 13a, 17). Still other riding instructors tell their students to lean back over the cantle and drive forward "in order to increase the horse's impulsion" — by which they really mean: "in order to raise the horse's forehand like the front end of a motorboat traveling at high speed."

Does the rider find his balance on a rocking horse in the same way that he maintains it on a live animal? This is one of the most important questions ever to be raised in equestrian science. The answer centers on the question of whether or not the horse's back is rigid. Despite the belief of some horsemen that lateral torso flexion — side-to-side bending — in horses is an optical illusion, study of film footage has shown that there is an important functional difference between horses of flesh and those of wood: that is, the back of a wooden horse is stiff, while that of a live horse is flexible.

By 1895, Federico Caprilli, an Italian cavalry instructor, had become dissatisfied with the "wooden horse" model of equine movement. He began a series of experiments with the object of developing riding techniques that would permit cavalry horses to jump higher obstacles with greater comfort (Figure 14). By 1907, Caprilli and his students had perfected the "forward seat," today acknowledged by all hunter and

Nineteenth-century riding instructors first used the rocking horse to explain to students about the location of a horse's center of gravity (CG). But the inflexible rocking horse's CG (indicated by the dot) is located at its geographical center (crossed lines), and a live horse's is not.

Figure 13a

Figure 13b

This horse's CG is indicated by the black dot, a point far from his geographical center (crossed lines). The weakest part of the horse's back is marked by the triangle. Because the horse's back is by nature a flexible chain, a rider cannot lighten a horse's forehand either by lifting the horse's head or by sitting far back. Neither do high-lifted knees *per se* indicate lightness. "Lightness" refers to the *whole* of a horse's forehand (see cover illustration and caption). Lightness comes not from a horse's head position or how he addresses the bit, but from engagement of the hindquarters, bascule of the freespan of the back and the "neck-telescoping" gesture. Does this horse show engagement (coiling of the loins)? Is he basculing? Is he making a neck-telescoping gesture?

jumper riders as the best technique for helping the horse to clear obstacles. Caprilli's technique helped the rider as well, for it smoothed the ride and eliminated the horrible jar upon landing. These things, in turn, helped the rider to "stick on" even if the horse pecked or stumbled.

Photographs of Caprilli's students showed them achieving unheard-of feats of horsemanship — such as jumping vertical fences more than 3½ feet high or clearing with aplomb a Rolls Royce convertible filled with dignitaries. They astounded the world, and military tacticians of other nations couldn't resist subjecting these photographs to analysis. Their findings showed what might have been obvious years sooner, had the world's cavalries been thinking less about wooden horses and more about live ones: the rider who rises to a forward seat as his horse thrusts over a jump is the one who keeps his CG in alignment with his horse's. *This is exactly the opposite* of what the rider of a wooden horse would expect.

Balance And Bendability

What factor present in live horses — but not wooden ones — accounts for this unexpected result? *Flexibility.* Caprilli emphasized to his students that they were to leave the horse's head and neck perfectly free over a jump. Left to use his body naturally as he thrusts over a jump, a horse will extend his neck and drop his head. Less obviously, he also will tighten his abdominal muscles, flex his lumbosacral (L-S) joint and bend the joints of the hind limb, coiling his loins and hindquarters for thrust. This coiling arches the freespan of the horse's back, pushing the pommel of the saddle up into the rider's crotch. As the horse prepares to jump and redistributes the parts of his body to form an arch, his CG moves up and forward (Figure 14d).

Caprilli's riders saw this happening in unmounted horses jumping "free" and then applied their observations in a two-step process, permitting the horse to arch his torso for jumping and then staying over the CG, wherever it feels as if it goes.

Yet convincing the world's riders to "stick with the CG" was not the most important result of Caprilli's work. The real advantage of his method lies in feel. Clearing a jump with the rider in the forward seat makes the horse feel comfortable and makes the

Steps In The Development Of The Forward Seat

Figure 14

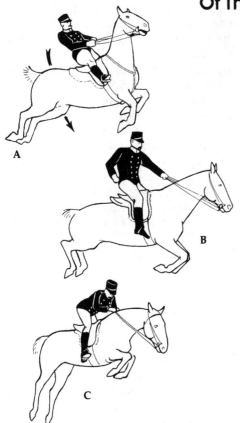

The traditional nineteenth-century cavalry technique for jumping an obstacle (A) had the horse stiffening his torso as the rider pulled back the neck. With a stiff torso, the horse conforms well to the "rocking horse" model: his head rotates up, his croup rotates down and his body spins about a line through his CG. As the technique was refined (B), the rider made a conscientious effort to yield the reins so that the horse could lower and extend his neck and head. Illustration C shows a full bascule and the neck-telescoping gesture, while a modern jumper (D) coils his loins for thrust.

rider feel secure. Why? Because Caprilli's method permits and encourages the flexibility inherent in the horse's torso.

Caprilli's most revolutionary discovery was that *bascule is important.* "Bascule" is a French term meaning "an arch that comes into being through movement." In horsemanship, this term is used to refer to a slight upward arching of the horse's back during movement. Of course, the horse's back also can be arched or flexed sideways. In order to move his best, especially when carrying a rider, a horse must be able to bascule and to flex around turns, for balance and bascule are intimately related.

The following two scenarios — the first at a hunter show, the second at a competitive trail ride — illustrate how important torso flexibility is to normal equine functioning.

Lateral Balance: Bending Around Turns

Close your eyes for a moment and remember the last time you watched a hunter schooling round. Imagine that the weekend had been damp, and although the course was laid out under the roof of the local indoor arena, water had begun to seep into the underlayers of the footing. By late afternoon, a few slick spots had begun to develop in the arena, especially near the end turns.

Now a junior rider enters and makes her courtesy circle. She is mounted on a school horse — one of those iron-jawed survivors who already has packed a half dozen other riders over the course this afternoon. Here is a horse that is going to move as much like a wooden horse as a live horse on terra firma ever does. The odd part of it is, when the horse holds his torso stiff like that of a wooden horse, his balance becomes very delicate; it is then that the wooden horse model applies with a vengeance.

The course is neither high nor technically difficult. The pair takes the first line — an inviting little brush and rail, then five strides to a rolltop — without difficulty, though you notice that the horse seems tired and perhaps looks a little off, with a certain slight jerkiness showing in his movement.

You observe from your vantage point that the horse corners like a fire truck; his back is held straight and his nose is turned continuously to the outside (like the horse in Figure 15). You notice again that the canter isn't smooth: it doesn't flow from stride to stride. Instead, the horse raises his head with each stride, using his neck to hike his forehand off the ground.

The next line brings the horse straight toward you: two jumps, an in-and-out to a vertical, followed by a left-hand bend to the last line. You notice, as the pair lands over the vertical, that the rider's torso leans to the right and that her right stirrup seems longer than the left one. Her horse has never stopped looking slightly to the right.

The horse lands on the right lead, his rider hoping that somehow he'll manage a flying change by midturn. But the horse isn't capable of bending to the left, let alone of making a flying change. Stiff in the torso, he can only lean left while looking right. Then begins the long, slow-motion fall...the rider franti-

Figure 15. This horse does not flex his torso to the right as he turns to the right. His nose and breast are not the first parts to travel around the turn; rather, the horse "leans in" over his right foreleg and shoulder. As a result of this "counterflexed" posture, he has a narrow base of support, especially behind. Since the horse is falling into the turn instead of tracing the turn, his obliquely swinging legs may even interfere with each other. The horse's twisted posture also displaces the rider; her buttocks point left over the horse's croup while her right shoulder leads. Her head tips to the right to compensate for her mount's lack of balance.

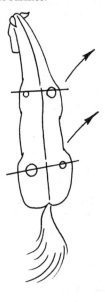

A bird's-eye view of this horse shows that he looks left while falling into the turn to the right. Unequal-sized circles indicate uneven weight distribution on the four feet.

cally tries to "climb the hill," to get back in the center of the horse's back, as her weight presses harder and harder into the right stirrup. While the horse's hind legs twist out from under him, he scrambles to spread his forelegs, to get a leg under his left side. Finally, all four of the horse's hooves slide out to the right.

How different this scene looks with a flexible horse (like the one in Figure 16). The next junior competitor enters, and like the first, makes her courtesy circle. You immediately notice the differences between this horse and the last one. Right from the first step of the circle, the horse gently arcs his neck and torso, looking into, not away from, the direction of his movement. Horse and rider seem so confident.

Figure 16. Handling a turn at speed in a jumper class, this pair is in balance because the horse is capable of side-to-side flexion of the torso. You can tell that the horse is flexing laterally because you can see both breast and hindquarters as he circles toward you. His lateral bend enables him to maintain space between his left and right pairs of legs, resulting in a broad base of support. This gives the rider some freedom to move without disrupting the horse's balance.

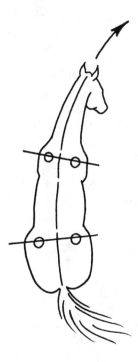

A bird's-eye view of this horse shows that he is tracing a right turn, nose first, shoulders second, hindquarters last. The vertebral column is in alignment and, as a result, the hinduarters are able to push the body straight around the turn (arrow).

You might think the girl would be worried about the greasy-looking streak left in the footing by the last rider's slide, but apparently unconcerned by the prospect of falling, she affords the mud hole not even a glance.

Through the first right-hand turn, you see that the horse continues to arc his torso in the direction of the turn. The many-jointed flexibility of the horse's sleekly groomed body reminds you of a well-oiled toy train negotiating a smooth turn on a track. Like a train, this horse is able to distribute his weight evenly between his inside and outside pair of "wheels."

This horse, you notice, canters smoothly, springing elastically from stride to stride. His rider doesn't

Drawing Rein On
The Wooden Horse

Figure 17

A

B

C

If you make a paper cutout of your resting horse (see p. 42 for directions), you'll find that his center of gravity (CG) is located about where the black dot is marked in the illustration of the live horse on p. 31. In live horses, the CG, the thoracico-lumbar (T-L) joint and the geographical center are three *different* points. Yet the old belief persists that they are the same point. How did this misconception arise?

The functioning of live horses often has been "modeled" by the wooden rocking horse. The CG of a rocking horse is located at the axis or center of a wheel. The rocker is just a segment of this wheel, and rocking motions are made by rolling forward and back on the rocker. The illustration on p. 30 shows that in the wooden rocking horse, the CG and the geographical center are located at the same point. Since a rocking horse's back is wooden, it has no T-L junction (or any other joint).

For these reasons, the pleasant head-goes-up, tail-goes-down movement of a wooden rocking horse is not usually produced by live horses. Because a live horse's back is flexible, his croup goes down when his head goes up only under special circumstances. One such time is when the horse swims (A), especially if the rider pulls at the reins. Another is when the live horse's back is unusually stiff (B).

The black lines in illustrations B and C trace the horse's spinal column. Both horses are in the second beat of a canter on the left lead, but the curves of the vertebral column of C are much smoother. The arrow shows the portion of the horse's neck at which the neck-telescoping gesture is made. Only horse C is cantering elastically, with a flexible torso.

Not all live horses move with the same degree of torso flexibility. In each illustration, compare the black lines which trace the horses' spinal columns. Horse B, who throws his neck back to hike his forehand off the ground with each stride, moves less smoothly than horse C, who is able to extend the root of his neck for more fluid forward motion. Torso flexibility also shows up in back: which of these two horses shows greater engagement of the hindquarters (coiling of the loins)? Is engagement of the hindquarters reflected in the positions of the hind feet?

have to pump her arms back and forth to avoid banging him in the mouth, because her horse's head remains almost still. Instead of throwing his head up with each canter stride, the horse uses his hind legs to push his withers up into the rider's crotch. His head, if anything, drops slightly downward with each stride.

The next line brings the horse straight toward you over the two jumps. You notice, as the pair lands over the vertical, that this rider is able to keep her hips and torso right on top of the horse; he's not "hollow" on one side. Her stirrups look even. While the horse is still in the air, the rider closes her hand on the left rein, softly encouraging her mount to look to the left and bend his neck in the same direction. Without moving her body off center, she subtly advances her left leg and hip to help him arc his torso to the left, too.

Inevitably, this horse lands on the left lead, his rider not even needing to worry about getting a flying change. While this horse's CG is in the same position as that of the last horse coming into the slick turn, this pair won't fall. His flexible torso has permitted this horse to keep his feet, torso and rider in alignment both over jumps and around turns.

Longitudinal Balance: Coiling The Loins

It's a lovely fall day for a competitive trail ride: 70 degrees, light breeze, the sky as high and clear as a clean china plate. You're out today not to ride but to help the horsemanship judge. In order to get a candid and clear view of rider technique, the two of you are posted in a blind halfway up a hill in the woods. The trail is two feet wide and fairly smooth as it comes over the crest of a hill and down a long slope. About halfway down, though, where some rocks jut out, it steepens abruptly. Not more than 60 feet farther down, at the bottom of the slope, a little stream runs in a trough-shaped channel.

You ask the judge why he's chosen this particular section of trail to observe — it doesn't seem to be too difficult or tricky. Though the gradient steepens, it's hardly a slide. Wouldn't something like a brush pile or a forked log test rider ability more severely?

"Nope," the judge drawls, settling his back in the fork of a tree and pulling out his clipboard and score-cards. "You see that spot where the trail changes slope? That's where you'll find out which horses are green. And I'm going to be watching how the rider sets up the situation — how he handles the crest of the hill. If that goes right, the rest of it has a chance of coming out right, too, even on a green horse. But it's the creek bed that'll be the real proof. Just you wait and see."

A

Figure 18. With the rider tugging at the reins, this horse can't seem to get his hocks under his body. He moves forward faster and faster until he and his rider have lost control.

B

This horse heads downhill by extending his neck and carrying his head a bit lower than the saddle horn. His rider helps — not hinders — his progress by leaning slightly forward.

You find that you don't have long to wait. Soon the head and shoulders of a rider, bobbing in time with his horse's trot, appear over the crest of the rise. The horse's nose is the first part of him you see, followed by a straight section of neck. Intent on "making time," the rider seems indifferent to the change of terrain and asks for no slackening of pace. As the pair begins to drop over the rise, however, the horse — seeming tired, although this section of trail is less than 10 miles from camp — breaks to a walk.

As the horse begins to sidle downhill, he leads with his right shoulder and seems to favor that foreleg. Within 10 steps, his rider has to tug his head around to the right in order to keep his quarters behind his shoulders; otherwise, it seems he might go downhill sideways.

Busy with the reins, the rider doesn't seem to notice that as the horse descends, he speeds up bit by bit, until, by the time they find themselves at the break in slope, the rider is trying frantically to shorten the reins to keep the horse from tumbling headlong toward the creek. Standing in the stirrups, the rider tips his torso backward in an effort to slow the horse down again to a walk (Figure 18a).

Now things start to happen in that same slow motion you remember from your own falls...the rider tugs mightily on the reins...the horse's head comes up and his neck and back hollow...although his rider is "helping him to slow down" by leaning back, the horse can't seem to get his hocks under his body. His hind legs seem unable to "catch up." He tumbles forward faster and faster, "chasing" his own balance, until he finds himself at the brink.

By the time the pair reaches the creek, mass and momentum have made it inevitable that the horse will either jump the creek or fall into it. Preferring to jump, he is hindered by the fact that his hind legs are out behind his body — not in a good position to propel him upward. Off-balance and crooked with the rider still tugging away at his mouth, the horse makes a mighty effort, doing his best to thrust off...your last vision before the pair parts company in midair and each splashes to earth. Although the horse manages to scramble up the opposite bank, the trip home for the rider will be an unpleasantly bruised and wet one. "Hmm," you muse, "guess there's more to this trail-riding business than I'd thought."

"Startin' to see what I mean?" says the judge, once he's helped the unfortunate novice to catch his horse and has settled down in the blind for a second time. "Let's watch this next rider, and see how he handles sloping terrain."

Again, you find that you don't have long to wait. Soon the head and shoulders of a rider, bobbing in time with his horse's trot, appear over the crest of the rise. The horse's ears are the first part of him you see, followed by a curved section of neck. This rider is a well-known competitor, but he's more intent on good horsemanship than on "making time"; it's the best-condition award he covets most.

At the top of the rise, the rider asks his horse to break to a walk, and the horse complies smoothly, within three steps. The rider immediately slackens the reins, which surprises you a little, considering how fresh the horse looks.

Still on a loose rein, the pair begins the descent. "Hey," you whisper to the judge, "it looks like that horse is in a posture to back up as he goes downhill." "Yep," whispers the judge in reply. "That horse knows how to lower his croup to go downhill. He bends the joints of his hind legs and digs his hind hoofs into the ground to use them like a safety brake. You can train a horse to do that by walking him downhill and stopping him every few steps. Later on, the horse will balance himself that way without your having to ask. Keep watching. Let's see what he does when he gets to the break in slope."

As the horse continues to walk downhill, you notice that his quarters track true behind his shoulders. The crest of his neck slightly curved, the horse extends his neck and carries his head a little lower than the saddle horn. Now you notice something really odd: the rider seems to be leaning the wrong way: slightly forward. Your indrawn breath draws the judge's sidelong glance. "I thought you were supposed to help a horse out going downhill by leaning back."

"That's just what the last rider did wrong," intones the judge. "Made it hard for his horse to coil his loins. Just keep watchin' t' see what I mean."

As horse and rider reach the break in slope, you can't help noticing the relaxed look of the horse's eyes and body as he descends, still on a loose rein. As he passes over the rocky ledge, the horse simply lowers his croup a little bit more, coiling his loins and hind limbs like a jumper about to spring. The rider leans forward over his own relaxed, bent knees just enough to stay with the horse's CG, and more importantly, to get off the horse's back, permitting his mount to bascule. "Just like a jumper rider," you notice. Far from speeding up as he crests the brink, the horse continues in a balanced and slightly slower walk (Figure 18b).

As the pair reaches the brink, the rider flicks his little finger, and the horse comes to a stop, softly chewing the bit. "Want to drink, fella?" you can hear the rider ask as he pats his mount's shoulder. "No? Okay, well, then let's walk this one," he says as they step off the brink and into the knee-high coolness of the stream. Three gurgling strides later, the rider rises from the saddle, grabs the mane with one hand and urges his horse — still at a walk — up the opposite bank. "No slow motion on that one, eh?" says the judge as he marks his card.

Falling Off: Breaking The Vicious Circle

Now that you've fallen off, now that you've "attended" a hunter show and a competitive trail ride with a new eye for torso flexibility, now that you've seen how Caprilli's "forward seat" is more than a question of following the CG, how can you improve your balance on horseback? Finally, by remembering the intimate connection between balance and bascule. Good balance is the *product* of torso flexibility. There are two kinds of situations in which you are likely to take a tumble:

• when you interfere with your horse's balance, by failing to align your CG with his

• when you're in balance, but you prevent your horse's back from flexing, either up and down or side to side.

These two situations are actually the two halves of a vicious circle, for riding a stiff horse requires all the delicate balancing skill of a surfing champion cutting rough breakers: a slight error in balance quickly results in a fall. Torso flexibility is indeed important for the comfort and safety of both rider and horse.

Finding Your Horse's Center Of Gravity

To find the location of your horse's center of gravity (CG) as seen from the side, take the following steps:

1. **Photograph the horse.** Put the horse in a paddock with short grass or in a dry lot, so that tall grass won't block your view of his legs and feet. Halter the horse and have a friend hold the line loosely. It is essential for the horse to stand squarely, and it is helpful if he is relaxed or even snoozing.

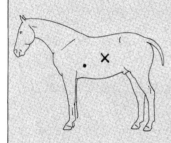

Load your camera with print film. Back away 10 to 20 feet from the horse. Then, standing exactly opposite point "X," snap the picture. If you stand closer to the shoulders, they will be artificially enlarged in the photograph; likewise, the hindquarters will appear too big if you stand too close to them. In either of these cases, the result of your search for the CG will be distorted.

2. **Enlarge the photo.** After the print is developed, take it to a photocopying machine that has the capability for producing enlarged copies. You probably will need to make several generations of enlargements. To do this, set the machine for maximum enlargement. Photocopy the print. Then photocopy the first photocopy. Continue doing this until the image of your horse measures eight to 10 inches from nose to tail (i.e., until it is almost too big to fit on an 8½-by-11-inch sheet of paper). Don't be concerned if the second or third enlargement looks dark; to find the CG, all you need is a crisp silhouette.

3. **Transfer the outline to heavy paper.** Take the photocopied enlargement and tape it to a sunlit window. Using a soft pencil, draw a wide band that covers the edges of the silhouette. This process is called "blacking the back." Then remove the paper from the window.

Now tape the photocopy to a sheet of heavy paper, penciled side down. Using a ballpoint pen and moderate pressure, carefully go over your horse's silhouette. Then remove the photocopy. (You also can use carbon paper to accomplish this step.)

4. **Cut out the silhouette.** Using a small, sharp pair of scissors or a razor knife, cut out the silhouette. Follow the traced outline exactly, with the following exceptions:

    a. cut off the tail at the root

    b. "trim" the mane if it is bushy

5. **Spin for the CG.** Using a long pin (a large sewing pin or a hat pin is ideal), poke a hole anywhere in the cutout silhouette. Enlarge the hole just enough to make the pin fit in it freely; this can be done by pushing the pin in and gently withdrawing it several times.

Holding the pin in one hand, tap or push the silhouette so that it spins around the pin. If the silhouette always stops in the same position or spins asymmetrically, the pinhole you've made isn't in the position of the CG.

It will be obvious after the first couple of tries which direction you have to go to make a better guess at the location of the CG. Keep poking holes and spinning the silhouette until you find a point around which the cutout spins with perfect smoothness and stops at random. The CG of most horses is located in the chest, at a point behind and above the elbow.

There's more to the high-school movement called *levade* (shown by the black horse) than just good balance. Contracting his abdominal muscles, the black horse coils his loins, engages his hindquarters and deeply bends all three joints of his hind limbs. The net effect of these efforts is to raise the withers — true "lightness." The gray horse, with thrown-back neck, sagging back and stretched hind limbs, is merely rearing.

Chapter 3

The Ring Of Muscles

Unlocking the unifying principle of riding

In the last chapter, we discovered that because live horses have flexible torsos, a wooden rocking horse does not make a very good model for explaining equine movement. In a normal horse, the back is only *relatively* rigid. Like a pole vaulter's pole, the horse's loins are designed to coil, storing energy, and then uncoil in a springy release that both complements and multiplies the efficiency of the movements of the hindquarters and the neck. The live, moving horse can both bend and bascule.

Earlier in this book, I emphasized the need to judge conformation with reference, not to our idea of beauty, but to the natural mechanism of the animal. The "ring of muscles," discussed in this chapter, is a description of the actual anatomy at the heart of this mechanism. The idea of "the ring" was first proposed in the late 1880s by German horse trainer Gustav Steinbrecht. Later, his student Waldemar Seunig presented the idea in his book *Horsemanship*. German breeder Gustav Rau applied the principle in judging halter classes and in making breeding decisions. In the 1940s, Dutch researcher E.J. Sleijper independently discovered "the ring" while studying how whales and dolphins swim. Sleijper apparently didn't read the equestrian literature and didn't call this subset of mammalian anatomy "the ring." However, his research subject was ideal for illustrating ring function because the major locomotory movement made by whales and dolphins, which swim by alternately raising and lowering their flukes, is "loin coiling." It is loin coiling and back arching which the ring of muscles controls, and in marine mammals there is little in the way of limbs to confuse the issue.

Whales and dolphins, however, have an incomplete "ring" because they have very short, straight necks which do not contribute much to locomotion Sleijper was unable to discover how the "ring" was closed until late in his life, when he turned his attention to torso function in hoofed mammals. The importance of the scalenus muscle, which powers the "neck-telescoping gesture," then became obvious.

This chapter contributes to a clearer understanding of equine function because in it the work of scientists (who didn't ride horses) and horsemen (who didn't study whales) are brought together for the first time. Steinbrecht, Seunig and Rau gave incomplete (and sometimes inaccurate) descriptions of the anatomy which forms "the ring." Here, the parts and functions of the complete ring of muscles are explained for the first time.

All the desirable qualities of the movement of riding horses — impulsion, collection, engagement, lightness, stride length, self-carriage — depend upon and flow from normal "ring" functioning. All horses, no matter what task they're bred for or are asked to do, move from their "ring." Without good "ring" functioning, a horse cannot perform athletically. *A well-conformed horse is the one so structured and so fitted that his ring of muscles is able to function most powerfully.*

The "ring of muscles" is the unifying principle of riding.

In this chapter we examine more sophisticated models of equine movement. While these models require the dedicated rider to take a close look at equine anatomy, the payoffs, for both you and your horse, will be tremendous.

The benefits you'll reap from understanding the "ring of muscles" are of two kinds. The first kind concerns the mechanics of riding — where on the horse's back you should sit and how to make it as easy as

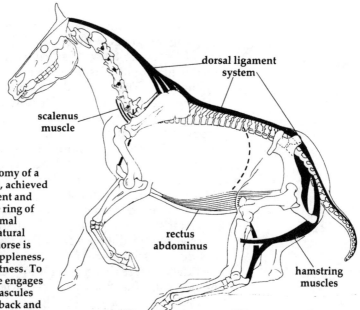

dorsal ligament
system

scalenus
muscle

rectus
abdominus

hamstring
muscles

Figure 20. The anatomy of a perfect sliding stop, achieved through full, efficient and powerful use of the ring of muscles. This maximal expression of the natural mechanism of the horse is characterized by suppleness, impulsion and lightness. To achieve it, the horse engages his hindquarters, bascules the freespan of the back and stretches to the bit by making the neck-telescoping gesture.

possible for your horse to move athletically while burdened with your weight. Did you ever wonder what such terms as "impulsion," "collection" and "engagement" really mean? Are they just part of the jargon found in the international rule books, or is their meaning somehow rooted in the horse's body? Yes, their meaning is real and flows from the way the equine body is structured to function.

The second benefit you'll reap from understanding the "ring of muscles" is even more important, and concerns your peace of mind. Has it ever bothered you that each riding instructor you've worked with has a different method? This is generally true even among instructors who are supposed to be teaching a single "style," such as stock-seat, hunt-seat or saddle-seat riding. Have you ever needed advice about training your horse and been amazed that every horseman you asked had a different answer? If you've ever longed for a unifying principle in riding, dig into the ring of muscles now.

There are two ways to achieve unity in movement between horse and rider. One is for the rider to refine his balance and his "feel" to such a degree that no matter what move the horse makes, or how suddenly, the rider can make a complementary movement, much as in skillful dancing. Physical training of both partners in this "dance" style tends to focus on suppling the joints of the limbs and torso as a means not of lessening but of *distributing* unavoidable jars over as many joints as possible and thereby smoothing them out. This is the "dressage strategy."

The other way to unify rider and horse is to make the horse's center of gravity (CG) remain still. This happens automatically at a halt. At a walk, oscillations of the horse's CG are slow enough that most people find no difficulty "dancing along." At faster gaits, however, the rider either must become a more skillful dancer, or he must induce the horse to stiffen his torso, thus damping the up-and-down oscillations characteristic of equines that originate or are expressed within the freespan of the back. When up-and-down oscillations of the torso are practically nil, the rider receives a smooth, gliding sensation no matter how fast the horse moves its legs. This is the "gaited horse" strategy.

In Chapter 1, you learned the unique anatomy of the horse's lumbosacral (L-S) joint and how it is adapted for loin coiling (Figure 7). The "ring of muscles" model of equine function is built upon the fact that, because of this structure, the equine torso functions like that of no other animal. While up-and-down oscillations are normal in the equine torso, stasis, which results in "that gliding sensation," can be — and often unwittingly is — imposed upon it by the mere presence of a rider.

Stillness of the horse's torso is obtained in two stages. The first is to inhibit or prevent bascule by sitting in the geographical center of the horse (i.e., over the weakest part of the horse's back, the thoracicolumbar [T-L] junction [Figure 13b]). Other techniques for obtaining a continuously flattened (or even sagging) back include lifting the horse's head while riding and selecting horses that have long backs or that have difficulty engaging the hindquarters.

The second stage is to induce the horse to hold his back rigid. Horses do this by muscular effort, continuously contracting the large longissimus dorsi muscles that lie along the topline. Contraction of these muscles has the effect of "locking the back down."

A stiff or "locked" back is normal for many other kinds of hoofed mammals but not for horses. A sagging, stiff or "downwardly locked" back position is a

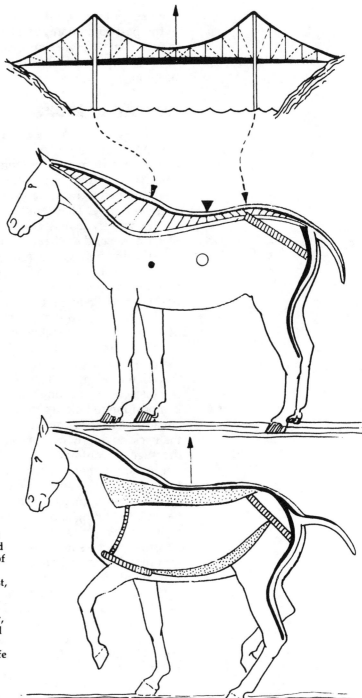

Figure 21. This "suspension bridge" model (top) is an aid in visualizing the function of the back in mammals. It correctly predicts that, at rest, the horse's back is held up not by any muscle lying along the topline but, rather, by a series of interconnected and stretched cables. The same horse executing a piaffe (just above) actively bascules, arching his back. The muscles of his topline stretch because those of his belly contract.

cowlike, not a horselike, spinal position. At no time in the past 55 million years has there been any horse whose spine was designed to operate — much less undergo the added stress of weight-bearing — in this position.

How An Unlocked Back Works

The vertebrae of the living horse's back are held together mainly by very short, very tough ligaments which pass from one vertebra to the next. Anyone who has ever had to separate spareribs has discovered these tough white bands as they appear in slaughter cattle. They look much the same in horses.

If you were to dissect a horse, removing the chain of vertebrae and the head intact from the carcass, the spine would behave like a wiggly snake. If you were to prop the head, the withers and the lumbosacral joint up on three poles, the neck and back would sag, despite their ligamentous connections.

Why, then, do these parts not sag in a healthy, live horse? A reasonable guess would be that the large back muscle (the longissimus dorsi) holds up the back and keeps it from sagging (Figure 22). Yet this is a wrong guess. Though some riding instructors still insist on it, the longissimus dorsi muscles are not in a position to hold up the back. Instead, as we have already seen, these muscles are in a position to "lock the back down" when they contract. The purpose of dressage — contrary to what is so often heard — is not to "strengthen the horse's back." Any technique that causes prolonged bilateral contraction of the longissimus dorsi muscles is antithetical to dressage or helpful to stilling movements in the horse's torso, whichever way you prefer to look at it.

If the longissimus dorsi muscle is not supposed to contract hard on both sides, how is it supposed to work? This large muscle is segmental in structure, with the segments arranged and separately innervated ("wired") like keys on the keyboard of a player piano (Figure 22). When this, the largest single muscle in the horse's body, is functioning normally, it "plays" a glissando from its "low notes" at the croup to its "high notes" at the root of the neck. A pianist plays a glissando when he sweeps his finger across the keys, playing all the keys in sequence. This is the musical counterpart of the undulation or "ripple" of

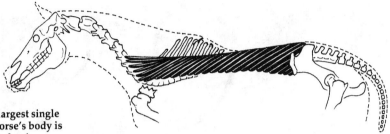

Figure 22. The largest single muscle in the horse's body is the longissimus dorsi. Segmental in structure, its fibers contract sequentially. The equine back is not designed to remain rigid in movement but to undulate up and down.

the normal equine back. By a similar analogy, an abnormal, "locked" back plays a discord — as when the pianist lays his arm across the keyboard (Figure 26a).

There are two complete keyboards in every horse, one on the right side of the back and one along the left. In a normally functioning horse, each keyboard plays its glissando in coordination with the hind leg on its side, so that the glissandos of the left side of the horse alternate with those of the right side.When functioning in this way, the longissimus dorsi acts to stabilize lateral curving of the back and to regulate and transmit energy flowing from the horse's hindquarters.

By contrast, it is normal in trotting cattle for the longissimus dorsi muscles to contract hard on both sides at once. This largely accounts for the vast difference in watching a calf bounce across a pasture after its mother — it looks like a ladder with legs — and the glorious, flowing, elastic, earth-spurning movement of any healthy horse.

Why The Back Of A Standing Horse Doesn't Sag

Clues to the identities of back-support elements in the horse lie in the bones comprising the back. In early members of the horse family, such as *Hyracotherium* ("Eohippus") and *Orohippus,* the spines of all the vertebrae are short and point straight upward (Figures 3a, b). In advanced members of the family, such as *Parahippus* and *Equus,* those that comprise the withers are tall and slant strongly to the rear. Those of the lumbar vertebrae and the sacrum are also fairly long. Those of the lumbar slant to the front, while those of the adjoining sacrum slant to the back (see last two pages of text). Slanting, elongated vertebral

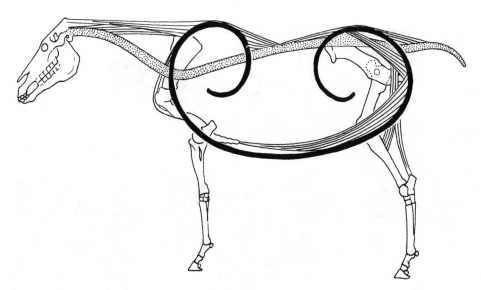

Figure 23. In this "watch spring" model of equine function, the black coil symbolizes the balance of tensional forces that hold up the horse's back. A dynamic balance exists, even at rest, among the vertebrae of the back, which is the cause of the arched shape of the row of vertebral centra (stipple). This model emphasizes the importance of the muscles and ligaments lying *below* the horse's topline.

spines look and function like tent pegs; where are the tent ropes? Unique among hoofed mammals, the horse possesses a "cable" system, a series of interconnected ligaments and ligamentized muscles that runs all the way along the horse's topline from the poll to the hock (Figures 20, 21).

The dorsal ligament of the neck, attached in front to the poll, anchors itself upon the backwardly slanting withers. Still more ligamentous fibers interconnect the separate vertebral spines forming the withers. The dorsal ligament of the back connects the withers to the center of the horse's back just in front of the thoracico-lumbar joint.

Tall withers topped by a well-attached neck constitute a lever advantage; each time such a horse lowers his head, the neck ligament pulls on the withers spines, which in turn pull on and raise the center of the back via the connecting ligaments. By contrast, when a horse with a badly attached or "ewe" neck, or a "hatchet" injury which cuts the neck ligament, lowers his head, the back rises little or not at all.

A second branch of the dorsal ligament runs from its attachment in the center of the back to the hindquarters. Passing over the V-shaped gap in the oppo-

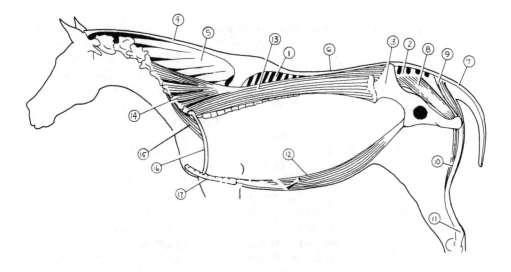

Figure 24. The ring of muscles actually is composed not only of muscles but also of bones, ligaments and tendons. Its anatomical parts include:

1. Dorsal spine or upwardly projecting "slat" of a thoracic vertebra
2. Sacrum bone
3. Pelvic bone
4. The cablelike portion of the nuchal ligament, which forms the crest of the neck
5. The sheetlike part of the nuchal ligament, which connects the withers and crest to the neck vertebrae
6. The dorsal ligament of the back
7. The dorsal ligament of the tail
8. The sacrosciatic ligament, a sheet of elastic tissue that connects the sacrum to the pelvis
9. The upper part of the semitendinosus muscle, which connects the sacrum to the pelvis and hock
10. The lower part of the semitendinosus muscle, which connects the rear part of the pelvic bone (ischium) to the hock
11. The point of the hock (just above it is the Achilles tendon to which the semitendinosus muscle attaches)
12. The rectus abdominus muscle, which connects the pelvic bone to the sternum (breastbone)
13. The longissimus dorsi muscle, largest single muscle in the horse's body
14. Division of the longissimus dorsi muscle found at the root of the neck
15. Scalenus muscle, which connects the first rib to the neck. This muscle closes "the ring" in a long-necked mammal and is vital to making the neck-telescoping gesture.
16. First rib bone
17. Sternum bone

site-slanting spines of lumbar and sacrum, it broadens and merges with the broad, tough fascia which pass over the lumbosacral joint. It acts as an elastic connector or "coupling" between the horse's back and croup. From there, a minor branch of the dorsal ligament continues out to the tip of the horse's tail.

While the main leverage point in the forequarter is the withers, the main leverage point of the hindquarter is the lumbosacral joint. Flexion of the L-S joint, the last joint in the horse's "loins," is the main cause of bascule. In the process of flexing the L-S joint, the croup angles downward as the horse coils his loins. The resulting arching of the back tightens the dorsal ligament passing over the croup and out to the tip of the tail. This is why, when a horse bascules, his tail is passively raised into a smooth arch (Figures 26b, c). A horse can, of course, stick its tail straight up in the air like a poodle's or curl it over its back, but these kinds of tail raising result from the active use of the tail muscles.

Below the croup, a new cable system, rooted in the hind limbs, functionally continues the dorsal-ligament system (Figure 24). At the top, the sacrosciatic ligament and a prolongation of the semitendinosus muscle span the gap between the sacrum and the pelvis. Below, the semitendinosus becomes a tough and fibrous "cable." This muscle attaches not just to the gaskin (shin bone or tibia) as in humans and cattle but branches and extends all the way down to blend with the Achilles tendon and terminates on the point of the hock (equivalent of the human heel).

The horse is unique in having this system of elastic ligaments and cablelike muscles, which are arranged in such a way that they stretch in a functionally continuous band from poll to hock. Because of their attachment to specially modified vertebrae, a pull on either end of the system has the net effect of raising the center of the back (Figures 20, 21).

Part by part, the horse's back corresponds pretty well with the components of a suspension bridge. This model correctly predicts that the horse's back is not held up by contractions of the longissimus dorsi muscles that form the top surface of the back. Like the slightly arched floor of a suspension bridge, the horse's vertebrae are held up by a series of interconnected and stretched cables. These cables are

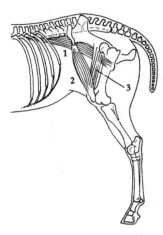

Figure 25. Why "striding up"
or "engaging the hocks" is
important: the protractor
muscles of the horse's hind
limb are not part of the ring
of muscles, but by helping to
draw the hind limb forward,
they make lumbosacral
flexion easier and thus assist
in producing both
engagement and bascule.

1 = iliopsoas muscle
2 = tensor fasciae latae muscle
3 = quadriceps muscle

stretched when the horse bascules. If he never bascules, this major support system is "cancelled out."

An even more sophisticated model for static support uses a watch spring to symbolize the balance of
tensional forces that hold up the horse's back (Figure
23). A dynamic balance exists, even at rest, among
the vertebrae of the back. The watch spring model
highlights the role of the joint capsules and ligaments
and of the epaxial muscles (the "stew meat" down
next to the bones), which passively and actively function to hold the vertebrae together. Its most attractive
feature, however, is its recognition of all the muscles
and ligaments lying below the horse's backbone in
maintaining a slight bascule, even at rest.

How A Horse Supports Weight On His Back

More than a passive cable system is needed when
a horse's back is loaded with a weight or when he begins to move. Muscles now must come into play —
not the muscles of the back, as we have seen, but the
muscles of the horse's *belly*. The effect of all dressage
exercises is, in whole or in part, to strengthen the rectus abdominus muscle of the horse's underline. A
horse with a deep, strong belly muscle — a horse
whose groin depth nearly equals his girth — can bascule, engage his hindquarters, achieve collection and
carry you athletically (Figure 26c).

Both the suspension bridge and watch spring
models predict that the weakest point in the horse's
back is the T-L junction, located at the center of the
arch. If a rider sits on or leans over this point, he
forces the horse to use his abdominal muscles more
strongly to maintain the arch and support his back.
Sitting near the "bridge pylons" or "spring curls"
(behind the withers or on the croup) lessens the effort
the horse must exert to maintain bascule.

In active, forward movement, the center of the
horse's back is raised primarily by the three groups of
muscles which complete the "ring":

● the rectus abdominus muscles of the belly (Figure 24). When these muscles contract, the pelvis is
drawn closer to the sternum, and the horse's back
humps up. You can observe this movement in most
horses when they urinate, in mares when they are

Figure 26a, b. A lofty head carriage is maintained in both these silhouettes, yet only in the horse on the right is the ring of muscles functioning. What are the clues? First, look at the whole topline. Is it arched? Are poll and croup falling together or stretching apart? Then consider the underline. Is it stretched or shortened and deepened?

Figure 26c. At the age of 16, this horse is still active at the highest level of competition. He shows all of the most desirable features of "ring" function: he flexes the lumbosacral joint, thus engaging his hindquarters. His whole topline is stretched, including the critically important area at the root of his neck. His stifle, hock and fetlock joints are deeply bent. His abdominal muscles are "on" (see apparent heave line, which is just the edge of the bulging rectus abdominus muscle). The smooth-looking loin area and the depth of the gelding from loin to groin is a typical development in horses that actively use the "ring." As a result of these efforts, the horse produces suspension — all four feet are off the ground during this extension of the trot. From suspension plus regular rhythm is born cadence, the very soul of dressage.

sexually excited, during the execution of a good piaffe or sliding stop or when you accidentally splash cold water up under your horse's tail when giving him a bath.

• the "protractor" muscles lying on the front of the thigh, between the point of the hip and the stifle joint (Figure 25). These muscles act to swing the thigh and all the rest of the hind limb forward.

• the scalenus muscles of the neck. These produce the "neck-telescoping gesture" — the extension and lowering of the head so ardently desired in the jumping horse (Figures 11, 14c, 17c, 18b, 20, 26c). A good place to view horses spontaneously producing this gesture is at the breeding farm, when the stallion simultaneously arches and extends his neck to sniff his lady love.

The Ring And Riders

The practical results and implications of the "ring of muscles" model may not be what you've heard from your riding instructor, nor are they stated in these terms in the handbook of the Fédération Equèstre Internationale. Yet they are grounded in the realities of anatomy and equine biomechanics, and they can help you to be a more knowledgeable rider and consumer. The next time you get on your horse just keep in mind:

• The most important quality in domestic riding horses is their ability to carry weight upon their backs. A horse's weight-carrying ability depends on well-structured, sound legs and feet, as well as his ability to achieve and maintain the slightly humped weight-carrying or basculed posture. Therefore, any anatomical structure or conformational feature that enhances a horse's ability to bascule is desirable.

• Bascule is the result of engagement of the hindquarters, which is flexion of the lumbosacral joint.

• Collection starts from and is always primarily the product of flexion of the lumbosacral joint. Collection is completed when the scalenus muscles produce the neck-telescoping gesture.

• Impulsion is the horse's willingness to use the propulsive muscles of the hindquarters to drive the basculed body forward. Whether from unwillingness, fatigue, laziness or clamping down of the back, a horse without a bascule is a horse without impulsion, and that makes for a very unsatisfactory ride.

Figure 27. This computer-generated mosaic image of a horse's head symbolizes the head as it really grows: a harmoniously integrated summation of thousands of separate parts. The shape and development of each part is separately inherited and is separately controlled by different genes or gene complexes.

Chapter 4

The Body Mosaic

How combining genes can produce an infinite variety among offspring

Bascule, impulsion, collection, engagement: these are the results of the horse's mechanism. Your understanding of how a horse is structured to move fits you to make choices concerning conformation.

The next step is to learn in concrete terms how to "see" the body structure. In the second half of this book, we now shift somewhat to the horse breeder's point of view, because our ability to produce good horses is a revealing measure of our capacity to analyze conformation.

Acquiring an "eye" for conformation is — or should be — a stepwise process. In this chapter, we'll consider the horse from a geneticist's perspective — as thousands of tiny phenotypic units. The development, appearance and functioning of each of these qualities — from coat color to ear size to cannon bone length — is controlled by a separate gene or complex of genes.

In the last two chapters of this volume, we'll consider seven "P"'s of conformation judging, learning to differentiate constructions which are Perfect or Primitive from those which are Pathological or Pathogenic. Finally, we'll talk about getting the most for your money in a horse purchase, establishing measures of value and excellence through a balance among **Pedi-gree**, **Performance** record and **Phenotype**.

If someone asked you why children look like their parents, you certainly would be right in replying, "because they have similar genes." But let's apply this question to a common scenario with horses: the breeder who says, "My stallion always passes his head to his foals." When you hear this, do you wonder if the owner might not be exaggerating? Can a stallion *really* pass his head — his *whole* head — on to every foal?

Is a stallion's head literally "stamped" on the tissues of the developing foal? Although this is what many breeders imply, what a breeder really means is that all the genes which his stallion carries for head shape and development are dominant over all those carried by the mares he's been bred to. Can this be true?

Experience informs us that human fathers don't usually "pass their heads." But to what experience do we refer when making judgments about the similarity of the heads of fathers and sons? It is, of course, the experience conveyed by careful, close observation, because even as babies we begin to scrutinize faces and hone our ability to tell them apart. Thus, within our own species, we are able to recognize differences between extremely similar heads, such as those of a father and his son, even a son who is a "chip off the old block."

Perhaps, then, we are tempted to say that a stallion "passes his head" because we are unable to notice and remember small differences in horses' faces; in other words, they all look alike to us.

This assertion is borne out by two lines of evidence: one, that we sometimes make this observation within our own species when referring to people of races different from our own; and two, that it takes years of experience to learn to notice and interpret even the most obvious facial expressions which horses may show. It is especially for this reason that breeders are able to use the "my stallion always passes his head" line as a sales pitch to first-time buyers.

The Power Of Observation

However, some horsemen really are able to tell

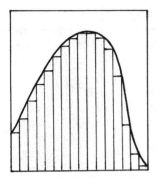

Figure 28 A. The integration of a curve in calculus merely means *approximating* **or** *modeling* **the curve by fitting a bar graph beneath it.**

one head from another and can pick out their stallion from a distance, even in a large herd. Such breeders also can tell you which foals in a given year's crop most resemble their sire or dam. The degree to which a breeder will admit to and describe small differences between a herd sire and his get is a good measure not only of his honesty but of his ability for observation and fine discrimination.

And this visual assessment should illustrate something about the practicalities of genetic study. *Genes don't have labels.* The only way that Gregor Mendel, father of the science of genetics, or a horse breeder can investigate what's going on genetically is to take careful note of the phenotype. The point of this "head story" is that the better and more detailed your observations, the more you'll ultimately discover about the genetics of your horses.

Holistic Vs. Analytic Ways Of Looking At Horses

This isn't to say that horses actually are composed of characters which work like zillions of tiny mechanical parts. All living things are composed both of parts and of interrelationships among the parts as they function and affect one another. When recognized as such a system, the whole organism is breathtakingly complex and cannot be atomized, for the whole seems to be greater than the sum of its parts.

An illustration of this concept is the difference between the integration of a curve, as modeled by calculus, and the curve itself (Figure 28A). To integrate a curve, the mathematician constructs a histogram or bar graph which fits under the curve. A more precise model of the shape of the curve then can be made by making the vertical bars of the histogram thinner and adding more bars.

Taking this to its logical limit, the mathematician mechanically can produce a curved shape infinitely similar to the actual curve. But if you looked at this shape with an infinitely powerful microscope, you'd see that it still is composed of zillions of tiny steps and that it really isn't a curve. An equation which *precisely specifies* most curved shapes cannot be written. Likewise, the total genetics of any horse never will be discovered.

Why not? Because a complete phenotypic and

genotypic description is still only a *representation* of a real horse. Like calculus, genetics models reality and tries to approach it with an infinite degree of similarity. Philosopher Alan Watts has observed that the practice of science in India, China and Japan was not traditionally constrained to the analytical mode. As a result, these cultures have developed holistic forms of medicine and medical treatment, such as acupuncture, which often seem mysterious to us.

Likewise, when speaking of their favorite stallion or mare, many breeders wander off into what seem to be rhetorical excesses. What they are trying to express is not gushy sentimentality but the ineffable qualities of their bloodstock. Insofar as those virtues are sincerely felt, breeders are justified in doing this.

By contrast, the study of genetics is undeniably analytical. Knowing that genetics models the totality of the "real," a breeder might fear that his feeling for an excellent horse might be diminished or destroyed if he became too analytical. But this is not so, for the most fruitful way of looking at the world integrates the analytical with the holistic.

While the whole indeed may be greater than the sum of its parts, still the whole would not exist without those parts! While the greatest racehorse in a field of greats might be superior in such unquantifiable

Figure 28 B

Five full siblings — yet no two alike! Diagramming these foals as pointillist paintings will help you to see each whole as the sum of thousands of individual parts. If you visualize the characteristics of the foal's sire as red dots and those of his dam as blue dots, you can diagram a unique genetic mix in each foal with red and blue felt-tip markers.

A B

Directions: A pointillist painting is made by applying hundreds of separate small dots of paint to a canvas. Foal A is a "chip off the old block" — symbolized by being dotted only with your red marker.

Foal E is "just like mama" — symbolized by being dotted only with your blue marker.

Foals B, C and D are mixtures. Foal B is three-quarters red and one-quarter blue — he "takes after" his sire. Be sure to intersperse his blue dots evenly throughout his body. Hold your completed work at arm's length, and this foal should appear to be a pinkish magenta color.

qualities as "heart" or "try," still he could not run without a muscular heart and straight, sound, bony legs.

Examining The Mosaic Model

For this reason, geneticists look at horses as if they were **mosaics** (Figures 27, 28 B). The mosaic nature of some organisms — such as an ear of Indian corn — is easy to see. And with an ear of corn, it's easy to make the conceptual leap from "one character" to "one gene or one gene complex" which controls the color, size, shape and development of each kernel. Though it's harder to see in a horse, the analytical model which infinitely approaches the truth about equine inheritance is this mosaic model.

The mosaic model encourages the breeder to look at the outside of the horse and mentally break it up into very small characteristics. Is this a mere imposition of Western logic, or is there evidence that genes actually control the phenotype, bit by bit?

Yes, such evidence does exist, for it appears that the molecule groups — sections of the DNA strands — which we call genes actually function like switches. Each gene, at any given time, can be switched "on" or "off."

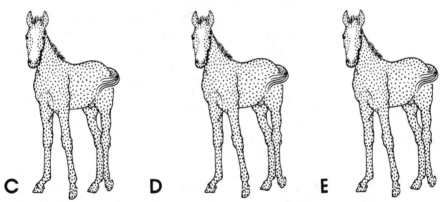

C   D   E

Foal D is three-quarters blue and one-quarter red — he "takes after" his dam. Be sure to intersperse his red dots evenly throughout his body. Hold your completed work at arm's length, and this foal should appear to be "blue-jean blue."

Foal C is a fifty-fifty situation. Be sure to distribute red and blue dots evenly throughout his body. Hold your completed work at arm's length, and this foal should appear to be purple.

Notice that neither this foal's sire nor his dam contributed "magenta," "blue-jean blue" or "purple" genetic material to the foal. However, the genetic contribution of sire and dam is associated and expressed differently in each and every offspring.

Figure 29. Barr bodies are found in half of all a filly's body cells. Nucleus of a cell with a Barr body (A) and one without a Barr body (B) are illustrated.

A

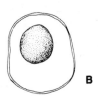

B

Mammals which most resemble mosaic ears of Indian corn are those whose skin and fur are marked with contrasting colors, such as tricolor horses and calico cats. In studying dividing cells of such mammals, researchers were surprised to discover distinct clumps of chromosomal material, detached from the main mass in the cell nucleus, called **Barr bodies** (Figure 29). Even more surprisingly, they noticed that these clumps appeared only in females. It was as if a certain portion of the genetic library had been shut up in a closet and not allowed to take part in the process of reduction division.

Why should this be so? Mares, with their XX genetic makeup, possess two *long* DNA strands, while stallions, with an XY makeup, possess one long and one short strand. This means that mares possess a higher total number of genes — a genetic no-no. When extra chunks or strands of DNA are present in body cells, the result is either lethal or debilitating; for example, babies with Down's syndrome have extra genetic material.

Consequently, even though it's perfectly normal for a mare to possess XX, the effect of a double dose of X must be compensated for, lest its effect be too strong. Barr bodies are formed in females early in embryonic life to isolate the genetic content of one X strand per cell.

The presence of Barr bodies in a female has far-reaching effects on her phenotype. A mare, like any other female mammal, inherits one of her X strands from her sire and the other from her dam. On the X strand reside genes which control many body functions and structures, including such easy-to-see items as coat color. The X strand a mare receives from her sire may call for one coat color while that from her dam may call for another.

Copies of both maternal and paternal X strands exist in each of a mare's cells, yet one X strand must be shut off. The selection is made early in embryonic life, when the developing filly consists of a colony of only a few tens or hundreds of cells. The "choice" made in a given cell is then imposed upon all the descendants of that cell.

Which X strand is shut off in a particular cell is random, and thus cells with an active maternal or paternal X aren't distributed evenly throughout a mare's body. As a result, all female mammals are mosaics consisting of patches of tissue in which either the maternal or the paternal X is active. When maternal X codes for red hair and paternal X codes for black, the offspring's phenotype is conveniently color-coded — like an ear of Indian corn — so that it is easy for researchers to see the mosaic.

But even when the mosaic is hard to see, it's still present. Again, consider the stallion's head, a composite of a large number of different parts. The development and shape of each part is controlled by one or more genes. Whether a filly's head looks more like her sire's or more like her dam's depends on which gene for each separate part of her head is dominant — i.e., able to express itself in the visible phenotype.

Chances are that only about 50% of all the sire's "head genes" will be dominant. In thousands of particular ways, the filly's head will be exactly like her sire's — because the genes she expresses for those characteristics of her head will be exact copies of her sire's genes. But in thousands of other ways, the filly's head will be exactly like her dam's.

For this reason, colts and fillies are *not* blends of maternal and paternal genes, and the phenotype resulting from a mating is not like a mixture of red and blue paint to produce purple. Instead, the visible phenotype is like a pointillist painting — composed of thousands of red and blue dots. If you stand close and analyze, you can distinguish the individual dots (pages 62-63). But if you stand far away, the "whole" painting will affect your senses and give you the impression that it's purple.

The whole really is greater than the sum of its parts, for purpleness — a new sensation — can be created from dots which are themselves pure red and pure blue. But the purpleness which delights you would never materialize if the red and blue dots comprising it were to be mashed together or blended. And the painting would lack liveliness and interest if it were *all* blue or *all* red.

The fun and interest in horse breeding does not lie in producing clones, to which a stallion really would "pass his head," but in selecting particular mares and stallions. The decision to bring a chosen pair together is an affirmation of accepting the universe as it is, for every mating produces one of an infinite variety of mosaics, each of which appears to be a shade different from *both* its sire and dam.

Figure 30. The importance of observation: since genes exert direct influence on development of the horse's body parts, selecting stock on the basis of accurate observation leads to the most direct control possible over the genetic constitution of your breeding herd.

Chapter 5

How To Look At A Horse

Is that really a fault, or is it the reasoning that's flawed?

In the last chapter, we visualized the horse's body as being broken up into thousands of tiny characters, each genetically determined and environmentally mediated. But we haven't yet been very specific about how a buyer or breeder is supposed to differentiate those parts. The patchwork photograph of a stallion's head transformed by a computer into thousands of small squares made the horse's head appear out of focus. Is this how a breeder is supposed to look at horses? Do geneticists see horses as composites of thousands of tiny bricks? In actual practice, a breeder must decide on more biological grounds where to draw the boundaries between characters. In this chapter, we will map those crucial boundaries and develop guidelines for understanding the origin of the characteristics of the visible body or "phenotype."

Biologists generally view large mammals such as horses as composed of large, nonuniform pieces — teeth, ears, cannon bones, nostrils, hindquarters and the hairs of the tail. Instead of subdividing the horse by a grid system, this way of finding the boundaries between characters treats the horse as if he were a model airplane or machine whose parts are glued or bolted together.

Veterinary surgeons have practical reasons for learning equine anatomy this way, since in the course of their duties they're going to be called upon to incise the body, and it is humane that they be taught how to sew its parts back together again. As a result, many textbooks of equine anatomy are available which demonstrate the horse's parts as the horse grows them; such books are worthy of the horseman's study also.

But since the horse's body is actually smooth, and since it came into being not by being assembled but by growing, a model-airplane view of the horse is, at best, incomplete. Therefore, one of the most desirable skills for a breeder to develop is the ability to notice not only beautiful individual parts, but how parts may fit together beautifully (Figure 30). Harmonious function is also genetically controlled.

Conformation And Movement

Most horsemen actually do not learn to see conformation by reading a book of anatomy. Instead, they develop their eye by watching live horses — perhaps in halter classes, perhaps at a local riding stable, perhaps at their father's side as they learn the ins and outs of ranching.

But despite the fact that in most of these practical learning situations the horses are observed in motion, many breeders eventually begin to focus on standing conformation as an end in itself. While this is the logical consequence of looking at a horse as if he were composed of separate parts, perhaps it is also the consequence of halter classes as they are conducted the world over. In these so-called breeding classes, the central necessity is to "stand the horse up" so that the judge can look him over and the photographer can take his portrait. Today more than ever before, breeders learn about horses other than their own by studying these static portraits.

A fascinating cycle is being completed here — a cycle of growth in becoming a perceptive breeder. The cycle begins with naive enjoyment of moving horses — the kind you had when you were a kid and saw horses moving in a green pasture or a dusty pen full of milling cattle or a floodlit show ring. The cycle moved on as you began to realize that some horses were "better" than others — better for certain tasks

and better at carrying out these tasks. As your investment in, and commitment to, horsemanship deepened, you began educating yourself further about
conformation, genetics and the reasons for selecting
some stallions and mares in preference to others.

But this process of maturation as a breeder is not
linear — it's circular, for the cycle is not complete until you return to the beginning and open yourself
once again to the pleasure of watching horses move.
With maturity, however, your pleasure is no longer
naive, for you recognize its roots in analytical appreciation of the equine phenotype.

Conformation studied in isolation is merely an
exercise in aesthetics. Every breeder wants beautiful
movement, but beautiful movement is a higher-order
function: it depends on the harmonious integration of
parts, as well as on the structural excellence of the
parts themselves. Since genes exert a direct influence
on the development of the horse's body parts, when
breeders select stock on the basis of accurate observation and analysis of body parts, they exert the most
direct control possible over the genetic constitution of
their breeding herd.

Structure For Horselike Movement

At the end of this volume, you will find an
"Equine Parts Inventory" illustrating dozens of the
horse's separate conformational parts. That figure
may seem high, but it represents a minor fraction of
all the separately identifiable and genetically influenced characters which biologists believe to be present in horses. Reviewing the inventory is not only fun
but instructive, for it will serve to illustrate the influence — both particular and great, immediate and
long term — which horse breeders can exert over
their stock.

You should move from study of the parts inventory to the "P's" illustrated in this chapter (pages 72
and 73). This figure invites you to learn to pick out
faults. But don't take this too far! Keep nitpicking in
perspective, lest you forget that all horses have faults,
and become blinded to structural strengths and harmonious functioning in individuals otherwise
flawed. It's important to know which faults really
matter. For this reason, in the following sections of
this chapter, each of the horse's body regions is sur-

veyed from the point of view, not of halter-class judge nor even of breeder, but from the broader viewpoint of mammalogy — the study of horses *as compared with* other kinds of mammals.

Are there characteristics in horses different from those of other hoofed mammals? Is there really anything special about horses? From the perspective of mammalogy, the most serious flaws a horse could possess are those which detract from his native "horsiness" — either in structure or in movement.

The Head

Since the time the horse species first began to be kept by mankind about 5,000 years ago, breeders have exerted great influence on the shape of horses' heads. Psychologists claim that our species — more visually oriented than any other — is drawn in a kind of biological mesmerization toward any head with a small muzzle (the human muzzle is one of the shortest in nature), a bulbous cranium and big eyes. The domesticated species of mammals, not only horses but sheep, goats, cattle and even pigs, support this assertion. *Every* species of domesticated mammal possesses a "cuter," rounder head, with a shorter muzzle and bigger eyes, than its wild relatives.

This observation helps to put many of the horse's so-called "faults" into perspective. Such features as a large and coarse head, a thick muzzle, big ears, small pig eyes, narrowness between the eyes, eyes set high in the head (i.e., long muzzle) and a convex nose are perceived by human beings as faults through a kind of species-based chauvinism, but they are of no proven functional consequence.

Other faults of the head are more accurately viewed from an evolutionary standpoint. These "faults" are merely primitive characters still capable of being expressed in living horses. For example, one million years ago, all horses were hammer-headed.

Hammer-headedness is present in the conformation of horses with a short distance in the skull bones between the back of the roof of the mouth and the back of the skull. The bone structure in this region in turn influences the conformation of the upper part of the neck. Partly through natural selection and partly by mankind's preferences, horses have acquired a more open bone structure in this part of the skull and thereby have gained a neck which makes for a long "turnover" or mitbah, a clean throatlatch and a more pleasantly arched crestline.

Some head conformations, however, are faults no matter how their development is understood. They are those which directly and immediately would interfere with the horse's ability to survive in the wild and include such features as bug eyes and gotch eyes (which prevent the horse's vision from functioning properly), parrot mouth, undershot jaw, scissor mouth (which could prevent him from procuring and chewing his food) and small nostrils (which inhibit his ability to breathe, and therefore to run from predators [Figure 31]).

Neck And Body

Following the explanation given above, faults and characters for this section of the body and of each section below will be classified simply as "primitive," "harmful" or "not harmful, but sometimes not preferred."

Primitive: thick throatlatch; short neck, bull neck; very large crest (a male secondary sexual characteristic which has been bred out of many modern horses); ewe neck, no turnover (both of these go with hammer-headedness); mutton withers (horses of a million years ago had lower withers than horses do now). Rough coupling or "widow's peak" is also primitive; mankind has succeeded in the effort to smooth the coupling, as this greatly enhances the horse's weight-carrying ability.

Harmful: neck too long (predisposes the horse to partial dislocations of neck vertebrae and damage to motor fibers of cervical nerves, resulting in faulty coordination or ataxia); roached back (when this condition indicates a misalignment of the lumbar vertebral centra); long loins, weak coupling or low-backed; horizontal or "tabletop" croup (when this is accompanied, as it often is, by upward tipping of the rear of the pelvis); wry tail (when present in young horses, it is often an indication of vertebral malformation and/or misalignment); narrow chest, small heart girth, tubular body; chest too wide (so that elbow and knee joints in front legs are deformed to a bowlegged conformation, or so that the horse appears to roll from side to side as he moves).

Figure 31
The Four P's

The "four P's" denote facets of conformation: "perfect," "primitive," "pathological" (injured or damaged) and "pathogenic" (structured so as to predispose to injury or damage). To structural features representing the first two P's — perfect and primitive — there is no biologically-based objection. You may not like the looks of primitive, but that horse is just as likely (maybe more likely) to stay sound through years of use as the model called perfect.

View A is PERFECT — in the author's opinion! This crossbred horse serves usefully as a model for a pleasure-riding horse: sound, athletic, easy to train; likely to live long, stay sound and perform willingly. You can change the ears, raise the set of the tail, add a full mane or put a dish in the face if that's your preference, but please — don't make him pathological or pathogenic!

The other images are re-drawings of the same horse. View B represents him with a preponderance of primitive characteristics; and View C, with a number of pathologies which are frequently mistaken for inheritable flaws in structure. View D, by far the most objectionable conformation from a biological point of view — and a haunting echo of a stylized 19th-century engraving — inflicts the horse with a number of inheritable structural weaknesses. In assessing B, C and D, the breeder — no matter what his breed — must hold a sound mental picture of "perfect" and make comparisons against that standard.

A. Perfect

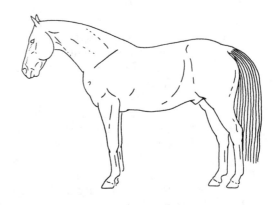

B. Primitive

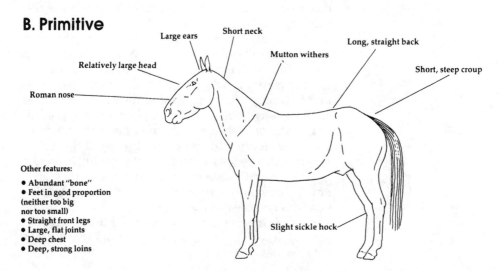

Large ears

Short neck

Long, straight back

Mutton withers

Relatively large head

Short, steep croup

Roman nose

Other features:

- Abundant "bone"
- Feet in good proportion (neither too big nor too small)
- Straight front legs
- Large, flat joints
- Deep chest
- Deep, strong loins

Slight sickle hock

C. Pathological

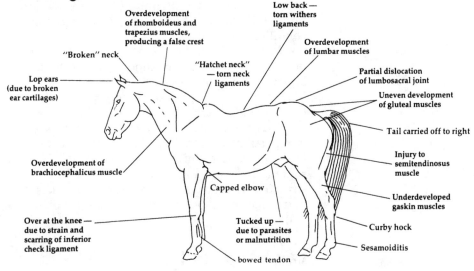

Overdevelopment
of rhomboideus and
trapezius muscles,
producing a false crest

Low back —
torn withers
ligaments

"Broken" neck

"Hatchet neck"
— torn neck
ligaments

Overdevelopment
of lumbar muscles

Lop ears
(due to broken
ear cartilages)

Partial dislocation
of lumbosacral joint

Uneven development
of gluteal muscles

Tail carried off to right

Overdevelopment of
brachiocephalicus muscle

Injury to
semitendinosus
muscle

Capped elbow

Underdeveloped
gaskin muscles

Over at the knee —
due to strain and
scarring of inferior
check ligament

Tucked up —
due to parasites
or malnutrition

Curby hock

Sesamoiditis

bowed tendon

Note: This horse is predisposed to none of these pathologies, but
every one of them can be induced in the course of training,
showing or riding across country — by "overdoing it," "doing it
wrong" or just plain bad luck.

D. Pathogenic

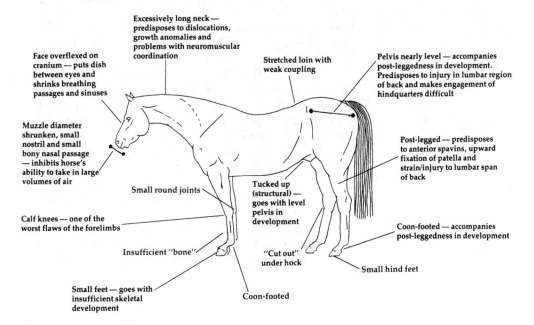

Excessively long neck —
predisposes to dislocations,
growth anomalies and
problems with neuromuscular
coordination

Face overflexed on
cranium — puts dish
between eyes and
shrinks breathing
passages and sinuses

Stretched loin with
weak coupling

Pelvis nearly level — accompanies
post-leggedness in development.
Predisposes to injury in lumbar region
of back and makes engagement of
hindquarters difficult

Muzzle diameter
shrunken, small
nostril and small
bony nasal passage
— inhibits horse's
ability to take in large
volumes of air

Post-legged — predisposes
to anterior spavins, upward
fixation of patella and
strain/injury to lumbar span
of back

Small round joints

Tucked up
(structural) —
goes with level
pelvis in
development

Calf knees — one of the
worst flaws of the forelimbs

Coon-footed — accompanies
post-leggedness in development

Insufficient "bone"

"Cut out"
under hock

Small hind feet

Small feet — goes with
insufficient skeletal
development

Coon-footed

Not Harmful, But Sometimes Not Preferred: knife-necked; dip in front of withers, hollow behind withers, ridge back, rafter hips (all indications of low-normal development, which can be changed through conditioning).

In addition, there are a number of "conformation" features which are almost always the result of injury. Such features can be debilitating in a riding horse but are not passed on genetically. These features include: topline not smooth (often from injury to base of neck or to back); hunter bump or racking bump; subluxation of lower back; saddle-backed; one hipbone carried lower; herring-gutted (fillies are sometimes fairly high-waisted due to their pelvic structure. In other cases, the tucked-up look is due to injury, disease, parasitism or malnutrition [Figure 31]).

Legs And Feet

Primitive: upright shoulder; pigeon-breasted.

Harmful: Insufficient "bone"; "tied in" below the knee; back at the knee; cannon with shrinking center diameter; coon-footedness; congenital club-footedness; toed-out; offset knees; lateral and medial carpal deviations; carpal rotations; lateral and medial deviations of pasterns; small, round joints; small feet; flat feet with weak walls and low soles; thin walls; small bars; tendons and sesamoids not well placed, large and firm.

Not Harmful, But Sometimes Not Preferred: front legs set too far forward; lack of definite armpit; long cannon bone; pasterns excessively long, short, upright or sloping, according to taste and intended use; stands close in front or behind (so long as it doesn't cause interference); pigeon-toed, so long as not severe (in mild form, this is actually an advantage for speed, as it frees the elbow from friction against the body and causes the shoulder joint to function more efficiently [Figure 31]).

Notice the disproportionate number of seriously harmful faults of the legs and feet. Horsemen should be tuned in to the importance of the legs as structural components. Through the 5,000-year history of equine domestication, the horse's torso — especially the neck, withers and loin coupling — have been improved, but the legs have lost 50 percent of their orig-

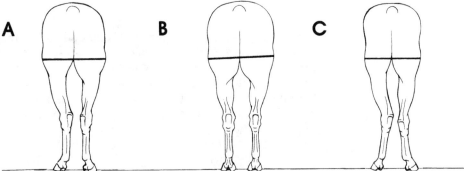

Figure 32. Illustration A (above) shows the *normal and desirable* condition for the equine hind limb as seen from the rear. Its characteristics: width between the stifles (horizontal bar); large, strong hock joints; parallel cannon bones; toes point out, not straight forward. *The hind toes should point outward to the same degree as the stifles* — never straight forward!

Illustration B shows "textbook straight" hind legs that will bow to the outside as weight passes over the hocks. The situation would be even worse if the hocks were less substantial or if the toes pointed inward. In our desire to model reality, this diagram has been touted as the "ideal" hind leg — but that is only true at rest. In movement, hind limb form A delivers thrust without wobble and therefore is less prone than this form to pathologies such as spavins.

Illustration C shows true cow hocks. A cow-hocked horse lacks width between the stifles (horizontal bars), often has small, twisted-looking hock joints and stands with nonparallel cannon bones. The toes point out *more* than the stifles, which look sunken-in or clamped to the body. Cow-hock starts in the hip and stifle joints and is expressed further down the limb by weak thrust, wobbly hocks, a narrow stance or hocks or fetlocks that brush each other in movement.

inal structural sturdiness (Figure 34). Buyers who are knowledgeable and particular about legs act as indispensible "watchdogs" for the entire horse-breeding industry.

Hindquarters

Primitive: short quarters; "steep" or goose-rumped; overangulated. The total length of the hind limb in a horse is essentially the sum of the lengths of the thigh + gaskin + hind cannon + hind pasterns + hind hoof. Overangulation simply equals long hind legs which bend in a "Z" shape to fit between the hips and the ground. Breeders (especially Thoroughbred breeders) have labored to straighten (i.e., to shorten) the total hind-limb length from its long, primitive condition.

Harmful: coon-footed (usually accompanies extreme post-leggedness, increases chances of strain of suspensory ligament or injury to fetlock when traveling over rough ground); shallow pelvis, narrow hips (especially in mare; increases likelihood of birth trauma, reduces area available for propulsive muscles); stands close behind (when this is a structural condition, it is caused by narrow pelvis); cat-hammed, camped-out (causes great increase in stress on stifle and hock joints and lumbar span of back during locomotion); overbent, sickle or sabre hocks; small hocks, "cut out" under the hock (weakens hock joint); wobbly hocks or bowlegs behind (Figure 31).

Most breeders would add cow hocks to the list (Figure 32), but this is incorrect. Horses are differentiated from other mammals precisely on the basis of the fact that horse hock bones (and stifle joint structure) force them to stand with their hocks pointing inward. In other words, a horse that is not cow-hocked is not horselike; in fact, a horse with "straight" hocks as seen from the rear (see Figure 32b) is likely to move with wobbly, pathology-generating hocks. There are degrees of cow hock: if extreme enough to cause interference (32c), the fault is a serious one, but hocks that face in are not a fault per se.

Likewise, many breeders seem to prefer "straight" hind legs (i.e., a short total hind-limb length) when viewed from the side. When straight hind legs get *too* straight, the animal is said to be post-legged (Figure 33b). This condition predisposes to upward fixation of the patella or "locking stifles" and subtle yet serious movement difficulties which are manifested in the lumbar span of the back.

A different argument applies to the mare in which the rear part of the pelvis (ischia) is so prolonged that it tips the vulva and causes her to require a Caslick's suture in order to carry foals to term. In nature such mares would not survive, and on strictly biological grounds they would be eliminated. However, the very prolongation of the pelvis that causes this reproductive problem also significantly increases the mare's speed and weight-carrying ability.

Other faults, such as hollow above stifles, under-muscled gaskins and some forms of standing close behind, look like structural faults but are merely evidence of low-normal muscular development which can be corrected with exercise.

Not Harmful, But Sometimes Not Preferred: apple-butted; upright hind pasterns. The alternatives — high/low stifle, short/long gaskin and high/low hock

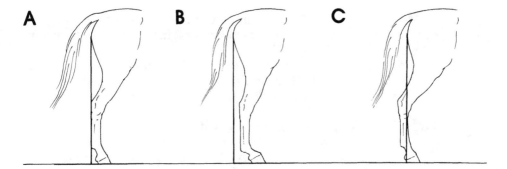

The Right Angle On Hind Legs

Figure 33. How much hind limb angulation is "good" depends to a certain extent upon the specific use you intend to make of a horse. Illustration A (above) shows a hind limb that falls well within the "good" range, one that would be a sound and useful hind limb in almost any current form of competition.

Illustration B shows a *short* or "post-legged" hind limb — one with wide-open angles. This degree of "straightness" predisposes the horse to bony pathologies of the front of the hock joint (spavins), to patellar dysfunction (sticking stifles) and contributes to difficulty in striding up and in loin-coiling at the trot.

Illustration C shows a *long* or "overangulated" hind limb — one with sharp angles. This degree of "crookedness" predisposes the horse to bony and ligamentous pathologies of the back of the hock (spavins, curby hock) and to stifle strain. If you are selecting a racehorse or jumper and must choose between a horse that is post-legged and one that is overangulated, choose the former. For any other activity, choose the latter. Best of all: find another horse that falls in the "good" range, between these extremes of hind-limb length.

— are actually manifestations of the lengths of the individual segments in a horse's hind limbs. Thus, high stifles really mean that a horse has short thighbones. Two horses with different thigh and gaskin lengths necessarily differ in the placement of the stifle and hock joints but might have identical *total* hind-limb lengths. Differently proportioned hind limbs are advantageous for different types of use, which will be explained in greater detail in Volume II.

Balance, Overall Impression

While horsemen tend to think of the "uphill" or "downhill" horse as a mere preference in appearance for horses registered in different breeds, a horse's size, weight and front-to-back balance are actually important summations of his overall conformation (Figure 31).

Primitive: "downhill" overall balance, with the withers lower than the croup (but not greatly lower); short (less than 15 hands); coarse (by today's standards).

Harmful: The withers greatly higher than the croup (extreme "uphill" balance; predisposes to stifle strain and injury); the withers greatly lower than the croup (extreme "downhill" balance; predisposes to injury in lumbar span of back and places undue stress on forelegs); massiveness (over 1,350 lb; it has been very difficult for breeders to produce a heavy horse with enough "bone" by biological standards); extreme height (predisposes to problems in skeletal development and in neuromuscular coordination).

How Much "Bone" Is Enough?

In nature, the weight of a mammal predicts its "bone" circumference (Illustration A). This relationship can be expressed as a mathematical ratio that relates "bone" to weight. For the horse species, the minimum acceptable amount of "bone" is seven inches per 1,000 pounds.

The seven inches/1,000 pounds ratio was developed by surveying the weight and "bone" of thousands of domestic individuals and then comparing the domestic average (seven inches) to similarly conformed and closely related wild equines. For example, the Plains Zebra (*Equus burchelli*) and the Przewalski horse (*Equus caballus przewalskii*) possess *twice as much "bone"* per pound of body mass as domestic horses. Over the last 5,000 years, domestic horses somehow have lost half the "bone" they started with! This is especially significant in light of the fact that no wild equine in its right mind spends a season on the hunter-jumper circuit or treks the length of the hemisphere over every type of terrain.

When averages for different types of domestic horses are studied, the results are even more disturbing. The average figure for what are now considered to be "small" horses —

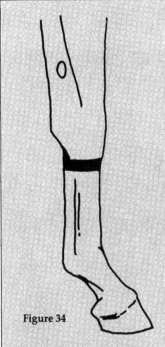

Figure 34

A. The term "bone" actually refers to the circumference, in the live horse, taken with a tape measure around the bone, tendons and skin at the point shown.

B. In 1932, this Argentine Criollo was ridden from Buenos Aires to Washington, DC, and back again, a journey of more than 15,000 miles. Abundant "bone" promotes soundness.

those standing under 15 hands and weighing under 1,000 pounds — nearly equals the "wild" figure. This is not surprising in light of the fact that there were *no horses on Earth larger than this until 500 years ago.* What we consider "small" horses actually defines the norm for the species.

At the upper end of the range of weights found in domestic horses, the average figure for horses standing taller than 16 hands, 2 inches, and weighing in excess of 1,350 pounds is only *five inches* per 1,000 pounds.

While "soundness" in horses depends on many internal and external factors, including muscle quality, circulatory efficiency, the laminar and trabecular structure of each bone of the limbs and hoof-horn quality, the amount of "bone" is itself a significant determinant of soundness. This is because structural stability and stress reduction in the support elements of a horse obey the same physical laws as the support elements of a skyscraper.

The ability of a support pylon to bear weight is a function of its circumference *but not of its density.* A very dense bone actually can be a brittle bone. Arabian horses tend to be sound-legged horses not because they have "dense bone" but because they rarely exceed Nature's limits — 15 hands, 1,000 pounds.

The lessons to be drawn from this discussion are of vital importance to today's breeder and consumer. They are:

● If you want a sound horse, avoid excessive "elegance" or "refinement" in the limbs. Make sure the horse has at least seven inches of bone per 1,000 pounds of body weight.

● If you want a sound horse, you'll be very wise to purchase one shorter than 16 hands, 2 inches, and weighing less than 1,350 pounds.

● Don't expect a draft horse (or any horse weighing more than 1,350 pounds) to stay sound in a career involving jumping or repetitive arena activities such as dressage. For the same reason, very large horses also are unsuitable for cross-country or endurance riding.

Figure 35. Behind each new foal lies a heritage that reflects the three key components of all breeding decisions: Pedigree, the history of the foal's ancestors; Performance record, the documented accomplishments of those ancestors; and Phenotype, the visible appearance and behavior of the sire, dam and other related individuals. Attention to all three facets gives the breeder the best opportunity for reproducible success in his program.

Chapter 6

In Order To Form A More Perfect Union

Pedigree, Performance, Phenotype: What constitutes a valuable horse?

Much as everyone might wish it, no one yet has been able to bottle and sell a magic formula guaranteed to produce champion foals 100 percent of the time. Nor is it likely that anyone will provide the potion to achieve that breeder's fantasy. Rather, the purpose of this chapter is to provide a balanced view of the various "angles" from which breeding decisions can be approached. If you're planning to buy a horse, you should understand the actual impact of these factors on the value of the individual horse being presented to you for sale.

Three main factors breeders most often consider in planning matings are a horse's **Pedigree**, the **Performance** record of the horse and his relatives and his **Phenotype**. We'll define each of these elements, discuss common misconceptions about them and then examine the utility and reliability of each — how easy it is to use and what it means in terms of heritability.

Heritability does not mean how likely a trait is to be inherited. Instead, heritability means what fraction of a trait seen or tested in an individual is due to environmental influence, and what fraction is actually attributable to the biochemical blueprints in the genetic complement of each cell (genome). The ideal criterion to use in making breeding decisions would give a perfectly accurate index of heritability and would be capable of exposing the actual genome of a horse. Knowing that, the breeder could optimize the environment and then would be close to obtaining the total potential of any foal. Can any one factor or combination of factors predict a foal's potential?

Pedigree

The pedigree of an individual is a written (or oral) representation of the sequence and degree of relatedness of its ancestors (Figure 36). Every horse has ancestors, but not every horse has a pedigree. Certified pedigrees, which usually bear some kind of official seal, are produced by political organizations called registries. The employees of a registry are experts in, and have ready access to, books or other documents which list the names, ancestry and relatedness of individual animals that are of special interest to them. Photographs or paintings of these horses often are included in this archival data base.

The earliest members of a designated bloodline, from which all or most of the horses of interest descend, are called "foundation" individuals. A foundation horse can be any sire or dam that the officials of a registry wish to designate. Some are recognized during their lifetime; many, posthumously. A number of foundation individuals have superior phenotypes, some have outstanding performance records, while others are distinguished solely by having been imported at a certain time from a specific remote or inaccessible locality and gain value by having the same kind of rarity that characterizes diamonds, the Mona Lisa or some breeds of dogs. Yet like a Ming vase, the rare or blue-blooded horse may be beautiful but physically fragile.

Owning a "papered" or "pedigreed" animal has a kind of snob appeal for some folks; for them, the mere possession of this political document implies that a pedigreed animal is better than a nonpedigreed one. In a slightly different sense, a pedigree is also an entry ticket because at certain horse shows (breed shows), only those animals possessing certified pedigrees can compete or be exhibited.

Degrees of relatedness: There are four methods

which a horse breeder can utilize in a breeding program: inbreeding, linebreeding, outcrossing and
crossbreeding. An *inbred* horse is one whose parents
are more closely related to each other than would be
expected for any two randomly selected horses. A
linebred horse is one whose parents are both more or
less closely related to some (usually famous) sire or
dam. Breeders like to market a horse as "double
Comet" or as having "three lines to Wing Com-
mander." Because the market value of a "famous"
name may be elevated only for a short time during
which everyone furiously breeds to the currently
fashionable stallion and his sons, linebred horses are
often the most inbred of all.

In genetic terms, the practices of inbreeding and
linebreeding are means by which horse breeders can
increase the degree of homozygosity in their bloodstock. Homozygosity means specifically that the two
information-equivalent copies (alleles) of one "volume" in the equine genetic library are identical. An
individual with a high degree of homozygosity has
many identical volumes.

To determine the degree of homozygosity of an
individual, a geneticist compares the two DNA
strands or chromatids that make up each chromo-
some and attempts to document how many base-pair
sequences (loci) are identical in both strands. In a tiny
minority of cases, this can be done directly by chemi-
cal means.

Practically speaking, however, a horse's genes
usually have to be inspected indirectly — by seeing or
testing for their presence in the body. The usual
method for doing this is the *test cross*, in which unlike
parents are mated many times to see what percentage
of offspring with outstanding characteristics they
produce. Of course, this method gives rapid results
only with organisms like fruit flies, which reproduce
quickly and prolifically. For "slower" animals such as
horses and cattle, a modified crossing procedure
called a *breeding test* can be performed (unfortunately
for the horse-breeding industry, such testing has
been performed far more often in cattle than with
horses, because unit production of such qualities as
meat and milk is easily measured and analyzed).

In a typical breeding test, a stallion is mated
every year for five years to the same group of 10 to 30
mares. Of the first 50 foals produced, if all have a de-

sirable characteristic (or lack an undesirable one), the stallion is considered statistically to be homozygous at the gene locus responsible for production of that trait.

More than one trait — indeed, every visible or testable characteristic — can be examined during a breeding test; the more like traits all of the first 50 foals possess, the greater the probable degree of homozygosity of the stallion.

An *outcrossed* horse is one produced by mating a sire from one bloodline to a dam from another. A *crossbred* horse is the same as an outcrossed horse, except that the term crossbred usually is reserved for the get of a sire registered as a member of one breed out of a dam registered in another.

Outcrossing is the horse breeder's main means of obtaining variability or of introducing desirable characteristics that are absent from an inbred bloodline. It is also the only means of obtaining that genetic-biochemical serendipity called hybrid vigor. Hybrid corn grows taller, resists disease better, has larger kernels and straighter stalks than the corn-plant lines crossed to produce it.

Among equines, mules have the same characteristic of being surprisingly superior to sire and dam (no puns about "ears" intended). A mule foal is produced by mating a jack and a mare, individuals whose alleles haven't met for more than a million years. Their common ancestor lived so long ago and their bloodlines are so unrelated that jacks and mares belong to two different species (for this reason, mules are usually sterile, just like hybrid corn).

Horse foals come only from horses; outcrossing within a species results in less hybrid vigor than seen in mules, but the positive effect of outcrossing on size, phenotypic quality, disease resistance, racing speed, etc., is nevertheless frequently documented.

Big names, top male and tail female: Despite the mesmerizing effect that sophisticated marketing or mere repetition of a name can have on consumers, every horse in a pedigree has a statistically limited effect on (that is, percent genetic contribution to) its offspring. The percentage effects of each individual in a pedigree are shown in Figure 36. The two ways to increase the likelihood that a given foal will be like a famous ancestor are either to repeat that name often in a pedigree or to increase the degree of relatedness of the famous individual to the foal (i.e., to bring it up close in the pedigree, as from grandsire to sire).

In a similar fashion, some breeders are fascinated by the effects of the tail-female or top-male line on foals. Just as with famous horses, when a breeder pays a lot of adulatory attention to details of the phenotype, behavior, prepotency or performance record of the tail-female line, he's likely to congratulate himself by discovering that all the things he expected to find are true. The problem is that facts or trends evident in the tail-female (or top-male) line are on average no more true or significant to the foal at hand than are the facts or trends characteristic of the top-female or tail-male line.

Prepotency: Not a few horsemen believe that prepotency in a stallion is related to the force with which he ejaculates or the volume of his ejaculate. Others believe that prepotency is a synonym for genetic dominance or the ability to settle mares. In actuality, prepotency is the ability of a stallion to get, or a mare to produce, foals that are uniform. It's good also if they are similar to the designated parent, but in judging a "get of sire" or "produce of dam" class, it is a greater fault for the foals to be of various builds, athletic capabilities and temperaments than for all of them to look alike but different from their parent.

The stallion that wins a get of sire class actually has won a prepotency award; he has proven that he is a consistent producer even if he doesn't get foals that look like himself. If such a stallion produces good-quality offspring, his services are easy to market; for the same reason, a prepotent broodmare of good quality is desired by every breeder.

Dominance: Dominance is nowhere indicated on a pedigree. Well-advertised or big-name horses are not dominant, except perhaps politically. Stallions are not dominant to broodmares, except in a behavioral sense (usually).

Genetic dominance is a function of frequency; the more often a certain trait appears in a population of horses, the more dominant is the allele or group of alleles that produces it. Dominance in the genetic sense is a word that properly can be applied to an allele but not to an individual. No individual possesses or expresses 100 percent dominant alleles.

The utility of pedigree in a breeding program: Utilizing pedigree information largely depends upon

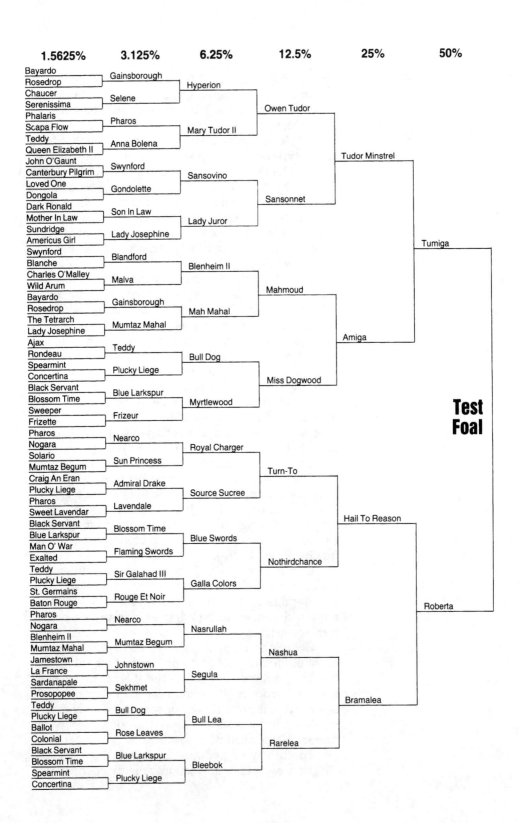

1.5625%	3.125%	6.25%	12.5%	25%	50%

Bayardo
Rosedrop
Chaucer
Serenissima
Phalaris
Scapa Flow
Teddy
Queen Elizabeth II
John O'Gaunt
Canterbury Pilgrim
Loved One
Dongola
Dark Ronald
Mother In Law
Sundridge
Americus Girl
Swynford
Blanche
Charles O'Malley
Wild Arum
Bayardo
Rosedrop
The Tetrarch
Lady Josephine
Ajax
Rondeau
Spearmint
Concertina
Black Servant
Blossom Time
Sweeper
Frizette
Pharos
Nogara
Solario
Mumtaz Begum
Craig An Eran
Plucky Liege
Pharos
Sweet Lavendar
Black Servant
Blue Larkspur
Man O' War
Exalted
Teddy
Plucky Liege
St. Germains
Baton Rouge
Pharos
Nogara
Blenheim II
Mumtaz Mahal
Jamestown
La France
Sardanapale
Prosopopee
Teddy
Plucky Liege
Ballot
Colonial
Black Servant
Blossom Time
Spearmint
Concertina

Gainsborough
Selene
Pharos
Anna Bolena
Swynford
Gondolette
Son In Law
Lady Josephine
Blandford
Malva
Gainsborough
Mumtaz Mahal
Teddy
Plucky Liege
Blue Larkspur
Frizeur
Nearco
Sun Princess
Admiral Drake
Lavendale
Blossom Time
Flaming Swords
Sir Galahad III
Rouge Et Noir
Nearco
Mumtaz Begum
Johnstown
Sekhmet
Bull Dog
Rose Leaves
Blue Larkspur
Plucky Liege

Hyperion
Mary Tudor II
Sansovino
Lady Juror
Blenheim II
Mah Mahal
Bull Dog
Myrtlewood
Royal Charger
Source Sucree
Blue Swords
Galla Colors
Nasrullah
Segula
Bull Lea
Bleebok

Owen Tudor
Sansonnet
Mahmoud
Miss Dogwood
Turn-To
Nothirdchance
Nashua
Rarelea

Tudor Minstrel
Amiga
Hail To Reason
Bramalea

Tumiga
Roberta

Test Foal

Figure 36. A pedigree documents the sequence and degree of relatedness of horses shown in it. An inbred horse is one whose parents are more closely related to each other than statistically would be expected for any two randomly selected horses. The "impact" or percent genetic contribution of any ancestor is strictly controlled by (1) where in the pedigree it occurs and (2) the number of times it occurs. In this pedigree, horses that are both "close up" and appear several times, like Plucky Liege and Bull Dog, make the greatest contribution to the foal's genome.

There are a number of methods for assessing the impact of any given ancestor. One is the "contribution" method. To calculate the impact of Plucky Liege by this method, simply scan the left-hand column in the pedigree for her name, which appears three times. This gives three "contributions" of 1.5625% (3 x 1.5625 = 4.6875%).

Next, scan the column with the next-highest value, and continue in similar manner until all columns have been checked. Plucky Liege picks up another two "contributions" of 3.125% in the sixth-pedigree generation (2 x 3.125 = 6.25%). Her name, however, does not appear in any other columns, so her total percent contribution to the test foal is 4.6875 + 6.25 = 10.9375%.

Another method is to utilize part of the output produced by the Inbreeding Algorithm written by Richard Trower of Richill Morgan Horse Farm in Adalanto, California. This program calculates the "contribution by ancestor" of certain horses whose names are repeated in a pedigree. For mathematical reasons, the "contribution" calculated for an ancestor by this program is lower than that derivable by the first method. For the moment, however, it is sufficient to note that both methods produce an identical ranking of the contribution of repeated ancestors.

Contribution to test foal, ranked in order of genetic impact:

Greatest Impact:	Second Greatest:	Third Greatest:	Fourth Greatest:	Fifth Greatest:
Bull Dog	Blue Larkspur	Blossom Time	Mumtaz Mahal	Bayardo⋆
Plucky Liege	Pharos	Gainsborough⋆	Black Servant	Spearmint
	Blenheim II		Mumtaz Begum⋆	Concertina
	Teddy			

⋆Not ranked by the computer algorithm

a breeder's ability to memorize and converse in terms of "names." Many breeders become as good at reciting pedigrees as baseball fans are at quoting box scores. Especially in breeds where initial letters, names or parts of names are consistently repeated in bloodlines, pedigrees become more useful because relationships are more evident. This is why Thoroughbred pedigrees are harder to learn and use than those of Warmbloods (which utilize consistent initial letters) or American Saddlebreds or Quarter Horses (whose names may incorporate those of famous ancestors, such as Peter McCue, Denmark, Stonewall or Leo).

The ability to quote names at bewildering speed, however, is not related to the ability or power to breed good-quality foals. The quality of a horse or foal is not a product of its pedigree; rather, quality and value only can be assessed *by looking at the horse or foal itself*. Statistically speaking, 25 percent of all foals fail to "live up to" their pedigrees, and another 25 percent make "usable riding horses." In other words, 50 percent of all foals are mediocre or poor *compared to their own ancestors.* The breeder who values every foal as a breeding animal just because of its pedigree is not only kidding himself but also doing a grave disservice to a species that is already extinct in the wild and whose future is entirely in our hands.

The words emphasized in the paragraph above are important because what matters in a pedigree is which ancestors are in it; not because they themselves were pedigreed individuals, but because they were individuals of good quality who were well conformed or who demonstrated in competition that they "had what it takes" to succeed.

A pedigree is not a tool for predicting the future; it is a historical document. But when the family tree of an individual is replete with well-conformed ancestors who had meaningful performance records, this represents the best expectation of genetic excellence that a breeder can obtain. In such a bloodline, even the 25 to 50 percent of foals who are culled may be of better quality than the best-quality foals of a bloodline founded on and propagated by phenotypically less superior individuals.

Performance Record

What's a meaningful performance record? There are many forms of equine competition today, especially in the US. The rules or the nature of some competitions make their results more "objective" or more "biologically meaningful" to horse breeders than others. To understand why this distinction in kinds of performance record is important, we must reaffirm our understanding of, and our commitment to, preserving the basic nature of horses.

A person might train a horse to hop like a bunny, pace like a camel or swim like a dolphin, and might then establish a breeding program that selected horses that performed best in the capacities of bunny, camel or dolphin; but he then would not be breeding horses. Rather, he would be merely manipulating the phenotype. The power of selective breeding is so great that with each passing year, it becomes more important for the majority of horse breeders to recognize "horselike activities" as the only justifiable basis for the establishment of performance, quality and value criteria.

Horselike activities: All equine competitions are artificial, but some retain, in greater or smaller measure, requirements that force successful participants to function as their wild ancestors did. The artificiality of competitions usually revolves around the simplicity or unidimensionality of the skill required. Therefore, competitions requiring diverse equine skills are more valuable in assessing horselike athletic capability than others. The following column lists such activities in descending order of diversity and "horselikeness":

1. Three-day event
2. Field hunter, point-to-point racer
3. Endurance, distances over 50 miles
4. Flat racer, distances greater than 1.5 miles
5. Competitive trail
6. Open jumper
7. Stock horse or "Western riding horse"
8. Dressage or reining
9. Polo
10. Cutting

Success in any of these activities is strong indication of equine athletic ability. (Success in some activities which are normally noncompetitive can also be used: stock work or riding fence, logging or plowing, police or ranger horse, pack horse.) On the other hand, examples of some activities that are not very "horselike" include gaited riding, harness racing, modern "park" and "three-gaited" competition, show hunter, sprint racing, parade work and pulling contests. Success in these activities doesn't mean your horses aren't valuable, only that these successes won't help you very much in evaluating your stock *as horses*.

Intensity: Some competitive activities require intense or prolonged energy output. Success in these activities gives indication of superior physiological capabilities. A list of intense physical activities includes:

1. Three-day event
2. Racing: sprint or "classic" distances, steeplechase or timed gymkhana events
3. Field hunter, point-to-point racer
4. Harness racing (especially heat racing)
5. "Park" competition
6. Five-gaited competition
7. Dressage competition, especially higher levels
8. Endurance, especially moderate distances, and open division competitive trail riding
9. Open jumper
10. Pulling contest

In contrast, some low-intensity activities include Western pleasure competition, pleasure driving and hacking or cubbing.

Objectivity: The value of some kinds of competition is greater because the results are determined objectively and reported as numbers which can be manipulated statistically. A list of usefully scored activities, in descending order of objectivity, includes:

1. Endurance (time, P&R scores/recovery times, soundness exams)
2. Flat racing, all forms, including gymkhana (time)
3. Harness racing, trotter and pacer (time)
4. Three-day event (time, recovery times, soundness evaluation, faults at jumping, dressage score)
5. Open jumper (time and faults, heights cleared)
6. Puissance (heights cleared)
7. European-style halter competition ("on the triangle" with a stringently applied point-rating system)
8. Dressage competition (detailed and fairly uniformly applied point-rating system)
9. Cutting (fairly uniformly applied point-rating system)
10. Reining (point-rating system)

Such events as show hunter, Western pleasure, "park" or three-gaited competition, by contrast, traditionally have been evaluated in subjective terms.

The value of a performance record thus depends upon the division of competition or type of athletic activity in which success is achieved, not merely upon whether an activity looks sufficiently active. When horselike, intense, objectively evaluated performance data are recorded in a pedigree, they achieve their greatest meaning and utility, for then such records stand in known degrees of temporal and physiological unity.

A performance superstar who stands at the head of a pedigree packed with consistent performers is doing what his breeder hoped for and is qualifying himself to carry on a reliable, good-quality bloodline. A performance superstar who stands alone or "comes out of nowhere" may represent a rare and valuable new matching of alleles.

Because a good performance record is worth more than a pedigree alone, such a horse is worth a breeding trial to determine to what degree he is prepotent. If the horse produces uniform, good-quality offspring, he becomes the founder of a new line, family or breed. The breeder who gelds a colt "because based on his pedigree he has no right to look that good or perform that well" is just as foolish as the one who saves every pedigreed foal.

Phenotype

The phenotype is the appearance of a horse's body or behavior which is visible or testable. *The phenotype is the only aspect of an individual on which selection can act.*

Natural selection: Mother Nature's way of breeding horses is to place all the live bodies in a more or less stringent environment and let the ones who survive to breeding age fight it out among themselves. Behavioral surveys show that in wild and feral horse herds, only about one in 100 fertile males actually ever breeds a mare.

The rules of this process — called natural selection — were discovered by Darwin and Wallace in the middle of the 19th century. Breeders who hope to make intelligent use of phenotype in their breeding programs must understand these rules also, because selection in the stud differs from that in nature only in that it is, potentially, far more efficient.

● There are a lot of different phenotypes, or as Darwin put it, "there exists variability."

● Some of the phenotypes are better suited for a given lifestyle or athletic activity than others. In other words, considering the whole of the animal kingdom, some body types are best suited for living in swamps; others, on mountains; others, in the desert. Some are structured to run; others, to hop, fly or swim.

● The phenotypes best suited to a given environment are possessed by the individuals who survive in that environment long enough to breed. Those with less suitable phenotypes either will not survive to breed or will do so, on average, less frequently than those structured ideally.

● The result of the foregoing process will be that, sooner or later, the majority of phenotypes living in a certain environment or committed to a certain lifestyle will be the descendants of the best-structured ancestors.

Sounds just like what a breeder would like to have happen in the marketplace, doesn't it? Wouldn't every breeder like his stallion to be the best-adapted "survivor" who gets all the mares? Breeding by selection on the phenotype is the most powerful technique for obtaining and improving athletic capability in horses.

The assumptions that lie behind this breeding strategy are first, that genotype is related to phenotype ("what you see is what you get," at least after a breeding test), and second, that athletic capability is detectable in and determined by the phenotype. There are breeders who don't believe one or both of these precepts, but the whole science of evolutionary biology accepts them as "givens." Many studies on other species have documented the reliability of these precepts, and the success of German horse producers, who for the past century have systematically followed this advice, first offered to them by Prussian stud master Gustav Rau at the turn of the century, is a case in point.

Breeding by phenotype: If you base breeding decisions purely on phenotype, you had better plan on outcrossing, because being forced to choose sire and dam from among suitable registered animals may prove too limiting. In nature, only physical or geographical barriers act to limit outcrossing. Where such barriers exist, regional forms called *subspecies* acquire distinctive phenotypes that adapt them specifically to the environment or lifestyle of a region. In parallel fashion, practical limits to horse transport still cause detectable and consistent differences in horses bred in Europe, Asia, Australia and the Americas.

One of the keys to the success of European horse breeders has been their openness to what most American breeders would consider very wide outcrossing or experimental crossbreeding. The mating of markedly different phenotypes always results in a hodgepodge of produce. Yet somewhere among a stallion's first 50 foals, one or a few may have just the phenotype desired. Breeders can greatly increase the likelihood of this happening — they can beat Mother Nature at her own game — when they:

■ Correctly analyze the conformation of sire and dam

■ Understand the specific relationships between conformational features and performance capabilities

■ Design phenotypically "interlocking" matings. In practice, this usually depends upon identifying a phenotypic weakness in a broodmare, such as upright shoulder or long back, and mating her to a stallion with a sloping shoulder and a short back.

Figure 37. You can turn to an advertisement in almost any equine publication to see a photograph of good or excellent bloodstock presented at its best. For comparison, this is an example of a "marginal" broodmare, one that falls just over the 50 percent cutoff into the "acceptable" range. There are no outstanding faults, and the mare's structural parts flow together harmoniously. However, there are also no outstandingly excellent features. For this reason, choosing a phenotypically complementary stallion for this mare will be difficult. He might be an all-around outstanding individual — but for such a stallion, a better broodmare probably could be found. Or he might possess one or two features, such as shoulder or loin coupling, that are much better than those of this mare. In that case, only some of his sons and daughters out of this mare could be expected to improve on their parents.

The crucial act of selection is culling. Even if only phenotypically superior foals are kept for the second round of breeding, their degree of homozygosity is still likely to be low. This means that they themselves are likely to produce a variety of phenotypes. At this point, the breeder has a choice. The quick route is to breed the phenotypically superior but heterozygous foal to a physically complementary individual from a bloodline known to be of much greater homozygosity.

The slow route is to continue to outcross and stringently select. This is what the European Warmblood breeders have done. Within a few generations, enough horses can be produced to make backcrossing (mating a stallion to its own granddam, for example) a possible means of establishing homozygous (and hopefully prepotent) lines. Phenotypically excellent horses, from whatever source, can still be brought in and are best used in phenotypically complementary matings. Meanwhile, the process continually upgrades the quality and athletic capability of produce, which in turn increases their market value.

When breeders consistently cull in response to stringently applied phenotypic standards, both upgrading and the establishment of prepotent lines is far more efficient than in nature. When performance as well as phenotypic criteria are utilized in establishing standards and in making culling decisions, the results are as biologically meaningful as breeders can make them.

"P's" In Perspective

All three "P's," **P**edigree, **P**erformance record and **P**henotype, are useful in horse breeding, but a pedigree that contains only the names of ancestors is the least important of the three. A pedigree becomes valuable to the degree that it contains performance records or shows phenotypes (a photographic pedigree).

Performance records, in turn, are most valuable when they are numerical, objectively derived, based on success in intense or physically demanding activities and biologically meaningful.

A photo pedigree in which every ancestor is represented by conformation shots — front, back and side — is the most powerful tool for analyzing patterns of phenotypic inheritance within bloodlines, families and breeds.

Appendix A

Equine Parts Inventory

External Points Of The Horse

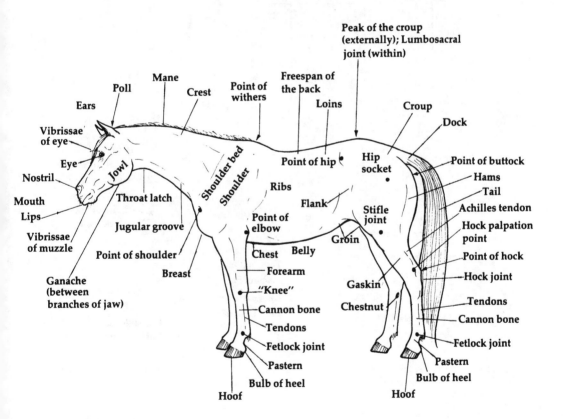

Note: "Hindquarters" includes all parts behind and below lumbosacral joint; "Quarters" includes all parts bounded by the lumbosacral joint, point of buttock, hams, stifle joint and point of hip.

Appendix B

Equine Parts Inventory

Internal Points Of The Horse

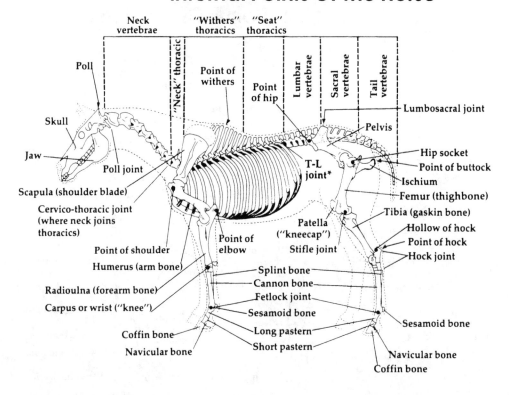

Note: In standard anatomy texts, divisions of the thoracic vertebrae are not recognized. The divisions "neck," "withers" and "seat" are functional categories useful to riders.

*Thoracico-lumbar joint

The symbols ● and ▼ mark "palpation points," where known bone parts lie just under the skin surface and are easy to see. The same points are marked on the companion figure. By using these points, you can "peg out" the skeleton in your own horse — no X-rays needed! This is also how the skeletal proportions of the horses shown in Figure 2 were found. Try it!

Principles of Conformation Analysis

Volume II

*For Sadie, my friend
and patient teacher*

Volume II

Figure 1. When palpating a horse's back, use the pads of your fingers, and cover the whole expanse from withers to loins. In these two photos, I am pressing firmly to demonstrate the effect of an ill-fitting saddle; when palpating to find "knots" and cold spots, you do not need to dent the flesh. In photo A, gouging the withers near or under the fore arch elicits fasciculation (vibrating waves of muscle contraction), even from this otherwise normal back. In B, gouging the loins elicits the same involuntary but debilitating reaction.

Chapter 1

How To Look At A Horse's Back

Examining the seat of equine performance

This volume of *Principles Of Conformation Analysis* continues the theme established in the first volume of this series — the functional importance of the horse's back. While the horse's forelimbs are the structural equivalent of the wheels and suspension system in an automobile, and his hindquarters are equivalent to the motor and drive train, his back acts as the transmission — the part which connects the motor to the wheels and which serves to regulate the amount of power that flows through.

Nobody wants to drive a car that has flat tires, bent rims or a sagging suspension, although in an emergency it is possible to do so. Likewise, a car without a motor isn't going to go far — unless you push it over the top of a hill, whereupon it will travel as far as gravity allows. However, a car without a transmission is truly nonfunctional: revving the motor or turning the steering wheel will get you exactly nowhere. In a similar way, it's important to realize that not all the weaknesses and lamenesses which afflict the ridden horse are native to the legs — the back is quite often literally and figuratively the "seat" of the problem.

A Feel For Tonus

Even before you begin to look at a horse's back, you should learn how to feel (palpate) it. There's no other way to determine the *tonus* — the natural muscle tone — of a given back. Physiologically speaking, tonus is the slight continuous contraction which is present at all times in live muscle tissue. You can feel the tonus present in your arm muscles right now simply by pressing your left forearm with your right index finger. See how the muscle tissue springs back to shape when you remove your finger? That's due to tonus. If you're seated and relaxed as you read this paragraph, it won't take very much force to dent your arm muscles. The slight contraction in your arm muscles, which results in a slight springiness, is called resting tonus. If you are sound asleep when tested for tonus, the dent in your arm would still spring back, but not quite as quickly as when you are awake. Tonus falls still further in a comatose person. A dead body has no tonus; pressure makes a dent, but the dent doesn't spring back.

At the other end of the spectrum lie excited and fearful states. Tense the muscles of your left forearm, and again try to dent them. Now it's much harder to make a dent, and when you remove your pressing finger, the muscles spring back to shape almost instantly.

You've just examined the wide range of tonus which your own body can produce. However, there are also variations in resting tonus, which is the starting or "zero point" of this range. These variations show up in comparing one person, or one horse, to another. Most important for judging excellence and suitability in a horse, increases in resting tonus tend to accompany increases in muscular *reactivity* — the ability of a given muscle to fire the instant it receives electrochemical stimulation. Just as some people have exceptionally fast reflexes, some horses have muscles which are able to react to stimulation exceptionally fast. Almost without exception, horses which have a high resting tonus show fast reflexes. Breeds which typically exhibit high resting tonus include the Arabian, Akhal-Teke, Thoroughbred and bloodlines of American Quarter Horses especially bred for sprint racing and cutting.

At the other end of the spectrum, the draft and

warmblood breeds usually show low resting tonus. The "buttery" back of the warmblood suits it for dressage, while the same series of exercises can be most difficult to execute on an Arabian. On the other hand, trying to turn back a steer with an American Saddlebred or a European warmblood is usually a losing proposition. In short, resting tonus and the accompanying reactivity form the physiological "background" for the suitability of each breed and individual for a given sport or activity.

With practice, you can obtain a good idea of tonus and reactivity simply by feeling your horse's back. What does tonus in the horse feel like? Tie or have someone hold your horse in a safe, quiet place. If you wish, go through your usual grooming routine. After you've finished brushing the horse, set your tools aside. Pat your horse on the shoulder and then slide your hand, palm down, up onto his back. Palpation is done with the pads of the fingers and thumb by sliding them along the skin with the same motion and the same amount of pressure that it would take to rub a glob of peanut butter off a countertop. This amount of pressure will dent the skin and muscles of the back without poking or gouging them (Figure 1).

Go over the entire back, from directly under the withers in front of where your saddle sits, all the way back to where the loins join the croup. Most horses' backs are fairly wide: feel from the widest point of the ribs of the left side, to the widest point of the ribs on the right side. By practicing back palpation this way, you'll accomplish several things at once:

1) You can compare the "quality" or "feel" of normal resting tonus from one individual to another. With practice, you will get an accurate idea of the characteristic tonus of different breeds.

2) You will become intimate with the bony and muscular anatomy of the horse's back. As a guide, refer to the anatomical drawings in Appendix A.

3) You'll be able to locate bony and muscular abnormalities and asymmetries.

Is This a Good Back?

The precise nature of abnormalities of the horse's back is best determined by a qualified veterinarian. However, from palpation you can develop a general idea of what may be wrong.

Abnormalities in the horse's back are revealed by the same standard signs seen in all other body zones — swelling, heat, pain and abnormal tonus. Swelling can be seen and felt; heat (or "cold spots") and zones of excessively high tonus ("knots") can also be felt. Pain is manifested by your horse's reactions to varying pressure — during palpation, saddling or even grooming. Such reactions range from pinned ears, rolling eyes, head tossing and attempts to bite or kick to the classic so-called "cold-backed" reaction in which the horse sinks down, even falls to his knees, in an attempt to avoid pressure on his back. A "cold-backed" horse may be impossible to saddle unless the tack is put on in a set order, and he may need to be longed in order to "get the kinks out" before being mounted. Such signs signify much more than "quirky behavior" — they are the horse's way of telling you that something in the saddle area is (or has been) causing him discomfort or pain.

Visual Inspection

Now that you've gotten close enough to the horse to give his back a thorough examination by feel, it's time to step back to take a look at his conformation. Based on the proportions you discover in this analytical look, you'll decide whether the horse's back is conformed correctly for the sport or activity you have in mind. Keep in mind, however, that a horse with a problem-free back still may not be suitable for you.

Look at a horse's back from three perspectives: the left side, the right side and the top. Viewing the horse from the top is essential, and can be done either by standing on a chair placed out of kicking range behind the horse or by standing on the hood of your car

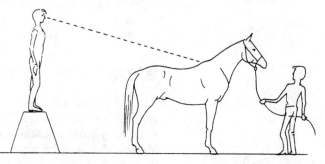

Figure 2. How to visually inspect a horse's back from above.

or a fence (Figure 2).

The most important feature to look for in top view is left-to-right symmetry. In order to accurately assess symmetry, the horse must stand absolutely squarely, with an equal amount of weight on all four feet. Once the horse's feet are "square," ask the handler to gently position the horse's nose exactly in front of the center of his chest.

From your elevated perspective, you should see a ruler-straight topline, all the way from the poll to the dock. In addition, the muscle masses of the left side of the horse should be equal to those of the right side. If they aren't, or if the horse's nose needs to be off to the left or right in order for him to look straight from the top, the horse is asymmetrical in build (Figure 3).

The severity of asymmetry varies. In making this judgment, remember that a slight amount of left-to-right asymmetry is normal for all animals, and people too. For example, the left side of your face is not a mirror image of the right side. Thus, in some horses, part of the mane falls to the left while the rest of it falls to the right. This is indeed a sign of asymmetry, but in most cases the degree of asymmetry which causes it is slight and has little or no effect on the horse's performance.

What you are looking for in this examination are obvious kinks, offsets or twists in the bony or muscular components of the topline. If you're pretty sure that that is what you're seeing in top view, refer to the front-limb section of this volume for further methods of detecting asymmetries.

The movement of the horse also helps to confirm a diagnosis of asymmetrical build. When led in hand, the horse with grossly asymmetrical build cannot move straight forward and will constantly drift, crab-like, to one side. In more subtle cases, the horse may consistently refuse to take one lead when longed in a circle. Under saddle, the asymmetrical horse feels as if he has a big hole on one side of him; he's always trying to bump or shift his rider into this hole. Canter departures and turns toward the side with the hole are easy; to the other side, they are much more difficult or impossible.

Severe asymmetries of this kind are congenital or developmental and may primarily affect either the vertebral column or any of the bones which make up the limbs. In most instances, such an individual

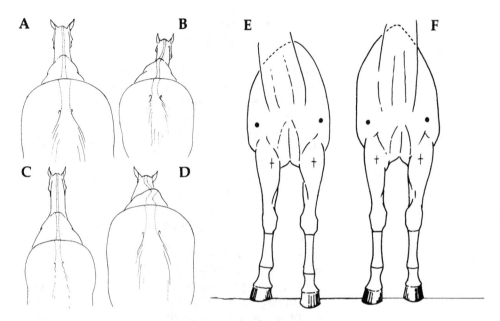

Figure 3. Visual inspection of the horse's back from above may reveal abnormalities. A, most horses look like this — when their feet are "squared up" below and the nose is positioned in front of the breast, the topline from poll to dock is ruler-straight. B, this 12-year-old Anglo-Arabian gelding's topline cannot be made straight even when his feet are square. Physical examination revealed that his right foreleg is about one inch shorter than his left. C, this is how the same gelding looked after physical therapy (a program of being stepped sideways over ground poles) and corrective shoeing by farrier Anthony Gonzales. D, an 8-year-old Arabian gelding with primary scoliosis (curvature of the spine). Despite his spinal deformity, he became a champion hunter-hack, though difficult to ride. His legs are all the same length. E, front view of 12-year-old Anglo-Arabian gelding before therapy and corrective shoeing. F, same horse after correction.

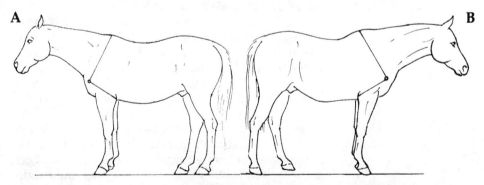

Figure 4. Left and right views of 12-year-old Anglo-Arabian gelding before correction. The gelding's right front leg is one inch shorter than his left. A, "normal" side of horse; the angle formed at the point of shoulder is 93 degrees. B, "short" side of horse; the angle at the point of shoulder is 88 degrees, indicating that this horse compensated for his deformity by compressing his right forelimb, which is evident in front view (Figures 3E, 3F). One of the goals of physical therapy was to stretch the muscles of his right arm and open the shoulder angle on this side.

should be eliminated from further consideration for purchase or breeding.

In Side View

If careful scrutiny of the horse's topline reveals — as it does in most cases — no abnormalities, you can step down from your elevated vantage point and walk around to the right side of the horse. From this angle, you're looking for four main features: the shape and condition of the loins, the shape and condition of the withers, the length of the back in relation to the length of the whole horse, and the internal proportions of the back. When you repeat this procedure from the left side, make one final ground-level check for symmetry (Figure 4). In the exercises that follow, you'll begin learning to judge conformation by example, as you examine the horse's back both from the top and from the sides.

The Back: Lab Exercise 1

A Look At The Loin

Its structure determines how well a horse can move

In "What Kind Of An Animal Is A Horse?" (Chapter 1 of Volume I), I discussed the evolutionary and functional importance of the loin area or "coupling" in horses. Figure 5 shows the horse's lumbosacral joint (LS), which is the bone structure that actually forms the coupling. This joint is *the* most important one in the horse's body for determining the ability to move well. That's why this book begins with the loin, instead of dealing with the horse's head or front legs.

Analysis

Horse #1: This mare's loin is short and strong; the topline over the lumbosacral joint is smooth; the joint itself is well placed. An ideally placed lumbosacral joint lies as far forward as is anatomically possible — on a line connecting the left and right points of hip. This makes the croup bone (the sacrum) as long

L-S joint in front view

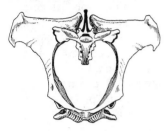

Side view of L-S joint

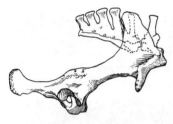

Figure 5. Front and side views of the bony anatomy of the horse's lumbosacral (LS) joint. Top, horse's head toward the viewer; bottom, horse's head to the right.

as possible which confers a great lever advantage to the horse when he is asked to shorten his underline and flex the LS joint during any movement or exercise requiring collection. At the same time, placing the LS joint far forward shortens the lumbar span of the back. This is good because while the lumbar span is necessary for coiling the loins during collection, it is also the weakest part of the horse's back. Only a minimum length of loin is necessary for loin coiling.

The view from above confirms our observations from the side. A short loin forms a broad triangle. From the side, a strong loin shows no peak or undulation in the topline overlying the LS joint. The upper profile of the back in this area is arched slightly upward.

Horse #2: This mare's loin is long and her back is long, too. The placement of her lumbosacral joint is poor, thus shortening her croup and lengthening a back that would have been long anyway. The longer a horse's back, the weaker and more likely to sag un-

(1) 17-year-old Hungarian-Thoroughbred mare
(2) 24-year-old grade mare
(3) 19-year-old Arab-Quarter Horse mare
(4) 14-year-old Appaloosa gelding

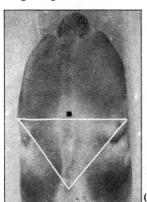

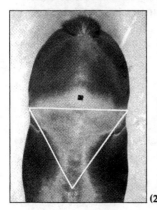

der a rider's weight it tends to be. As a result of her
conformation, this mare gives a smooth ride and is
good at turns and lateral movements that require her
to bend her long rib cage. Movements and exercises
that require collection are, however, very difficult for
her. In top view, her triangle is longer than it is wide,
and her LS joint is located far behind the line connecting her left and right points of hip.

Horse #3: At first glance, in side view this mare's
loin appears to be very short. In top view, it is certainly broad. From the side, she visually conforms to
an old rule of thumb in conformation judging — that
the horse be divisible into three approximately equal
masses (neck and shoulder, back and belly, and quarters). However, because her lumbosacral joint is located behind the line connecting the left and right
points of hip, this mare's lumbar span is actually as
long as Horse #1's (in top view, the lumbar span is
measured from the apex of the triangle to the black
dot). Because of the rearward placement of her LS

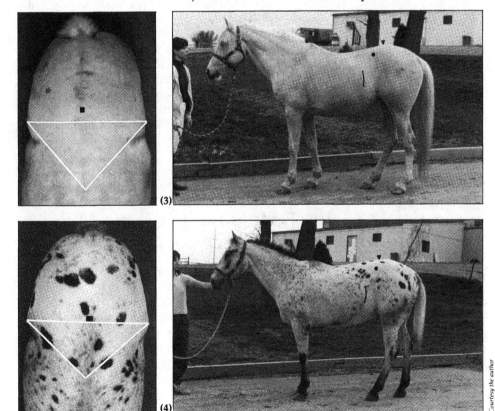

(3)

(4)

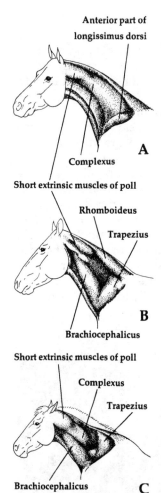

Anterior part of
longissimus dorsi

Complexus   **A**

Short extrinsic muscles of poll

Rhomboideus

Trapezius

B

Brachiocephalicus

Short extrinsic muscles of poll

Complexus

Trapezius

Brachiocephalicus   **C**

Figure 6. Desirable and undesirable muscle development in the equine neck. A, ideal development; the complexus muscle dominates. B, a stiff-necked horse that pulls and throws his head up during transitions. Here the rhomboideus, trapezius, brachiocephalicus and short extrinsic muscles of the poll are all overdeveloped. C, pathological development in a horse with a dislocated atlanto-occipital joint (the joint between the skull and the first neck bone).

joint, her croup is also shorter than that of Horse #1, even though her pelvis and quarters are equally large. For these reasons, this mare is doubly disadvantaged: she lacks the lateral flexibility of Horses #1 and #2, while at the same time lacking the croup length and leverage of Horse #1 or #4. Moving the LS joint backward changes this mare from a potentially superb performer — a horse that should have been brilliant in collection — to one having only average capabilities.

Horse #4: Like Horse #3, this gelding shows a short back and a short, broad loin. However, because his LS joint is ideally located (top view), the profile of his topline in side view appears high, smooth and arched slightly upward like that of Horse #1. Although this gelding has neither as nice a neck nor as good a set of legs as Horse #3, he is the superior performer because the good placement of his LS joint shortens his lumbar span and lengthens his croup. This gives him the leverage he needs to shorten his underline and flex the LS joint for collected work.

Functional tradeoff: A short but level coupling like the Hungarian mare's is so strong that it's nearly indestructible, but horses with this structure can be stiff-backed. They usually trot better than they canter. A short but slightly peaked coupling like the half-Arab mare's is harder to preserve without pathology. However, horses possessing this construction tend to canter fluidly, with a supple loin.

The Back: Lab Exercise 2

The Telltale Topline

Years of use determine its shape

Conformation judges often speak of looking for the horse with a "smooth topline." But how smooth is smooth enough? Certainly, you wouldn't want a horse with the sort of topline you could lay a ruler on in side view: that kind of silhouette belongs on a beef steer. The horse's topline, in contrast, naturally forms a curving profile. But if the topline is "wavy," which of those curves is desirable? How much curve is acceptable?

The horse's topline is formed by the bones of the

Figure 7. The lump-hollow-lump characteristic of the rough-coupled horse. Ideally, the topline over the loin is high and convex, not concave and sagging. This structure predisposes the horse to muscular back strain.

spinal column and its overlying layers of ligamentous and muscular tissue. Ridden horses often acquire muscle strains in the lower back and enlargements of the bony pieces (vertebrae). Ligaments hold the chain of vertebrae together. If they tear, the bony pieces may not stay in perfect alignment. Likewise, abnormal or excessive development (hypertrophy) of the muscles along the topline makes the topline lumpy and can stiffen and reduce the movement of an otherwise flexible structure.

As you examine these four horses, check the topline of each for hollows that represent partial dislocations of vertebrae, dips that signal ligament tears, peaks formed by bony enlargements, and isolated, pillow-like bulges that indicate muscular hypertrophy.

Analysis

Horse #1: This horse possesses the best bone structure in the group, but he also has the lumpiest topline. This means that the soundness of his torso is not a sure bet — not nearly as good as that of his near-perfect set of legs.

The lumpiness in this topline arises entirely from muscular hypertrophy. This particular set of muscular bulges (Figure 6b) is characteristic of dressage horses that have been incorrectly schooled in devices which tie down the head (such as draw reins, standing martingale, chambon, de gogue, etc.) and which encourage them to strain upward. In actuality, strong and shapely muscles develop by alternately stretching and contracting which, like good gymnastic practice, will produce full, smooth topline muscling.

Horse #2: This mare has very good legs and pelvic structure. However, her back is "letting down," due to the gradual tearing of its ligaments at two key points — the withers and the point where the spine joins the croup (lumbosacral joint). The lump-hollow-lump at her coupling (Figure 7) is characteristic of muscle strain here. At least half of all ridden horses sooner or later acquire this trait, which, depending on its severity, diminishes the effectiveness which flexion of the joint (engagement of the hindquarters) has in raising the center of the back. Strengthening the horse's abdominal and iliopsoas muscles (Figure

8) act both as prevention and therapy for this condition.

Horse #3: This gelding shows "hatchet neck," a slash in the topline that results when the ligaments that bind the crest to the withers are torn. (Compare this nine-year-old to the 18-year-old gelding, who shows a dip but no "hatchet line.") This pathology can result from a bad fall, during which the horse slides on his face, or from the horse panicking and going over backwards while in a device that ties down the head. All such devices put pressure on the poll in order to bring about a lowering of the head.

This horse also shows a peaked enlargement of the dorsal spines of the first several lumbar vertebrae (Figure 9). Such an enlargement results either from repeated concussion (improper saddling and posting technique) or from moving or landing "hollow" so that the dorsal spines bump and grind together. The

(1) 18-year-old Thoroughbred gelding
(2) 20-year-old Thoroughbred mare
(3) 16-year-old Thoroughbred gelding
(4) 14-year-old Appaloosa gelding

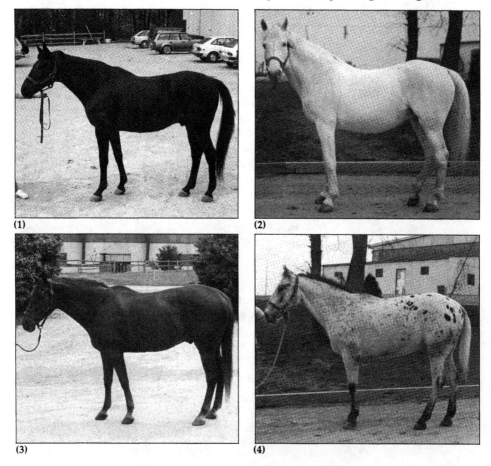

(1)

(2)

(3)

(4)

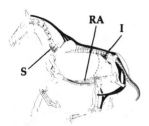

Figure 8. Bascule (arching) of the back and the neck-telescoping gesture are produced as the result of effort by the rectus abdominis, scalenus, and iliopsoas muscles, all of which lie below the vertebral column. The muscles above the vertebral column merely have to remain stretched and relaxed.

Figure 9. Peaked enlargement of the lumbar spines looks similar to the lump-hollow-lump characteristic of rough coupling (Figure 7), but in this case actual bony pathology is present. Consult your veterinarian to obtain a correct diagnosis.

shape of this horse's topline probably resulted from changes in his way of going subsequent to the neck injury.

Horse #4: High knees (long fore cannons) and somewhat slight bone in the front legs are this gelding's primary weaknesses. His nicely crested neck ties on to his prominent withers a bit low, forming a dip in the topline, but this is no cause for concern. Through his back and quarters, this horse's topline is smooth and strongly built. His back is as straight as it can be in side view and still be within the normal range for the equine species.

Functional tradeoff: Compare the 25-year-old Thoroughbred mare with the 18-year-old Appaloosa gelding. Which would you rather have — good legs or a good back? I would have liked to have owned the mare when she was younger, before the days and years of "little ligament tears" that add up to a low back at her age. On the basis of his back, the Appaloosa gelding rates slightly higher for durability, but the mare has the bone structure for greater speed and flexibility and is more harmoniously conformed.

The Back: Lab Exercise 3

Evaluating The "Transmission"

How the length of a horse's back determines the efficiency of his movements

In the standing horse, the free span of the back, measured from the highest point of the withers to the junction of the spine and croup (LS joint), serves to support the rib cage and to connect the fore- and hindquarters. But in the moving horse, it becomes something more: a dynamic transmission that functions to transfer the thrust or impulsion generated by the hindquarters to the forehand.

In the first two lab exercises, we've scrutinized the horse's back for anatomical signs of weak or damaged structure. Now it's time to look at overall back length and at proportions within the back, because these factors determine how efficiently a horse's back can function as a transmission.

Overall back length is determined by comparing it to total *body* length, measured in a straight line from the point of the shoulder to the point of the buttock

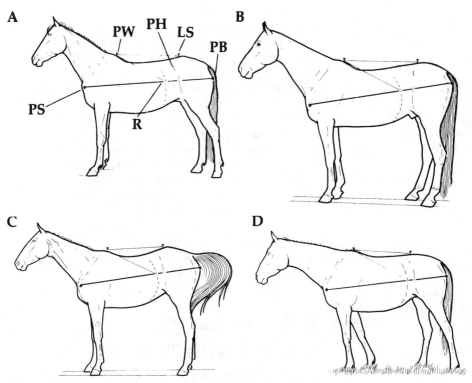

Figure 10. How to calculate the proportional length of a horse's back. First, measure the distance between the point of withers (PW) and the lumbosacral joint (LS) — this is the absolute length of the back. Secondly, measure the distance between the point of shoulder (PS) and the point of buttock (PB) — this is the total body length. Then calculate the proportional back length as follows:

Proportional Back Length = Back Length X 100 ÷ Body Length

Likewise, to calculate the proportional length of the rib cage, measure the length of the rib cage between the point of withers (PW) and the last rib (R). Then calculate the proportional length as follows:

Proportional Rib Cage Length = Rib Length X 100 ÷ Back Length

In the case of mare A and gelding B, who share very similar proportions despite a great difference in height, the back as a whole is too long (near 50% of body length) while the rib cage is too short (there is too much space between the last rib, marked by the dotted line, and the point of hip marked PH). Mare C is rough-coupled but has much better proportions; the whole length of her back equals 47% of her body length, and her rib cage carries well back to total 95% of her back length. Mare D not only has an ideally placed, smooth coupling, but has very desirable proportions: her back totals 47% of her body length while her rib cage equals 105% of her back (a percentage higher than 100 indicates that the rib cage is deep as well as long). Despite some limb faults, good axial body posture will be easy for this mare to maintain while being ridden and, as a result, she will be able to collect, extend and turn athletically.

Courtesy the author

(1) 24-year-old grade mare
(2) 8-year-old German
    Warmblood gelding
(3) 17-year-old Thoroughbred
    mare
(4) 6-year-old Thoroughbred
    mare

(Figure 10). Which horse pictured has the longest back? Does a good loin coupling shorten or lengthen the back span? Consider also the internal proportions of the torso. Which horse has the most space between the last rib and the point of hip?

Analysis

Horse #1: This mare's lumbosacral joint is placed far back, causing her to have a long back, a long loin and a short croup (see Figure 10a). This is a horse whose "transmission" is no more than a connector, even in movement.

This mare earns her keep by carting young hunter-seat riders over their first courses. She has survived because of a sturdy set of legs and a placid temperament. Her long back actually makes her good at her job: she jumps "flat," just stepping over fences. Her total lack of back flexion (bascule) wouldn't interest more advanced riders and prevents

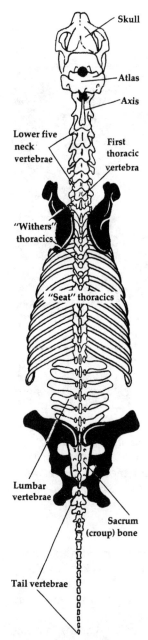

Figure 11. Bones of the horse's axial skeleton (the skull and vertebral column) seen in top view. The pectoral and pelvic girdles (shoulder blades and pelvis) are black.

Labels on figure:
- Skull
- Atlas
- Axis
- Lower five neck vertebrae
- First thoracic vertebra
- "Withers" thoracics
- "Seat" thoracics
- Lumbar vertebrae
- Sacrum (croup) bone
- Tail vertebrae

her from succeeding at more demanding activities. The stillness of her back builds confidence in beginners who cannot keep their seat on a well-conformed horse whose back undulates up and down in movement.

Horse #2: This gelding is nothing more than an enlarged version of Horse #1 (Figure 10b). Like her, he has a long back, rather crooked hind legs and a short pelvis. He differs from her primarily in possessing a better loin coupling. As a result, he moves with a more elastic, undulating back. Because of his proportionally short pelvis, he isn't very powerful, and Horse #1 has legs with larger, cleaner joints and pasterns with better slope.

Horse #3: This mare's conformation is much nicer than either Horse #1 or Horse #2. Her lumbosacral joint is peaked and not ideally placed, but this is partly compensated for by a long pelvis which simultaneously lengthens the croup and greatly increases her thrusting power. Her overall back length is shorter than either #1 or #2, and the lumbar span within it is also short. The space between her last rib and the point of hip is ideal: not more than eight inches — a hand span (Figure 10c).

She stands over good legs, showing relatively little wear and tear. The left hind seems too smooth because it is stocked up, but this swelling, in her case a normal sign of age and stall confinement, should pass after a few minutes of free movement.

Horse #4: This is a mare with much the same torso as Horse #3's, and one thing more: a perfect lumbosacral joint. The reader who sent this photo asked whether the mare is suitable for competitive dressage, and the answer is a qualified "yes." Her excellent coupling guarantees that the impulsion generated by the hindquarters will be transmitted smoothly forward (Figure 10d). The mare is somewhat low withered, and her neck is also set somewhat low on her body. Her rider, therefore, will want to work her "long and low" — otherwise, the mare will learn to resist at the root of the neck, hollowing it there and blocking the flow of impulsion from back to front.

This mare's head is prettier than Horse #3, but her legs are not as good. She's slightly tied in below the knees in front — her flexor tendons appear to be too close to the cannon bones in those areas — and

Tish Quirk

Figure 12. Nicole Uphoff of West Germany and Rembrandt, a beautifully conformed, short-backed Warmblood gelding. The pair earned the gold medal in dressage at the 1988 Olympic Games in Seoul, South Korea.

cut out (narrow) under the hocks in back. Teaching her to move anatomically straight and developing a clear canter cadence will protect her somewhat vulnerable hocks in movements such as the pirouette, which might otherwise damage them by twisting.

Functional tradeoff: The internal proportions of the back are important. A long lumbar span (a long loin) weakens a back, no matter what the back's overall length. For this reason, Horse #2's back is stronger than Horse #1's. A long rib cage predisposes a horse for side-to-side (lateral) flexibility, while the lumbar span is almost incapable of lateral flexion (Figure 11). Thus Horses #3 and #4 are actually more capable of bending around turns than Horse #1 or #2. The argument that dressage horses should be long backed for flexibility is pure nonsense: a survey of nonexported European champions reveals that the best-structured backs tend to stay at home (Figure 12).

The Back: Lab Exercise 4

Of Mutton And The Mighty Camel

How the withers get their shape

Most of the "coffee table" books on equine conformation inform the reader that high withers are desirable in horses to keep the saddle from slipping to one side and from creeping too far forward. This is not, however, the most important function of the withers.

The ridge that riders call withers is composed of the long neural spines of the second through about the eighth to the twelfth thoracic vertebrae (Figure 13). The neural spines line up like the slats in a picket fence. The slats are not all of equal length, giving the withers their characteristic arched shape.

Besides being of different lengths, the neural "slats" lean backward. This braces them, like tent pegs, against the forward pull of the muscles and ligaments that form the crest of the neck. Thus, the withers serve two biomechanical functions: first, to anchor the neck and second, to provide a point of leverage, like a fulcrum, so that when the horse lowers and extends his neck, the center of his back rises. If the withers act as this kind of fulcrum, should they be high or low? Might their shape make a difference in function? Your answers to these questions will determine how you rate this set of examples.

Figure 13. Bones of the withers and their relationship to differently proportioned neck structures. A, "ewe neck" type 1, in which the lower curve of the neck bones is wide and deep, but the upper part of the neck (mitbah, or "turnover") is short. This makes the horse hammer-headed as well as ewe-necked. B, ewe neck type 2, which still shows the wide, deep lower cervical curve but also has a long upper curve. This type of ewe neck is harder for the untrained viewer to detect, especially if the crest of the neck blends nicely into high withers. C, a straight neck, in which neither cervical curve is very deep. The lower curve of the neck usually lies low on the neck in this type, but especially in certain bloodlines of American Quarter Horse, may lie higher. D, the ideal neck structure, in which the lower curve of the neck is shallow and lies high relative to the shoulder, and in which there is a long mitbah. This is the easiest neck to train.

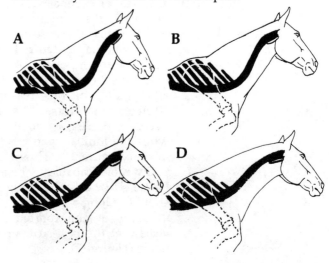

Analysis

Horse #1: This gelding is analyzed first because he has a beautiful neck and withers ideally conformed for a riding or sport horse. From such an example, the leverage role that the withers play in connecting the crest of the neck to the center of the back becomes obvious. The neck looks as if it springs from the center of the back. The neck attaches to the very top of the withers, and the withers are prolonged to the rear, smoothly blending into this horse's short back at nearly 50% of the distance from the point of shoulder to the loin coupling.

This gelding's faults are slight. His pelvis is a little short and steep and his "bone" a tad lighter than ideal. Overall, though, he is a beautiful example of an American Quarter Horse. This animal can do almost anything requiring toughness and athletic ability. He's a natural for cutting and stock work but could also be tried in reining or dressage, where his ability to pivot the forehand around the hindquarters, and his Andalusian-like nobility of carriage, would shine.

Horse #2: This mare has prominent withers, but the crest of her neck doesn't take advantage of them. This is not entirely because she was born with a "dip" in front of the withers. The muscular development of a horse's neck also depends upon the conformation of the back and loin coupling. Where the back and loin are as long as this mare's, the back tends to sag instead of rise under the rider's weight. A full or "double" back and crested neck do not develop in mares or geldings with sagging backs. A skillful rider who could effect engagement of the hindquarters (flexion of the lumbosacral joint) with the neck low and extended could fill in the "dip" and put a full crest on this neck. This is possible because the necessary bone structure is present. Because of her long back and loin, however, engagement of the quarters will always be more difficult for this mare than for Horse #1.

Horse #3: This stallion shows the same long back and loin as Horse #2 but has much poorer conformation in five other ways: a more peaked loin coupling; long, crooked hind legs that force him to stand rump-high and tip his balance to the front; and low (mutton) withers. The stallion also shows very light bone, and many structural weaknesses of the limbs — up-

(1)

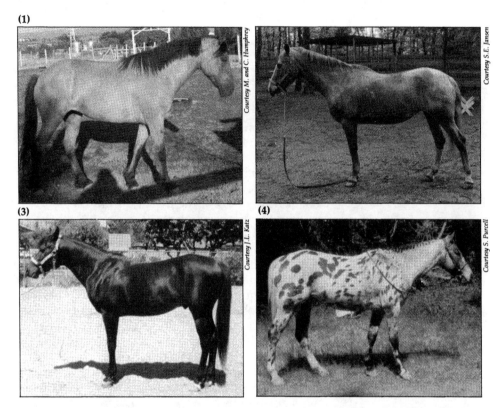

Courtesy M. and C. Humphrey

Courtesy S.E. Jansen

(3)   (4)

Courtesy J.L. Katz

Courtesy S. Purcell

(1) **Aged Quarter Horse gelding**
(2) **18-year-old Quarter Horse mare**
(3) **7-year-old Arabian stallion**
(4) **11-year-old Appaloosa-Thoroughbred gelding**

right pasterns, small round "knees" and hind cannon bones offset to the rear ("cut out under the hocks").

Because of his low withers, this stallion is limited in his ability to raise his back when he lowers and extends his head and neck. But with this loin, back and withers structure, why does this fellow have such a well-shaped neck? Every stallion develops a better-looking neck than he would have had as a gelding, partly as a secondary sexual characteristic, and partly as a result of the passage and piaffe-like movements that all stallions practice. Thus a pretty neck is no special distinction in a stallion, and in light of this horse's overall weak structure, his owners might seriously consider gelding him.

Horse #4: This gelding exemplifies "camel withers," the opposite of mutton withers. As in the case of Horse #2, excellent riding can do something to fill out the knife-thin crest of his neck and to raise the line of the crest to the top of the withers. However, camel withers drop off abruptly to the rear; even Horse #2's withers are prolonged farther to the rear than this fellow's.

Like Horse #3, this gelding has crooked hind legs and a poor loin coupling. His pelvic length is short, too. Nevertheless, he has enough bone, good feet and large, angular "knee" and hock joints, and these will go a long way toward keeping him sound through the period of training necessary to improve the shape of his neck and topline.

The Back: Lab Exercise 5

Ropes And Ladders

Building flexible, not rigid back muscles takes more than just good riding

Riding instructors are forever reminding their students that "dressage develops the horse's back." Yet from a biomechanical point of view, this statement is false. The muscles that such exercises as "striding up," turns and transitions really strengthen are not those of the back but the rectus abdominis of the horse's *belly* and the iliopsoas of the belly side of the back (Figure 8).

Desirable results for every riding discipline, including engagement of the hindquarters ("sticking his tail into the ground"), the neck-telescoping gesture ("going onto the bit" or "looking through the bridle") and the maintenance of bascule (a raised back or the weight-carrying posture), are effected by contractions of these muscles. Thus, the truest statement that a riding instructor can make is that "excellent riding strengthens the horse's underline."

What, then, about the back? When functioning normally, the longissimus dorsi muscles of the back (see Appendix A) act to *regulate* back movements and postures, but not to cause or *dictate* them. They perform their normal function by alternately stretching and contracting. In a horse that will not or cannot relax the large muscles of the back — paradoxical though it may seem — these muscles do not develop a full and rounded shape but instead become thin and flat and feel stiff or wiry. Thus, relaxation and stretching of the topline is more important in developing a full or "double" back than any technique that seeks directly to develop the back muscles.

When the back muscles fail to relax and are partially "on" all the time, the horse's back not only fails

Figure 14. Therapeutic exercise for horses can take many forms; these photos show several different, effective techniques. A, a 7-year-old American Quarter Horse showing tremendous impulsion and excellent overall body posture while being longed on one line. When used therapeutically, longeing is more than just a way to let a horse blow off steam. The beneficial effect of longeing is enhanced still more by the use of cavalletti. For more information on the proper use of cavalletti, see Reiner Klimke's "Cavalletti" (J.A. Allen, 1969) or Bertalan DeNemethy's "The DeNemethy Method" (Doubleday, 1988). B, the author longeing 21-year-old Arabian/Quarter Horse mare with two lines. This technique is a simple modification of line driving. The outside line, which goes from the left side of the horse's mouth, around her quarters and thence to the driver's left hand, simultaneously stimulates the mare to produce more engagement of the hindquarters while it keeps the quarters from deviating outward. C, the same mare at age 19 being longed over cavalletti. She is wearing a surcingle and longeing cavesson and, in (C), side reins. Poles can be used to lengthen the stride (C) or make it loftier (D). In C, the left hind leg carries all the weight for a split second. E, the author riding the same horse at a left-lead canter on a straight line while slowly flexing the mare's head left and right in rhythm with her gait. The head is held to the right for one or two strides before being straightened for a stride and then bent left. The mare responds easily to the request to flex laterally ("translate") at the poll; note

to fill out but becomes very stiff (abnormally high tonus) or even rigid, like a ladder. One quick way to stiffen a horse's back is to tie up his head and neck with a checkrein and then ask him to trot fast. This produces an efficient gait for horses involved in harness racing but does not promote an elastic ride. Another way to stiffen a horse's back is to tie his head *down* and ask him to trot fast. A third way is to tie the head in any position at all — up, down or to the side — for long periods of time (the "dumb jockey" approach).

As you assess these examples, look at the upper surface of each horse's rib cage. In which horses does this surface look hard, flat and angular? Such an appearance indicates a stiff back. Extra credit: three horses in this group are of the same breed. Which horses are they and what is the breed?

Analysis (page 29)

Horse #1: This young woman is clearly pleased with her 11-year-old Standardbred gelding. She writes to say that he was given to her after his career

A

B

the loose rein. To perform this exercise at the canter requires much gentle, persistent work. First attempts should be made at the halt; later, perfect the exercise at the walk and trot before trying it at the canter. F, just plain good riding can also make a world of difference. My heels could be farther back! Nevertheless, the mare carries me with generous impulsion. Good quality movement is evidenced by the wide "V" formed between the mare's two hind legs and her desirable axial body posture with neck-telescoping gesture and obvious engagement. The lively attitude of her tail is a cardinal sign of a relaxed and swinging back. Seeing this mare move, most people think she's a decade younger than she is.

as a racing trotter. The gelding has successfully learned to canter and has won some prizes at hunter competitions, all to his owner's credit. The photo, however, shows a classically undermuscled back. I hope his young owner will find the time for plenty of flat work with her equine companion and include the following simple exercises (Figure 14):

- leg yielding
- trotting and cantering a 20-meter circle, alternately flexing the horse's head and neck in and out
- walking six-meter circles and figure eights
- stretching the neck down and forward at trot and canter
- various forms of longeing.

All of these exercises will not only improve the quality of the gelding's canter, but will fill out his back.

The gelding has the Standardbred's typically good front legs and feet and excellent coupling. This individual is unusually straight in the hind limb for his breed, and this is what has made it easier for him to learn to canter. He also has an unusually long and well-formed neck for a Standardbred horse (#4's is

C   D

E   F

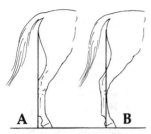

Figure 15. A perfect hind limb (A) compared to a crooked one (B). Depending on how the horse is posed, crooked hind limbs are also sometimes referred to as "overangulated," "camped out" or "sickle-hocked."

more typical), so that his new owner has had less of an uphill battle than others who try to help these horses have a second, mounted career.

Horse #2: This aged Standardbred gelding has the longest neck I've ever seen on a horse of his breed — so much so that one is tempted to think he's an American Saddlebred instead. Like Horse #1, this gelding also came from the harness track and shows the usual flat, angular, stringy back of a horse that has spent years trotting with his neck stiffly erect.

The job of making him into a riding horse will be harder than in Horse #1's case, because his pelvis is more level and his hind legs are more crooked, the hocks lying behind the buttocks when the hind cannon is vertical (Figure 15). Both these conformational features make it difficult for a horse's belly muscles to effect engagement of the hindquarters and consequent stretching of the back muscles. Cantering, by the way, is impossible unless the horse can coil the LS joint between canter strides.

Like Horse #1, this gelding has wonderful front legs and joints and an unusually nice shoulder. Trying the above-mentioned exercises with this fellow would certainly be a worthwhile project, but permanent changes in his musculature will probably not be confirmed for at least a year after beginning work.

Horse #3: The lighting in this photo of a seven-year-old Thoroughbred-Quarter Horse mare points up another characteristic of the stiff-backed horse: lacking fullness in the back muscles generally, there

Figure 16. A, with the rider tugging at the reins, this horse can't seem to get his hocks under his body. He moves forward faster and faster until he and his rider have lost control. B, this horse heads downhill by extending his neck and carrying his head a bit lower than the saddle horn. His rider helps — not hinders — his progress by leaning slightly forward.

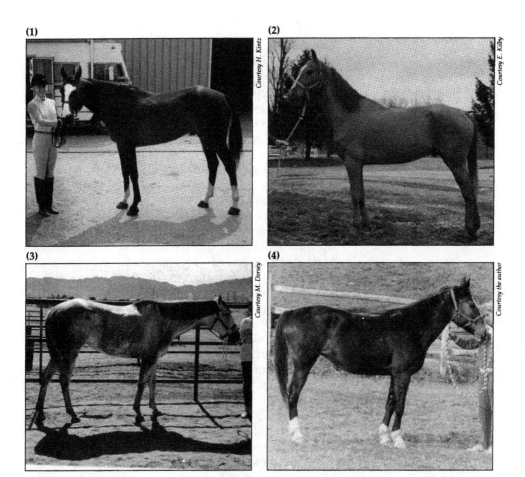

Courtesy H. Kintz

Courtesy E. Kilby

Courtesy M. Dorsey

Courtesy the author

(1) 11-year-old gelding
(2) Aged gelding
(3) 7-year-old mare
(4) 14-year-old mare

is a hollow behind and below the withers. This mare's coupling is the worst of the group, and as a consequence I see more evidence of low-back strain in her than in the others, i.e., a little more angularity in the surface over the loin and lumpiness in the topline itself.

This mare has excellent hind legs, and doubtlessly has always known how to canter. But when she canters, does she move freely in a bascule, bringing the inside hind leg well forward? Her knife-thin, uncrested neck and lack of fullness in her back make me suspect that she four-beats at the canter, shuffling along short strided; she probably picks up the canter by throwing her head back.

Her owner writes to ask whether she's suitable for endurance work. With care for her somewhat light front legs, the answer is yes, but this mare needs a year of arena work in addition to trail riding before competing. Endurance horses, like racing trotters, frequently develop a "ladder" back. This is caused by riding the trot indiscriminately over rolling terrain. The mare will benefit from the same exercises suggested for Horse #1. On the trail, trot her uphill and walk her down. Don't trot downhill until the horse can hold a bascule all the way down a steep grade at a walk (Figure 16). When the mare gets to the point that she doesn't rush or tumble forward as she approaches the bottom of the slope, she'll be ready to try trotting over terrain.

Horse #4: It's easy to pick faults in this 15-year-old Standardbred mare's conformation. She has an upright shoulder (exactly like Horse #3's), crooked hind legs (structured like Horse #2's, though posed differently), a long back and short, thick neck topped off by a hammer head. Her structurally good points are, however, functionally important: a close-to-perfect, short loin coupling, good length of croup and pelvis, and absolutely tremendous bone, short fore cannons, excellent joints and exemplary feet.

The photo conceals a particularly stiff back, which is just to point out that a photo does, sometimes, make a horse look better than he or she actually is. Since I happen to know this mare's history, I will share with you that she, too, came from the trotter track and when she first arrived at our barn, had a back that looked exactly like Horse #1's. Horse #4, however, could not canter and was so stiff that she

This mare is Horse #4, who appeared on page 29 in a 1985 snapshot. This photo was taken in 1987, after two years of steady practice of the exercises recommended above. She was also worked on the trail (but not trotted downhill).

fell down trying to turn a 20-meter circle at a trot. Her crest muscles (rhomboideus and trapezius) were so stiff that she could not stretch her neck down and forward. Her underneck was so thick and her poll so stiff that her "mouth" was like concrete. Her trot, too, was wooden, with no suspension and no hint of cadence.

All this was in the summer of 1985. The accompanying "after" photo shows this mare's appearance in August 1987, after two years of exercises. The mare can now canter, trots elastically in a bascule and goes readily forward from the leg to the bit. She has a second life as an all-around pleasure and trail horse, and an owner who takes as much delight in her daily progress as in looking forward to their first appearance before a dressage judge. 'Nuff said?

The Back: Lab Exercise 6

When The Ring Of Muscles Breaks Down

Understanding the source of a horse's structural sags and bags

The relationships between the horse's back, belly, loins and neck are the product both of conformation and habits of movement. This chapter's photos have been chosen to enhance your understanding of the all-important "ring of muscles," the chain of bony as well as muscular and ligamentous structures that allow the horse to move with unrestricted agility while burdened with weight from above.

As you glance over each of these examples, focus on the shape of the horse's abdomen. Is there a relationship between how stretched and sagging a horse's belly is and the shape of his topline? What happens to the shape of a horse's neck after his belly and back begin to sag? Does the slope of the pelvic bones depend on abdominal fitness?

Analysis

Horse #1: I chose this equine senior citizen not to criticize her conformation after a long life of service, but because she shows the muscular development of a horse whose ring of muscles no longer functions.

This horse's breakdown probably began with strain of the muscles overpassing the loins and lumbosacral joint. Stretching of the loin ligaments and straining of its muscles made this mare adopt a defensive habit of continual low-level "clamping" of the back muscles, resulting in the characteristic *flat, shiny* look of a "dead" back — one that has become very stiff or even rigid like a ladder. This habit of back rigidity in turn made it difficult for her to effectively contract her belly muscles. Eventually she lost all tone there, resulting in a potbelly. When the mare's abdominal tone fell below a certain level, her back also began to sink behind the withers. At the same time, her pelvis became more horizontal and her stifle joints more open. Then she began to have trouble cantering, and began to carry her neck nearly vertical at the trot, resulting in overdevelopment of the rhomboideus muscles of the neck (see Appendix A).

Horse #2: This gelding is in regular work under skillful, knowledgeable riders. Thus, although he, too, has a stretched loin and sagging back, the muscular strain is less and irregularities in his body out-

(1) 32-year-old grade mare
(2) 12-year-old Lipizzan-cross gelding
(3) 19-year-old Morgan gelding
(4) 13-year-old half-Arabian gelding

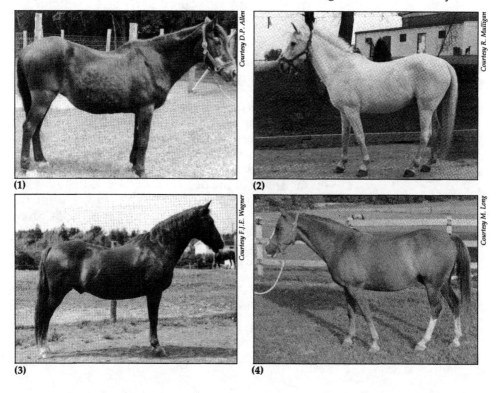

Courtesy D.P. Allen

Courtesy R. Mulligan

Courtesy F.J.E. Wagner

Courtesy M. Long

(1)

(2)

(3)

(4)

line and muscular development are less evident. Still fairly obvious is the fact that his neck sags rather than arches at the root, but his fit underline saves him most pain and dysfunction. Note the smooth, level profile of his underline and the vertical depth from loin to groin.

Horse #3: Conformation can predispose a horse for a lifetime of harmonious function or to athletic mediocrity. This fellow is very long in the back (remember that a horse's back extends all the way from the peak of the withers to the peak of the croup). As a result, he needs absolutely tremendous fitness and strength to move with engagement, bascule, lightness and impulsion.

Except for being tied in below the knees, he appears to have good legs and feet. Because this gelding has difficulty producing suspension or cadence, he is a guaranteed comfortable ride; there's little work for a rider when the horse executes a "stepping trot." In fact, it wouldn't surprise me at all if this fellow could produce a nice fox trot or running walk.

Conformation produces habits of movement, and habits of movement in turn produce characteristic muscular development. The reason this gelding's neck is so cresty is not due to his breeding as much as to the fact that — like Horse #1 — his "ring" isn't fully functional. I believe, however, that with proper conditioning and riding, any horse can produce springy, suspended gaits.

Horse #4: Now that you can identify the characteristic look of a horse with a partly or wholly non-functioning "ring," do you just retire or pass up horses with this problem? If you're a competitor and feel you must win, the answer to that is "yes." If, however, you're interested in horse training — that is, in developing a horse's weight-carrying and athletic abilities to their fullest capacities, read on.

There is essentially nothing wrong with this gelding's bone structure. He has a long, well-shaped neck, a well-placed coupling, a medium-length back with short loins, good length and depth of quarters and excellent feet. He's a bit rump-high, but his biggest problem is that he needs "belly therapy" *now*, before his lumbosacral joint and loins become damaged. Longeing over cavalletti (Figure 14) is the most effective technique I know for strengthening a horse's abdominal muscles and improving "ring" function.

Figure 17. This relatively short-necked pony has no trouble flexing his neck to curve around the barrel. In equine necks, short does not equal stiff.

Chapter 2

How To Look At A Horse's Neck

Of length, balance and the paradox of flexibility

By beginning with the horse's back, we have literally chosen to start studying conformation from the horse's "center." Branching outward from the horse's trunk are five parts which function as major appendages: the four limbs and the neck.

Anatomically speaking, the neck is the forward continuation of the vertebral column which also structures the horse's back. Unlike the bones of the back, however, the neck bones are unencumbered by ribs. Because of this and because of the unique designs of the individual neck bones, the neck is the most flexible of the horse's appendages.

Length, Flexibility and Balance

Almost all species of mammals have the same number of bones (seven) in their neck. It may come as a surprise to discover that the very long neck of the giraffe and the camel, and the long neck of the horse, as well as the shorter necks of cattle, dogs, pigs, cats and people are all supported by the same number of neck bones. Whether in nature or in the context of selective breeding under domestication, to make a longer neck means to make the individual neck bones longer, not more numerous.

This fact leads to insight as to the true functional capabilities of long vs. short necks. Horses with very short necks rarely have thin ones, but contrary to popular mythology, despite their bulk, such necks usually remain flexible: just think of the average 4-H or Pony Club "games" pony, who has no trouble zipping around flags, poles or barrels (Figure 17). Close-up photos of gymkhana horses and ponies show that even short-necked specimens curve their necks as they pass at speed around obstacles. At the opposite extreme are horses with very long necks which are often thin, poorly muscled and stiff. Long-necked horses have several physical "strategies" at their disposal to resist curving their necks in the direction of the desired turn under saddle (Figure 18). At first glance it would appear that the long-necked horse, who is more attractive to look at, would have the more flexible neck, but this is not so. Why?

Flexibility depends upon the horse's ability to bend his neck at each of his joints. Given seven bones in the neck, there are eight joints, of which seven will permit lateral and longitudinal bending. All side-to-side and arching movements in a horse's neck must occur at one or more of these joints.

Let's imagine one horse with a neck seven feet long, and another one of the same height with a neck 3½ feet long. On average, the long-necked horse has one joint for every foot of neck length. The short-necked horse has one every six inches. Because he possesses twice as many joints per foot of neck length, the short-necked horse has a neck with *twice* the potential flexibility of the long-necked horse!

The horse species has been domesticated for five thousand years and, from the very beginning, in every European, Asian and American horse culture, breeders strived to select and breed horses with necks longer than the original wild bloodstock. This is because the neck has a second important function to perform: it is the horse's major balancing organ, a sort of oar which he can throw to the side or up or down to compensate for shifts in the balance of limbs or torso during turning, stopping, climbing or jumping. While the big cats use their thick tails for this, the horse uses his neck.

The purpose of breeding horses with longer

Figure 18. The lateral S-bend is a resistance that comes naturally to the stiff-necked, long-necked horse. In this scenario, the rider approaches a corner of the arena and pulls back on the right rein to induce the horse to turn right, following the track. Instead of allowing the bones of his neck and thorax to flow smoothly around the turn like boxcars in a toy train, the horse faces right but also leans right and leads right with his right shoulder, producing the lateral S-bend. The cure? The rider should (1) shift to an opening rein, taking the right rein well away from the neck; (2) release with the left rein, permitting the left shoulder space to move left; and (3) kick (with the right heel) or slap (with reins, romal or bat) the horse's right shoulder, to induce him to displace weight from the right shoulder to the left one.

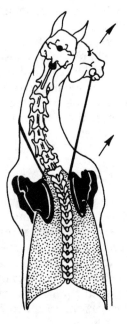

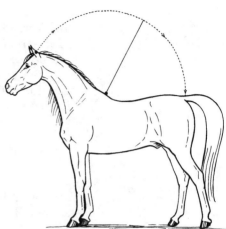

Figure 19. The "long-necked" show horse of this turn-of-the-century photograph doesn't look particularly long-necked by today's standards. Fashions in conformation may change — but our idea of how a good quality horse is built should not. A little more neck length would not have hurt this fellow, but at most he should conform to the proportions shown in Figure 20.

Figure 20. This top-quality Arabian stallion demonstrates the maximum neck length for athletic performance. Necks that exceed the body length tend to be stiff (see Figure 18) and add nothing to mounted balance. This individual was a champion eventer in Europe, on one occasion beating a field of 14 Thoroughbreds. After importation to the U.S., he became a champion "park" horse.

necks is to produce athletic horses who can turn, stop, climb and jump even while carrying the burden of a rider. But as we have seen, extremes in neck length trade off against flexibility. I once heard an experienced conformation judge declare: "You can't bring me a Quarter Horse with too long a neck." He then used the example of the circus tightrope walker, who uses a long pole to balance himself, just as a horse uses his neck to balance himself. No tightrope walker uses a 3½-foot-long pole; that's too short to be useful. But equally disastrous would be the use of a 200-foot-long pole! The big cat's tail is neither bobbed nor so long that it drags on the ground while he runs.

Unfortunately today there are many horses whose necks are at — or beyond — the upper limit of usefulness in balance and well into the range of absolute length which promotes stiffness and resistance to turning. Today's fashion — not function — calls for such long necks. Our idea of "long" has gotten longer and longer over time; the long-necked horse of only 80 years ago (Figure 19) would be considered medium- to short-necked today.

Considering all the functional tradeoffs, what is the best length for a horse's neck? Figure 20 shows how to "see" the ideal neck length. A neck of good length harmonizes with body build as a whole, giving an impression of overall balance.

Shape

Thus far, we have considered the bones of the

Figure 21. The S-shaped internal chain of neck bones does not follow the horse's crest.

horse's neck as if they were spools of uniform shape. However, each and every neck bone has a different shape. The differently shaped articulations between neck bones cause the bones to fit together to form an S-shaped chain. However, the crest of the horse's neck does not follow the curve of his bones (Figure 21); that's why a horse's neck does not look like that of a goose, deer or camel, whose necks exactly parallel their curved internal structure.

Because of the superadded crest, the S-shape within a horse's neck is harder to see than in un-crested animals but by no means impossible. The proportions of the upper, middle and lower curves of the vertebral S determine the shape of the neck which is visible from the outside. The following chart shows how the internal S dictates familiar variations in external form:

Some Common Neck Forms And Their Functions

Description Of Internal "S"	External Form	How It Functions
Short upper curve Medium middle segment Long, deep lower curve	Short upper curve produces "wrong," "hammer-headed," abrupt attachment of head to neck and acute angle at throatlatch. Long, deep lower curve produces external appearance variously termed "ewe neck," "upside-down neck," "hollow crest" or "fallen crest"	Horse tends to carry head too high or "stargaze;" note that a neck that is too *low* at the root produces head carriage that is too *high*. Hard to get horse to lower head and stretch neck forward for suppling or correct transitions. Muscle development thin and hard above, too thick on underside
Medium upper curve Medium to long middle segment Long, deep lower curve	"Common neck" or "rubber neck." Its appearance is similar to the above, but the neck is less upright and may be longer; the angle at the throatlatch is more open	Similar to above, although head may not be carried as high. In heavy-bodied individuals, the neck may have a heavy, ungainly or "rubbery" feel when bitted. This is the horse most likely to learn how to overflex his neck and "run through his shoulder"
Medium to long upper curve Medium to long middle segment Short, shallow lower curve	Neck goes "straight out the front" or appears horizontal; the horse has a build like the Greek letter "Pi" — two legs supporting a long horizontal bar (the torso and neck) on top	Ideal structure in a stock, endurance, race, three-day event, hunter or polo horse. Efficient, athletic; bridles and supples easily. Horse does not "stargaze," "run through his shoulder" or "ball up"
Medium to long upper curve Medium middle segment Short, shallow lower curve	"Arched neck" or "turned-over neck"	Ideal structure in a dressage, bullfight, reining, park, parade horse or a jumper. Showy without loss of athleticism; bridles and supples easily. Horse does not "stargaze" or "run through his shoulder," but may "ball up" (curl his neck down until his nose is pressing against his chest)

As the chart above makes clear, horses' necks come in all shapes; any combination of short, medium or long in any of the three segments of the vertebral S is possible. However, the most important part of the neck from a functional standpoint is the shape of the lower curve. If the lower curve is short and shallow — in other words, if the base of the neck is set high on the chest — the horse will be easy to train and ride, even if he also happens to be hammer-headed. If the neck is set low on the chest, as in the ewe-necked horse, training becomes much more difficult even if the head happens to be set on well. The upper curve, mitbah or "turnover" area of the neck is second in importance to the root. The longer the upper curve, the better the head is likely to be set on the neck, and the cleaner and more open the throatlatch area will be.

The Neck-Telescoping Gesture

To understand why the lower curve of the neck is more important from the standpoint of training and function than the upper curve, horsemen must understand what physical movements the horse makes with his neck when he is said to "go onto the bit," to "look through the bridle" or to "stretch to the bit." Most training manuals emphasize the necessity of inducing a horse to "release" or "yield" or "flex" at the poll, thus making a "yes" gesture with the head, bringing the forehead nearer to the vertical and closing the angle at the throatlatch. While this movement is necessary for good equitation, it is governed by the neck-telescoping gesture that originates not close to the poll but at the *root* of the neck.

Although the neck-telescoping gesture is rarely mentioned in the equestrian literature (the best description is by the French master General De Carpentry), it is easy to understand how it works, since people can also make this gesture. Sit comfortably in a chair or in your saddle, with your weight squarely on your seat bones. Shrug your shoulders several times to relax them; be sure you aren't holding them up in an endless shrug. Look straight ahead. Now, make your neck longer — push your head straight upward toward the ceiling. That's the neck-telescoping gesture made by the human physique. When a horse

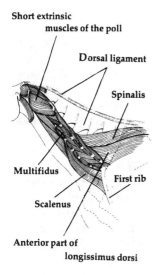

Short extrinsic
muscles of the poll

Dorsal ligament

Spinalis

Multifidus

First rib

Scalenus

Anterior part of
longissimus dorsi

Figure 22. Deep dissection of the horse's neck, showing the scalenus and other muscles that effect the neck-telescoping gesture. Contraction of the left and right scaleni flattens out the lower curve of the horse's neck and tends to push the neck bones upward. These movements are aided by simultaneous contraction of the spinalis and anterior part of the longissimus dorsi muscles. When these three muscles contract, the rider feels that the horse's neck and rib cage suddenly become "all of one piece." The multifidus muscle and the overlying complexus muscle (not shown here) are composed of many short slips that "lace" the separate neck bones together. During the neck-telescoping gesture, these muscles fill with blood and bulge.

produces the same gesture, he makes the same movement with his neck, except that his forehead is pushed forward, not upward. This is because the equine neck lies in the horizontal plane, not the vertical plane like ours (Figure 14f).

People and horses can both produce a neck-telescoping gesture because the neck bones of both species curve at the base. It is not actually possible for muscles to directly push your head up or the horse's head forward; an important rule of physiology states that *muscles don't push*. When a muscle does anything, it contracts or gets shorter. When you make a neck-telescoping gesture, you make it because specific muscles in the base of your neck contract. But if muscles contract, how in the world can your head go *up*? If the same mechanism operates in the horse, how can contraction *lengthen* a horse's neck?

The neck-telescoping gesture works because the scalenus muscles, which lie close to the underside of the bones forming the lower curve of the neck, act to *flatten out* this curve when they contract (Figure 22). Straightening out the lower curve of the neck is much easier if the lower curve is already short and shallow; that's why horses with this build have the advantage over ewe-necked ones. However, the scaleni can be strengthened through proper therapeutic exercise in any horse, no matter what his build. By teaching and training this gesture, the appearance and function of almost any horse's neck can be greatly improved.

Since the scalenus muscles lie deep within the neck of the horse, down next to the bones, their action cannot be directly seen or felt from the outside. However, the neck-telescoping gesture produces three effects easily seen from the outside:

1) It *raises the root of the horse's neck*, making the lower third of the crest fill up and rise higher relative to the top of the withers (Figure 23b,d,f);

2) It pushes the horse's forehead away from its chest. The reins of a "green" horse with weak scaleni must either be loose or instantaneously lengthened in order to permit the gesture;

3) It causes the complexus muscle of the horse's neck to bulge and become visible. Prolonged practice of this gesture will bring the bulging lower edge of the complexus all the way down to the level of the horse's shoulder, completely "remodeling" the shape of the neck (Figure 14f).

Figure 23. External effects of the neck-telescoping gesture demonstrated by horses participating in three of the four major American riding disciplines. A and B are "saddle-seat" horses, and could be American Saddlebreds, Arabians, Morgans or National Show Horses competing in a park, three-gaited, English Pleasure or five-gaited class. Horse A is not making a neck-telescoping gesture; in fact, he is "sucking the root of his neck down," which he accomplishes by contracting his brachiocephalicus, rhomboideus and trapezius muscles, which bulge as a consequence. Saddle-seat specialists refer to this horse as "elk-necked." Horse B exemplifies the ideal; he neither leans over his right front leg nor pulls at the bit. As a bonus, he also has higher, more brilliant knee "action." C and D are dressage horses, and could be of any breed competing at any level. Lacking the strength to make a neck-telescoping gesture, horse C lies on the bit, hollows his neck, raises his head, jams his shoulders, leans over his right front leg and "flicks" the extended left fore hoof. Horse D exemplifies the ideal. The toe of the extended forefoot should point down toward the ground and should not extend farther forward than the projection of the plane of the horse's forehead. E and F represent "stock-seat" horses, and could be of any breed. In addition to lacking a neck-telescoping gesture, horse E shows a "broken neck," which indicates that he does not flex at the poll joint. Horse F exemplifies the ideal. This horse can be stopped from a dead run by aids of the seat alone, because he has the strength to

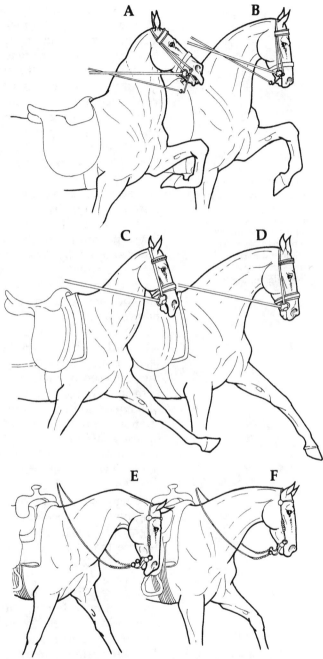

maintain good axial body posture, and therefore has good balance. In such a case, there is never a need to hang onto the bridle reins. In all six cases, notice that the desirable or undesirable action of the forelimbs is the RESULT of the axial body posture.

Figure 24. "Showing the horse the way to the ground" — doorway to higher levels of performance. The horse cannot do this and will not respond this way to the action of the snaffle bit and reins until he can make a neck-telescoping gesture.

There are two forms of the neck-telescoping gesture: elementary or gravity-aided, and advanced or anti-gravity. Correct therapeutic "stretching" to the bit — the way most horses should be ridden most of the time — involves the elementary neck-telescoping gesture. To make this gesture yourself, first make your neck longer as you did before. While still actively lengthening your neck, tip forward, allowing gravity to gently pull your head forward and downward. You will feel a strong stretching not only in the back of your neck, but extending down the center of your back past your shoulder blades. The stretching sensation produced this way is much stronger, and different in quality, than if you simply relaxed your neck and let it hang forward. This is why the very low, "peanut-roller" head and neck position sometimes adopted by Western pleasure horses is no indication of athletic achievement; relaxation and a low head carriage without the neck-telescoping gesture enhance neither a horse's appearance nor his performance ability.

In dressage parlance, "showing the horse the way to the ground" (Figure 24) *presupposes* the neck-telescoping gesture. In this exercise, the reins are neither released nor lengthened. Rather, the horse has sufficient strength in the scaleni to first raise the root of its neck and then, while maintaining the effort, to stretch down and forward. The horse does not lean on the snaffle bit — he pivots his mouth around it. The ability to perform this exercise is the doorway to higher levels of performance.

The advanced, anti-gravity form of the neck-telescoping gesture is the one you perform if you simply lengthen your neck straight upward against the pull of gravity. This form of the gesture is much harder for a horse than for a person: great strength in the scalenus muscles, developed from long conditioning which also stretches the muscles along the top of the crest is required before a horse can push his neck straight upward from the root (Figure 25). As explained in Chapter 3 of Volume I (pp. 56-57), collection of the form required for success in upper-level dressage, reining, park and three-gaited work requires that the horse be able to make the advanced neck-telescoping gesture. For example, the upper-level dressage movement called *passage* is impossible unless the horse first is able to make a very strong

A

B

Figure 25. These two photos show the essential similarity of dressage and reining. A, U.S. Olympic team member Jessica Ransehousen and Orpheus executing flying tempe changes during the 1988 selection trials. Orpheus takes up the rein because he seeks the bit through engagement of the hindquarters, bascule of the back and the neck-telescoping gesture. B, Dick Waltenberry beautifully slides to a stop on The Material Girl, who shows the same cardinal signs of collection as the dressage horse. Notice the bulging complexus muscle in the neck of each.

neck-telescoping gesture of this advanced type.

As the anti-gravity neck-telescoping gesture raises the root of the neck, it benefits the function of the neck's upper curve as well. When collection is achieved this way, the neck-telescoping gesture acts to *open* the throatlatch, even if the horse's forehead is held in the vertical plane (Figure 26). Opening the throatlatch opens the horse's windpipe and frees his voice box (larynx) and assures that there will be plenty of space for the base of the tongue, even if he is performing in high collection. If collection instead is forced by merely pulling the horse's head back so that the forehead comes into the vertical plane, the excessive flexion at the poll that this causes (Figure 23a,c,e) will close the throatlatch, crushing the muscles of the lower surface of the neck up into the ganache. This constricts the horse's breathing, making it sound raspy, and painfully crushes the voice box up against the root of the tongue. The tongue then seeks to find space in the only place remaining — outside the lips.

The cure for a hanging tongue, therefore, does not lie in a tongue-tie, but in inducing *and allowing* the horse to make a neck-telescoping gesture. Since this is not a book on training, little will be said here about how the rider is to induce the horse to contract the scaleni, except to note that tight reins will prevent the horse from making the gesture, especially in the beginning of training, when the scaleni are weaker than an average man's arms. Horses naturally offer the neck-telescoping gesture in response to squeezes of

A

B

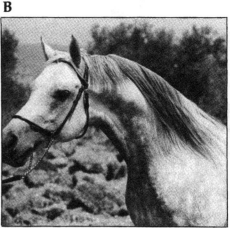

Figure 26. This stallion shows what a horse looks like before (A) and after (B) he makes the neck-telescoping gesture. Stallions naturally produce the gesture when they smell a mare, but the ridden horse also produces it in response to squeezes of the rider's calf.

the rider's calf, so long as they are ridden either on loose reins (American Western style) or with a "following" hand, which knows how to yield the instant the gesture is offered.

Applying these new concepts of neck function will enhance not only your ability as a rider and trainer but also your eye for a good neck. In the next exercise, you're invited to practice spotting the "easy to train" neck — the one that just naturally wants to make the neck-telescoping gesture.

THE NECK: LAB EXERCISE 1

A Menagerie Of Necks

How the chain of vertebrae determines the structure's shape

The most important fact to know about a horse's neck is the precise shape of the bone structure supporting it. Whether your horse has a "ewe," "swan" or "bull" neck or something in between is largely determined by the proportions of the neck's internal "S" (Figure 21).

To assess the size and shape of the important lower curve, first check the point at which the base of the throat enters the horse's chest. Next look for the widest point in the lower half of the horse's neck. Are these points located low or high relative to the chest?

Muscular development also can be a giveaway, but don't be fooled by length; a short neck can be just as well-shaped as a long one.

Analysis

Horse #1: This is a classic example of a "swan neck": long, slender and shapely. Its shapeliness does not derive from an excess of length but from the most desirable internal bone structure. The lower curve of the S is short, shallow and placed very high (higher than halfway up the line of the shoulder). There is also a long upper curve or mitbah. Structurally, the only changes that might benefit this horse would be a shorter back and a stronger loin coupling. The hind legs are a bit crooked, but all four legs, all the joints and the hooves are well structured.

Delicately beautiful, this fellow is especially suitable as a lady's horse — especially a lady with very light hands. Every conformational feature is a trade-

(1) 8-year-old Anglo-Arab mare
(2) 4-year-old Thoroughbred gelding
(3) 13-year-old Quarter Horse gelding
(4) 12-year-old Palomino mare

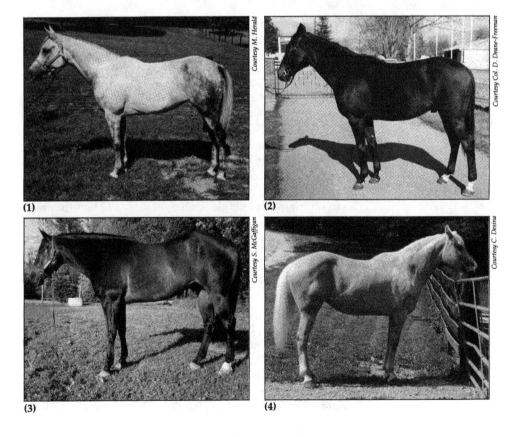

(1)   *Courtesy M. Herald*

(2)   *Courtesy Col. D. Deane-Freeman*

(3)   *Courtesy S. McGuffigan*

(4)   *Courtesy C. Desina*

Figure 27. Reins attached to a non-leverage bit, such as the snaffle, can act as a crutch for the scalenus muscles only when they pass level with or below the lower curve formed by the neck bones. If they are adjusted higher, the green horse will merely drape his neck in the reins like a vulture. With training, as the short extrinsic muscles of the poll (SEP) and other muscles of the topline become loose and supple, and as the scalenus gains strength, the reins can be fixed at position A and the horse will still be able to make a neck-telescoping gesture. Higher rein positions are justified to the extent that scalenus contraction is capable of raising the root of the horse's neck.

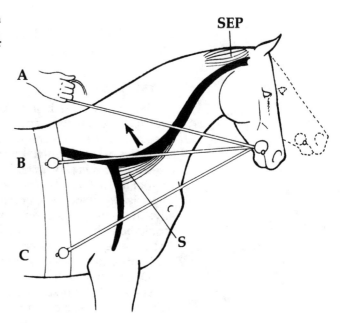

off, and a perfect neck is no exception. Horses structured like this are easy to put "on the bit" — but all too easily they can learn to roll their noses down to touch their chests, evading contact by getting behind or under it. With careful, intelligent handling, this fellow will be a winner in hunter, hunter-hack, dressage, or even Western pleasure.

Horse #2: Like many of his relatives at the racetrack, this fellow is ewe-necked and hammer-headed. Otherwise his conformation is good, especially for hunter competition. He has exceptionally good hindquarters and his slightly upright shoulder will actually help him to fold well over fences. The fore pasterns are as long as they well can be but appear upright only because of the pose.

The opposite of Horse #1 in neck conformation, this gelding has no mitbah and a lower curve that is long, low and deep. Although ewe neck results from a low placement of the lower S-curve, many people erroneously think that these horses have their necks "set on high" because they tend to *carry* their heads high. Ewe-necked horses almost always stargaze, poking their noses up and out and getting above or over the bit.

Snaffle-bit contact can be used successfully to train a green horse only when the line formed by the reins cuts level with or below the lower S-curve (Figure 27). If the reins pass above the curve, contact merely induces the horse to drape his neck on the rider's hands — something like trying to rein a vulture. The purist who tries to train this horse might wish she were an orangutan until the horse gains enough strength to carry his head lower and the root of his neck higher. Meanwhile, longeing with side reins attached low on the girth, while working the horse through many transitions, will help.

Horse #3: In contrast to the two horses just discussed, this is a classic example of a short, "bull" neck. Internally, this fellow's neck bones form a wide, deep lower curve, but a very short upper curve. The base of the lower curve (the widest part of the neck from side to side) lies much lower than halfway up the line of the shoulder. Internally and externally, therefore, this neck is the opposite of Horse #1's. While this type of neck is unattractive, as discussed in Chapter 2, it is incorrect to assume that it will be stiff. Its disadvantage does not lie in stiffness, but in the fact that such a short neck cannot act effectively as a counterbalance to the mounted torso.

Horse #4: This example is a "fooler," for here is a mare with nearly as good a bony neck structure as Horse #1, the only difference being one of overall length. She certainly is not bull-necked like Horse #3. However, like Horse #3, this mare's thick lower neck muscles reveal that she pokes her nose out and leans or pulls on the reins. To cure this, and at the same time improve the neck's appearance, I recommend that her rider try a mild snaffle or rubber mullenmouth bit with no leverage properties. Then it would be best for the rider to take her courage in her teeth, and drop the contact — ride "on the buckle" at a slow jog trot, gradually taking up light contact again as the mare finds her balance in a jog.

The thick rhomboideus muscle developed along the mare's crest shows that she needs to stretch her topline; she probably has to spread her legs far apart to get her nose down to graze. Her rider can teach her to stretch her neck down at a jog trot by first establishing light contact, then bumping or hugging her with her legs as she gradually feeds the rein out. The game is to get the mare to "follow the bit down." Later, she can learn "the way to the ground" (Figure 24). At least five minutes of stretching near the beginning and at the end of every ride would be beneficial.

This mare has a good back, loin, quarters and exceptionally good pelvis. Her hamstrings tie on high and her gaskin is a tad long compared to Horse #1 and Horse #3, indicating that she'll tend to move with short, rapid hind strides. Her rider will need to teach her to obey a slow rate of posting to counteract this tendency.

The trade-off between lower S-curve height and a tendency to get behind the bit has already been mentioned. The equivalent trade-off for the horse with a low-placed lower S-curve is speed at the racetrack, where horses are taught to pull against the rein and where the very act of galloping tends to flatten and raise that loopy lower neck. Animals like Horse #1 tend to float up in front when they gallop. This is considered beautiful in the dressage arena, but it does not predispose to speed.

THE NECK: LAB EXERCISE 2

The Long And Short Of Equine Necks

In the final analysis, shape is more important than length

A horse's neck is, perhaps, the most obvious feature of his conformation. Even those who are new to horsemanship will have little difficulty in telling which of this month's examples have long necks. While shape is more important than length, there is still such a thing as a neck that is too long and fine.

In each of these examples, the horse's neck ties into the withers well, each animal has normal neck muscling, and each torso shows evidence of a functioning "ring of muscles" (see Volume 1, Chapter 3). Yet one of these horses has a longer, weaker loin, a shallower groin and less powerful hind limb muscles, and as a result, a weaker "ring."

Analysis

Horse #1: This good-quality Thoroughbred gelding has had a history of injuries to the deep layers of the skin of his back and to the hamstring muscles (those that run from the point of the buttock down toward the hock). Though these structures are not major components of "ring" function, the damage to them has acted to diminish somewhat the horse's otherwise very high potential. He's not quite as deep from loin to groin and not quite as smooth behind the withers and over the croup as he could be.

(1) 13-year-old Thoroughbred gelding
(2) 2-year-old Appaloosa gelding
(3) 9-year-old Tennessee Walker-Quarter Horse gelding
(4) 7-year-old American Saddlebred mare

He does, however, have a beautiful neck and head (tongue and all). The neck has a straight shape at rest, narrow at the base, but shows no muscular maldevelopment due to his owner's sound training techniques, which include lots of hill work. As a result of the effort over physically challenging terrain, the gelding has well-rounded quarters with a nicely balanced development of the protractor muscles (the mass between the stifle and point of hip) and the hamstrings. Additionally, the gelding's slightly toed-

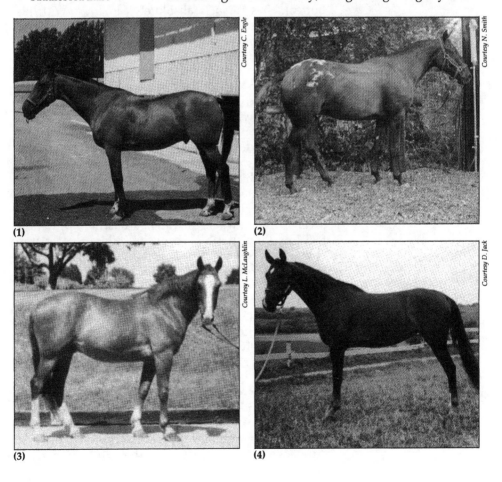

Courtesy C. Engle

Courtesy N. Smith

Courtesy L. McLaughlin

Courtesy D. Jack

(1)

(2)

(3)

(4)

in stance in front is a functional advantage and acts to compensate for his high "knees."

Horse #2: This gelding is only two years old but he looks older to me; I would have guessed that he is six. Despite his mature outward appearance, however, internally his bones and joints are far from fully grown. They won't be completely developed until he reaches the age of five to eight years, and the last to mature will be the intervertebral joints — those we sit upon when we ride. For this reason, I strongly discourage riding two-year-olds. Early riding has two pernicious effects: it shortens the horse's potential life span and induces an early, subtle habit of defensive "back clamping."

This gelding has a short but beautifully shaped neck. His pelvic angle is steep, but there's plenty of length from the point of the hip to the point of the buttock. His torso is absolutely fabulous. With his strong hocks and short gaskins, this fellow would make a terrific reining prospect.

His one major flaw, however, is "calf knee" (see p. 85 of this book). As a result, I recommend *not* jumping him and keeping his front heels fairly high. That way, his owner will minimize the chances of carpal arthritis which can be the result of this structural fault.

Horse #3: In a letter accompanying this photo, this gelding's owner states: "I was concerned about the lump in his loin area when I bought him, but his temperament was so sweet I decided to take a chance on him. I'm glad I did! It turns out the animal has a lovely running walk...he runs barrels...jumps to four feet (my limit, not his), babysits children and at the end of a three-hour ride, begs for more. The moral of my story is, he may be odd-looking, but the horse is a winner!"

My question is — what lump in the loin area? The gelding has a short, strong, smooth coupling flanked by well-developed gluteal muscles. If all grade horses (let alone fully registered animals) were "odd looking" like this fellow, Americans in both domestic and international competition would more often be winners. I know that gaitedness in a bloodline scares away many riders, but such concerns are groundless. Over a din of objections and the snickers of those who have forgotten that the Andalusian was the first "dressage breed," I encourage them to try American

Saddlebreds, Tennessee Walking Horses and their crosses when they are conformed like this gelding.

Horse #4: This mare, though she probably has never taken a "gaited" step in her life, is not suitable for dressage or for any type of general purpose riding. There is such a thing as too long and fine a neck. This limit is reached when neck length is more than about 1½ times the length of a horse's back. This mare is at that limit. In addition, her head is too big for the length and refinement of her neck.

Her coupling is all right but the series of lumps on the croup reveal: (1) less-than-perfect bone structure with overlying muscular strain, (2) excessive development (hypertrophy) of muscles which erect the tail, and (3) hypertrophy of the upper part of the hamstring muscles, where they root on either side of the tail. This development is not balanced by development of the protractors as in Horse #1.

The mare is not as crooked ("angulated") in the hind limbs as Horse #3. Normally this would be good, but as a three-gaited mare, she will be required to produce the type of hock action typical of crooked hind limbs. To get that kind of motion, this mare will have to be ridden very hollow and disengaged. This is what her owner is probably doing, as indicated by the profile of the horse's topline, underline and the muscular developments already discussed.

This mare is a little weak-legged all around and "cut out" under the hocks. The grass does not hide the excessive length of her front feet. The developing dish visible on the left fore reveals the beginning of a mechanical rotation of the coffin bone that will eventually result either in the fetlock knuckling forward or in a clubbed foot.

THE NECK: LAB EXERCISE 3

Getting To The Root Of Ewe Neck

How the lower curve in the chain of vertebrae gives rise to an "upside-down" crest

Ewe-necked horses are usually defined as those possessing a "sunken" or "upside-down" crest, but the ewe-necked condition goes deeper than that, back to the bones. When the lower curve is deep and wide — no matter what the size and shape of the upper curve may be — the horse has the bone structure for ewe neck.

Depending upon the quality of a horse's training, his fitness and the skill and knowledge of his rider, a ewe neck can be minimized. Such horses do, however, have a special need for their riders to provide effective leg and seat aids. Because of the low, wide shape of their lower neck curve, in the early and middle stages of training, these horses must be ridden with the poll no higher than the withers in order to make the neck-telescoping gesture effective or even possible.

Here we present three examples of horses who possess the bone structure which results in the external appearance known as ewe neck. Since this characteristic is often hard to recognize, these examples are particularly helpful. The group includes one horse who lacks the bone structure for a ewe neck; see if you can tell which one it is.

Analysis

Horse #1: A more obvious example of the bone structure supporting a ewe neck could not be presented. The mare's shoulder is fairly upright and meaty, which could be forgiven if her neck didn't loop, vulturelike, forward and upward from it. Fortunately, the neck possesses an equally generous upper curve, which enhances the mare's "turnover" or "mitbah" and saves her from being hammer-headed as well as ewe-necked, a common combination.

It is probable that this mare is either ridden well or infrequently, for her neck shows no muscular bulges in excess of the minimum dictated by her bone structure. Although ewe-necked horses are often said to have their necks "set on high," this is not true of their bone structure. Instead, it is true of their head *carriage* when they are ridden, for they typically become "stargazers," poking their noses up and out and getting over or above the bit.

Horse #2: The woman who owns this gelding writes to say that he cast himself in a stall as a four-year-old and displaced a vertebra in his neck. As a result, the gelding carries his head cocked to the right and has lost some of the vision in his left eye. Despite the fact that this type of neck injury usually renders a

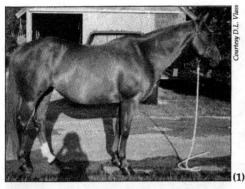

(1)

(2)

(3)

(4)

(1) **20-year-old Quarter Horse mare**
(2) **10-year-old Appaloosa gelding**
(3) **18-year-old Quarter Horse mare**
(4) **6-year-old Tennessee Walking Horse gelding**

horse dangerously uncoordinated, his owner reports that he is very sure-footed and is shown in English and Western pleasure, in sidesaddle and hunter classes and is trail ridden in the mountains. Recently, she has begun to school him in dressage.

In compensating for the neck injury, which is probably located at the junction between the skull and the first neck vertebra (the poll joint), the short extrinsic muscles of the poll (see Appendix A) have become overdeveloped, causing them to appear swollen. When these muscles are contracted, they act to lift the horse's nose. If the horse activates them during dressage, he will seem to be hard-mouthed or will pull against the reins.

The fact that this fellow is in the early stages of dressage training is indicated by the lack of muscular development in the lower triangle of the neck and by the fact that the tubelike complexus muscle, which extends back from his bulging mitbah, is prolonged only halfway to the shoulder. Although somewhat better in neck structure than Horse #1, the gelding is still ewe-necked, and his training needs are similar to those of other horses with this conformation.

Horse #3: Though the muscular development of this mare's neck is strikingly different from that of Horse #2, the proportions of the S curves of their neck vertebrae are similar. Like Horse #1, both Horse #2 and this subject show a prolonged "dip" in front of the withers, a telltale sign of a wide and deep lower S curve.

The muscular development of this mare's neck is typical of ewe-necked horses ridden by riders with average skills: the short muscles of the mitbah and the brachiocephalicus are well-developed, and a strong rhomboideus, which adds a "false crest," is evident (see Appendix A). At the same time, the tubelike complexus is nowhere to be seen, and the lower triangle of the neck is hollow. This horse is a bit "hard-mouthed" and probably does not make the neck-telescoping gesture when ridden.

Some strain is likewise evident in the musculature of the mare's loin area. Her coupling, although well-structured by nature, is uneven in profile and appears somewhat "stretched." Neck structure and function tend to parallel and predispose loin structure and function.

Horse #4: This "fooler" is actually a straight-necked horse. He lacks the characteristic dip in front of the withers shown by the other three. His bone structure becomes clear when you compare his neck to the equally long but differently shaped neck of Horse #1.

This is a nice riding horse, with a back that is short, well-coupled, broad and strong. The quarters are spectacular: long from front to back (point of hip to point of buttock) and deep (from point of hip to stifle). The hocks are low, not because the gaskin is long, skinny and wobbly as is so often seen, but because the stifle joint lies lower than the horse's sheath. This simultaneously deepens the quarters and lowers the hock. The weakest aspect of this gelding is his front legs which, though substantial, show steep pasterns and overstraight knees.

The generally correct muscular development of this horse's neck is the product of the depth and strength of his underline. The fact that the circumference of the horse's torso from loin to groin is nearly equal to his heart girth enables him to carry himself athletically and almost guarantees correct neck carriage as a secondary result. Work over cavalletti and allowing the horse to stretch down and forward at the beginning and end of each session will put the finishing touches on an already good structure.

THE NECK: LAB EXERCISE 4

The Ideal Equine Neck

Why bone structure, not crestiness, is the critical factor from a functional point of view

In terms of shape and contribution to a horse's performance capability, the four necks presented here are the inverse of the ewe necks discussed previously. Although all of these horses' necks are well crested, crestiness is not the critical factor in creating these desirable shapes. Rather, as always it is the bone structure at the root of the horse's neck that forms the basis for a high arch.

In a ewe-necked individual, the upper curve of the S-shaped chain of neck vertebrae is short, while the lower curve is broad and deep. Measuring from side to side, the base of the lower curve is the neck's thickest point. (This point can be palpated in a live horse by pressing the palms of your hands against the sides of the neck.) While the widest point of a ewe neck lies lower than halfway down the shoulder bed, the thickest point of an arched neck, as illustrated by the horses presented here, is located relatively high. This is a reflection of the underlying bone structure; in an arched neck, the lower curve of the S is relatively shallow.

The desirability of an arched neck goes far beyond beauty. The shape and proportions of the chain of bones within make it easy for the horse to perform the neck-telescoping gesture. This important ability is powered by the contraction of the scalenus muscles, which connect the first rib to the neck (Figure 22). In a ewe-necked horse, these muscles are less likely to develop their leverage capacity. In a horse whose neck is arched, however, the potential for muscle development is great. Contraction of the scalenus muscles acts to raise and steady the root of the neck, to establish unity in movement between the neck and the torso, to stretch the topline and to cause the horse to go willingly and *thoroughly* onto the bit (Figure 25).

Each of the following horses is not only an excellent specimen of his or her breed, but also a useful, sturdy, sound and well-moving riding horse.

Analysis

Horse #1: This stallion is exceptionally well proportioned and possesses a beautiful head. Like most other structurally excellent horses, he is sound and therefore comfortable, unworried and trainable. His easy disposition is evidenced by the interested, but not intensely pricked attitude of his ears, and by the relaxation of the small muscles of his face, especially around the eye.

(1) 12-year-old Morgan stallion

(2) 6-year-old American Saddlebred mare

(3) 15-year-old Appaloosa gelding

(4) 11-year-old 7/8ths Arabian gelding

The stallion's neck is not only beautifully shaped and just the right length, but the crest carries back over his well-shaped withers, making it look as if the neck springs from the center of the back. This conformation increases the neck's leverage capabilities,

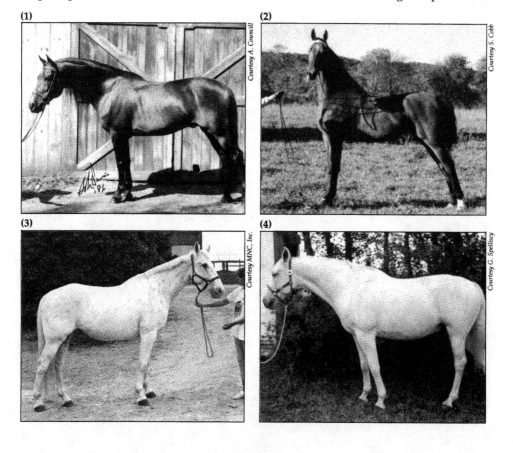

(1)   *Courtesy A. Councill*   (2)   *Courtesy S. Cobb*

(3)   *Courtesy MNC, Inc.*   (4)   *Courtesy G. Spelliscy*

which maximize the effect of the neck-telescoping gesture upon the back.

This fellow's conformation is further enhanced by a topline that carries smoothly back over the loins; a coupling that is ideally placed, broad and short; well-sprung ribs; and sufficient length in both the croup and the pelvis.

Horse #2: The mare's neck is well shaped and "set on" her very laid-back shoulder as high as is possible. Her withers end more abruptly than Horse #1's and aren't positioned so far behind the shoulders. The conformation of this mare's shoulders, withers and crest is very similar to Horse #4's despite the difference in their poses.

The rest of the mare's topline is smooth, her coupling is short and strong, and the ribs carry well back in a torso that is exceptionally deep through the heart girth.

Horse #3: This gelding's "uphill" build stems from three main factors: his straight, open-angled (and therefore short) hind legs; his long forearms (compare Horse #2; contrast Horses #1 and #4); and the high placement of the root of his neck. Though his neck is not as cresty as the others', its thickest part is still placed exceptionally high. The topline flows from the poll down over very tall withers which end a bit abruptly but still well behind the shoulders.

The gelding's worst feature is his coupling, which is peaked and set back, lengthening the loins and shortening the croup. He also needs conditioning: ideally, the gluteal muscles on the top of the pelvis, the rectus abdominis of the belly and the complexus of the neck would be larger in a horse possessing such excellent bone structure (see Appendix A for muscle location). With conditioning, his groin will drop and his neck will acquire more crest.

Horse #4: This gelding's bone structure is also excellent, though at first glance he seems somewhat light of leg and unusually thick through the base of the neck. The explanation comes from his owner, who writes to confess that he's gotten "a bit chubby" since she has been unable to ride him regularly. The gelding is not only pudgy about the neck, but around the tailhead as well, which produces an undulating topline at his hind end. Incidentally, these can depict a type of hypothyroidism — a condition seen with low output of the hormone thyroxin from the horse's thyroid gland. A veterinary examination and hormone assay would indicate whether this is the case. If so, the remedy will depend on the condition's extent. Simply reducing the horse's grain ration while increasing his exercise may compensate for his condition if the effect is only slight. In more serious cases, however, thyroid hormone supplementation may be necessary.

Significantly, however, this fellow isn't showing a lot of excess poundage from the underline: as his trim tummy shows, despite too many groceries and not enough exercise, he continues to move well, continually utilizing his ring of muscles. This is also indicated by the vertical depth of his body from loin to groin (contrast Horse #3).

His head is well shaped, with a chiseled look and prominent bones. Again note the relaxed, self-possessed expression. Especially pleasing is the depth of the muzzle, which does not look as if it had gotten stuck in a pencil sharpener.

Chapter 3

How To Look At A Horse's Forequarter

Standing or in motion, it's what's up front that counts

In the history of horsemanship, more has been said about this part of a horse's anatomy than any other. The importance of the forequarter is in direct proportion to the degree to which the horse is required by its use to travel "on the forehand." It is important to neither misunderstand nor overinterpret this term.

At rest, the average horse carries 65% of his weight on the forelegs, so when the Romans named the horse *equus* — meaning the animal which carries itself in balance, with equal weight on all four legs — they stretched the point with regard to the standing animal.

In movement, however, their observations were correct, for when a well-conformed horse engages his hindquarters (i.e., flexes the lumbosacral joint), thus activating his ring of muscles in movement (Chapter 3, Volume I), he *does* carry his weight equally on all four legs. The horse is the only hoofed mammal which is naturally and effortlessly able to raise his whole forequarter by engaging his hindquarters, rounding (basculing) his back and making a neck-telescoping gesture. These are the three biomechanical components or cardinal signs, not only of "ring" function, but of collection.

Figure 28. All gaits from trot to pace are merely points on a timing continuum. The fundamental difference between different gaits is not the pattern of hoofprints in the sand, but the timing relationship between front and hind feet. For any given hind limb position (left half-circle), an infinite number of corresponding right forelimb positions are possible. Three possible forelimb positions (right half-circle) are shown here. When the forelimb is in position A, the horse is trotting. When the forelimb is in an intermediate position (B), the horse is producing one of the ambling gaits, such as the rack, one of the paso gaits, or the running walk. When the forelimb is in the extended position (C), the horse is pacing.

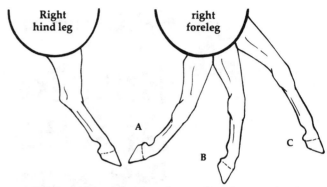

While a horse cannot be said to be on the forehand at rest, he travels that way when in a state of zero collection — that is, when he makes no effort to flex the lumbosacral joint and thus produces no basculed back posture and no neck-telescoping gesture. Just as there are degrees of collection, depending on how strongly and thoroughly the horse's "ring" functions, so there are also degrees of traveling on the forehand.

The horse travels most on the forehand when his hindquarters are *dis*engaged (when he opens instead of closes his lumbosacral joint, thus permitting his stifles and hocks to trail behind). As a corollary to disengagement, the horse's back sags instead of arching up into a weight-bearing bascule. Likewise, instead of making a neck-telescoping gesture, the horse on the forehand raises his poll and appears ewe- or even elk-necked. Despite appearances, pulling the horse's head and neck up or back does *not* lighten his forehand. Instead, by preventing the horse from making a neck-telescoping gesture, basculing the back and engaging its hindquarters, pulling the horse's head and neck back actually forces him to carry more weight on his forequarters than while standing at rest (Figure 23a,c,e). Due to the horse's unique anatomy and functional design, the belief that live equines work like wooden rocking horses is entirely erroneous (see Volume I, page 36).

Speed, as well as ill-founded theory based on fashion, also forces horses to the forehand. This is because the efficiency required for high speed requires that the horse stiffen his neck and torso. This stiffening does not completely prevent engagement of the hindquarters, but it does prevent or inhibit bascule and the neck-telescoping gesture.

While flat, harness and endurance racing are all examples of motion that sacrifice torso flexibility in the interest of speed, it surprises many to find that gaited riding also falls into this category. Surprising because, from the rider's point of view, gaited riding is very smooth and gives the impression of a light, fluid gliding. However, to the degree that a horse's footfall timing approaches that of a pace, the stiffer the horse must hold its torso in order to produce that gait. All the ambling gaits lie on a footfall-timing continuum from those closer to a trot, such as the foxtrot, to those closer to a pace, such as the rack (Figure 28). The fact that ambling gaits tend to stiffen a horse's torso and neck has been recognized for a thousand years by trainers of Spanish Jennets and the Caribbean and American varieties of Paso, who emphasize neck-bending and turning exercises as an indispensable part of training as well as proper maintenance for the finished horse.

Besides observing the three cardinal signs that reveal whether a horse is using his "ring" when he moves, thus relieving his forehand of weight, there are two other simple ways of deciding whether a horse is traveling on the forehand.

The first way is simply to observe the degree to which a horse's fore-pastern angle changes as weight passes over a given forelimb as he performs under saddle. How far does the fetlock joint descend to the ground? Is this distance the same for both front legs? Compare this distance to the height of the fetlock and the angle of the pastern when the horse is halted. The horse whose front fetlocks descend least toward the ground *compared to their resting state* travels least on the forehand.

Notice that many horses appear to travel lighter while being circled in one direction than in the other. Likewise, a horse might be lighter at trot than at the canter. The heaviness while performing one gait or one direction indicates that to be the gait or direction in which the horse stiffens his torso.

The second method requires making a movie of the horse in action. Traveling on the forehand is not just a function of weight on the forelimb; it is also a function of time. Filming your horse from the side can tell you how much time the horse spends weighting each of his legs. The amount of time corresponds proportionally to the amount of weight.

The method is simple. First, clip out a strip of frames that document one complete stride. One complete stride, or cycle, is counted from the first contact of the right foreleg with the ground to the next contact of the same leg. For simplicity's sake, let's say that this cycle occupies 100 frames of film.

Next, count the number of frames in which the horse stands on one or both front legs, but on *neither* hind leg. This number ranges from about 80 (in the case of a weighted big lick 'Walker) to 15 (in the case of a stallion of the Spanish Riding School of Vienna executing piaffe). Measuring "on the forehand" as a variable of time rather than weight clarifies its physiological effect on the horse. Being on the forehand to the horse is analogous to climbing rope for us. It involves the overuse of the muscles of the pectoral girdle: the same muscles of your chest, armpits, shoulders and neck which you'd feel straining if you were climbing rope. At the same time, it underutilizes the muscles of the lower back, abdomen and hind limbs (Figure 29).

Do not mistake this discussion as a plea to discontinue racing or gaited riding but an invitation to understand these activities for what they actually are. It is time to stop kidding ourselves that the majority of our park, three-gaited and dressage horses are light on the forehand. They're not.

The final lab exercises in this book give a systematic and detailed set of criteria and methods to enable you to recognize excellent front legs. If you're engaged in racing, three- or five-gaited riding, park, saddle-seat equitation or endurance, you simply will not succeed with anything less than excellent front legs. The same warning applies obviously to those in three-day eventing, jumping and hunting.

Polo, cutting, reining and dressage mounts can

Figure 29. A, a weighted "big lick" Tennessee Walking Horse doing the running walk. The horse stands on one or both front legs in 75% of the frames and stands on front legs only in 25% of frames. By any measure, this horse is "on the forehand." Dressage horses at extended trot frequently do no better; a horse at trot should never be caught standing on only one front leg. **B,** a stiff-backed and high-headed dressage horse. Like the Walker above, he stands on one or both front legs 75% of the time. However, in four frames out of 12, this horse stands on no front legs; in frames 5 and 11 the horse momentarily achieves self-carraige, in which he propels himself forward by means of hind legs alone.

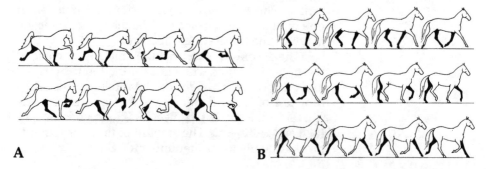

A   B

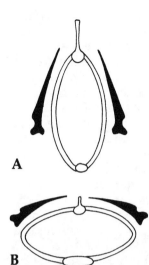

A

B

Figure 30. A, the horse's rib cage is elongated vertically and flattened from side to side; his shoulder blades work "against his sides." B, the human rib cage is elongated from side to side and flattened from front to back; our shoulder blades work "against our back."

get away with less structurally excellent front legs, because when well-executed, the horse works almost exclusively off his hocks. But a master horseman will tell you that he would rather not settle for anything but the best in forelimbs. For the rest of us mortals, who have to repeat movements or exercises or may have trouble obtaining collection because of our own lack of competence, excellent front legs are necessary insurance.

Now that we've concluded that all horses need excellent front legs, let's find out exactly what superb forequarters look like.

THE FOREQUARTER: LAB EXERCISE 1

The Right Angle On Shoulders

Upright or laid back, their position determines how the horse's forelimbs move

So far in this volume, we've thoroughly examined the structure and function of the equine topline. Now it's time to move downward to take a look at the bony elements of the forelimb, the uppermost of which is the shoulder blade, technically known as the scapula.

The horse's shoulder blades rest against his rib cage. Viewed from the front, the equine rib cage forms a more or less flattened oval shape, which is narrow from side to side. This is in marked contrast to the shape of the human rib cage, which is shallow from backbone to breastbone or back to front (Figure 30). As a result, a person's shoulder blades are positioned in a different manner than a horse's. If you bend forward at the waist so that your spine is horizontal like your horse's, you'll find that your shoulder blades lie horizontally, as if on a tabletop. By contrast, the horse's shoulder blades are set in a near-vertical position.

The orientation of each species' shoulder blades determines its basic capabilities for arm movement. People, like other primates, can grasp and hold things with their long, mobile arms and hands. We can easily swing from a branch. Horses obviously cannot. Their vertically oriented scapulas are designed for only one movement: gliding rotation in a fore-aft plane, a motion which can be compared to

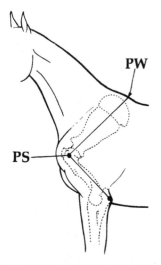

Figure 31. The shoulder line is measured from the point of withers (PW) to the point of shoulder (PS).

the path a soapy sponge follows when you wash a window.

The shoulder can rotate in every horse, yet in some individuals the shoulder blades rest at a steep angle. In others the angle is much more sloping, "low" or "laid back." You can estimate the angle of a horse's shoulder by finding the peak of his withers and the point of his shoulder. A line connecting these two points, when compared to the horizontal, defines the shoulder angle (Figure 31).

Many books on conformation indicate that the lower the shoulder angle, the better. Yet this generalization is inaccurate. Every structure has some desirable capabilities, but no structure is all good or bad. As always, in biomechanical study, everything is a trade-off.

The muscles that move the horse's scapula are rooted along the rear edge of the bone. When these muscles contract, they rotate the top of the shoulder blade down; this in turn pulls up the horse's knees (see Appendix A). Thus, an upright shoulder predisposes a horse for greater knee action (in a gaited or park horse context) and also to carry his knees well (in a hunter-jumper context). The flip side of an upright shoulder is that a horse so endowed may give an inelastic, rough-feeling ride; be less able to absorb forelimb concussion and thus exhibit diminished soundness; and possess a tendency to "stand under" or to be pigeon-breasted (have a prominent sternum).

At the other conformational extreme stands the horse with a low shoulder angle. Low shoulder angles were "invented" by breeders who wanted draft and carriage horses that could more easily and comfortably carry their work collars. Later, horsemen noticed that a laid-back shoulder is useful in other ways, but contrary to the information presented in many books, high knee action is not one of them. If a horse with a low shoulder angle has high action, he derives it either from training, the addition of artificial appliances, or through other forelimb components. As a hunter-jumper, such a horse can fold prettily but is not the one who can "put his hooves in his ears" to get his rider out of a tight spot going cross-country. As a dressage horse, he tends to have low, slightly round action carried out in front of the breast. When a Morgan Horse — a breed that frequently possesses a very low shoulder angle —

moves out at a road trot, he exhibits this weather-vane-like form in the extreme. The flip side of this attractive way of going is that horses with very low shoulder angles tend to first strike on the toe, slam the heel and frequently do not grow heel as fast as they grow toe.

As you examine the horses in this section's photos, check not only for shoulder angle but also for a shelf-like shoulder bed that defines where the neck enters the chest. A clean shoulder bed indicates correct muscular development at the root of the neck and on the shoulder blade, and is a sure sign of a mobile, free-swinging shoulder.

Analysis

(1) 17-year-old Thoroughbred gelding
(2) 5-year-old Arabian gelding
(3) 4-year-old Arabian-American Saddlebred gelding
(4) 12-year-old Thoroughbred gelding

Horse #1: This is an unusually low shoulder angle for a Thoroughbred horse. Notice that the farrier has maintained plenty of heel on this gelding, and that the angle of the fore hoof is steeper than that of the shoulder. This hoof trim contributes to maintaining correct alignment of the pastern bones, thereby reducing stress on the pastern, fetlock and knee joints. In hoof trimming, it is more important to mini-

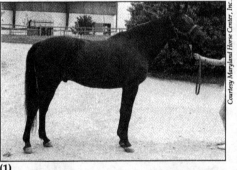
(1)

Courtesy Maryland Horse Center, Inc.

(2)

Courtesy L. Darnell

clean shoulder bed

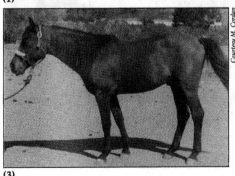
(3)

Courtesy M. Cordan

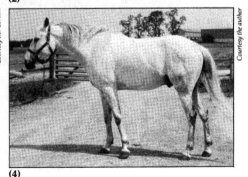
(4)

Courtesy the author

mize joint stress than it is to meet any arbitrary rule about shoulder angle.

An owner may, however, want to measure a horse's shoulder angle in order to assess performance capability. In this horse, the withers carry exceptionally well back into the free span of the back, and the shoulder blade is centered on the line connecting the withers to the point of the shoulder. This gelding is used as a dressage schooling horse and does very little jumping.

Horse #2: This horse shows a shoulder angle that is neither too steep nor too laid back. The clean, shelf-like shoulder bed implies a mobile shoulder, something that a hunter-jumper or three-day-event rider would be grateful for. So freely does this fellow's shoulder slide over his ribs that, even at five years of age, he often lies down with both forelegs stretched out parallel in front of him, like a dog (Figure 32). He can raise his knees high enough to "put his hooves in his ears", and when he gets bored with the view from his stall, he steps up to put both front feet on the stall door to peer out from on high. You may agree that this is a bit hard on the stable furniture, but it's a sign of athletic ability nonetheless.

This fellow is especially suitable for use as a show hunter and is an all-around excellent horse, despite minor shortcomings (his pelvis could be slightly longer; his coupling slightly farther forward; his bone slightly more substantial). However, as a wise breeder once said, "For every thousand people who can pick faults, you'll find hardly one who can pick a

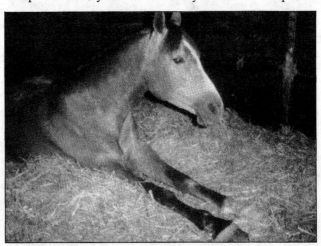

Figure 32. A five-year-old Arabian gelding lying down in his stall with legs extended to the front, like a dog. Such extreme shoulder flexibility is rare in horses and is an indicator of athletic prowess.

horse." This gelding scores high in the harmonious integration of his parts and in overall balance (compare him to Horse #3).

Horse #3: A long and shapely neck is this gelding's one outstanding conformation feature. His shoulder lies at about the same angle as that of Horse #2. However, compared with any of the others, his neck posture is poor — it's carried quite low at the root. Overall body balance is as important as shoulder angle in determining this.

Standing rump-high, this gelding has hind legs that are too long to match his front legs. The resulting downward slope of the topline will cause a plethora of difficulties, starting with saddling. Moderate withers prevent the saddle from actually sliding up onto the neck, but keeping the buttons of the fore arch from gouging the shoulders with every posting stroke will be a challenge. Since this gelding is underweight and out of condition, as well as narrow-backed with the coupling set fairly far back, his whole topline is in jeopardy under saddle. A graduated program of regular, physically challenging exercise as well as larger rations may help him.

This horse is balanced like a wheelbarrow. It's easy enough to make him move forward, but very difficult to get his front end up off the ground. Without expert training, this gelding will offer a suspensionless "stepping trot" and a four-beat canter. In changing from walk to trot or trot to canter, or if asked to jump something, he'll throw his head up and may even hit his rider in the face. Adding a tie-down device is no solution; it will just imprison him on the forehand.

This gelding's teenaged owner can help him most by enlisting a professional horseperson to advise her in feeding, conditioning and training. For any type of showing or athletic endeavor beyond hacking, this gelding's great physical limitations are likely to be beyond the owner's ability to remedy.

Horse #4: This horse has high, steep withers that peak far forward (compare them to those of Horse #1). His shoulder angle is remarkably steep, and as a result his neck extends more forward than upward. The shoulder bed is vague and meaty-looking, indicating restricted shoulder movement. What saves this gelding is his overall body balance — his topline, the opposite of Horse #3's, rises from back to front.

With powerful quarters, a nice deep chest and an upright shoulder angle — implying an ability to raise the knees — this gelding might be able to compete successfully as a jumper. However, he's light of bone all around, has small, round joints, and a grade-B coupling. Therefore, he's not likely to stay sound in that division. He's used in dressage, but paddles and has unfashionably high knee action. Moreover, he's a somewhat rough ride. His head and neck "rattle" and it is difficult for him to stay on the bit. With all their shortcomings, horses like #3 and #4 provide great learning experiences for their owners; horsemanship develops through working with teachers like these.

THE FOREQUARTER: LAB EXERCISE 2

The Lesser-Known Arm Bone

Its length and angle dictate the style of a horse's front-end movement

The previous exercise served as an introduction to the whole of the horse's foreleg, because the higher in a limb a bone is located, the greater its overall influence on the swing of that limb. Moving down the foreleg, the bone below the shoulder blade (scapula) is the humerus, or arm bone.

Although the length and resting angle of the humerus are of great importance in determining how a horse moves in front, this bone is often overlooked by all but the most astute judges of equine conformation. Perhaps neglect of the humerus (and of the femur, the equivalent bone of the hind limb) is due to the fact that in horses these bones are bound up in flesh and are therefore difficult to visualize clearly. Once you know where to look, however, the humerus is easy to find; it connects the point of the shoulder to the elbow.

Of all the joints in the horse's forelimb, only the broad ball-and-socket joint located between the scapula and the humerus is capable of side-to-side movement. This allows the humerus to swing not only from back to front, thus raising or lowering the elbow, but also allows the front limbs to cross each other for lateral movements.

While the shoulder blade governs the entire fore-limb, the humerus determines the way in which an individual horse folds and unfolds the elbow, knee and fetlock joints. Whether long and steep, long and horizontal, short and steep or short and horizontal, the humerus determines the style of a horse's front-end movement in the following ways:

• **The longer the humerus, the more "scopey" the horse's gait** since swinging a long humerus results in a greater arc, or scope, at the elbow end of the bone. Scope is defined as the ability to move the elbow away from the torso, either toward the front, as in a jumper clearing a spread fence, or to the side, as in a dressage horse executing a fluid traversale. Scope enables a cutting horse to crouch in front, spreading or crossing his forelegs as necessary to head the calf. Scope is a very desirable characteristic. It has saved the neck of many a fox hunter, trail rider and three-day eventer, enabling their horses to recover from a mistake after committing to an obstacle, whether it be a log, a slide or a Normandy bank.

• **The shorter the humerus, the more choppy the horse's gaits will be**. A horse with a short humerus moves with correspondingly short, stiff strides, has difficulty with lateral work and is frequently dangerous to jump. Choppy-gaited is the opposite of scopey.

• **The steeper the resting angle of the humerus, the higher the horse can raise his knees.** This is of obvious importance in choosing a three-gaited, fine harness or park horse, especially when the owner adheres to a policy of natural trimming and shoeing and eschews appliances in training and showing. The most spectacular natural action is possessed by horses with the following combination of characteristics: a moderately upright shoulder angle (near 60 degrees); a long, steep humerus; and moderately long cannon bones with high knees.

The same combination of factors produces the hunter-jumper who not only folds nicely but can virtually "put his hooves in his ears" in negotiating a grand-prix course. The only difference between the successful jumper and the three-gaited horse is that the jumper needs to have short cannon bones, low knees and substantial bone to preserve soundness through repeated landings.

• **The more horizontal the resting angle of the**

humerus, the less natural ability a horse will have for high action or tight folding. A horizontally oriented humerus guarantees that the horse will be a "grass clipper" — when asked to jump, he will have difficulty raising his forearms to level and may hang his knees.

In scanning the examples, first locate the horse's humerus. Then compare its length to that of the scapula. To be considered long, the humerus must be at least 50 percent as long as the shoulder blade. Then look at the resting angle of the humerus. Ideally, the angle between the line of the humerus and the line of the shoulder will be wider than 90 degrees. In which of these examples is this not the case?

Analysis

Horse #1: This mare is especially useful in illustrating the principles under scrutiny in this lab exercise because she is one of those Thoroughbreds who simply doesn't pack a lot of body fat. As a result, nearly every muscle in her body is visible and this, in turn, makes the location of the bones easy to see. The humerus, demarcated by the dotted line on Figure 33, is short; it only covers half the length of her shoulder. The angle between the shoulder and arm at the point of shoulder is just acceptable at 90 degrees.

The muscles of the mare's neck are thin along the upper side but thick along the lower side; the lower triangle of the neck is hollow. The desirable complexus muscle is not at all evident. The incorrect muscling of her neck and the rather thick, stiff-looking muscling of her shoulder and arm have developed together. These are the signs of a horse that travels on the forehand.

The structure of her back, loins, croup, hindquarters, gaskins and hocks leaves me wondering why she travels so badly, because she has excellent structure everywhere behind the withers. Her front legs are also OK, although I don't like the over-straight knees. Perhaps her lack of self-carriage is due merely to youth and light use. Her short humerus and close shoulder angle indicate that she does not have spectacular scope, but she is nevertheless well worth someone's time to teach her to go correctly onto the bit in self-carriage.

Horse #2: Like almost all other members of his

Figure 33. The line of the arm is measured from the point of shoulder (PS) to the point of elbow (PE). The shoulder angle is formed by the shoulder line and the line of the arm joining at the point of shoulder.

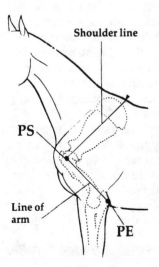

breed, this American Saddlebred gelding shows a very long, steep humerus that forms a wide-open angle with the shoulder blade at the point of shoulder. This conformation guarantees that the horse will be scopey and free-moving. I'm also pleased to see such a good hindquarter on a Saddlebred. The shadow on this photograph draws a perfect picture of the horse's pelvis. The shadow stretches from point of hip in front, dips as it crosses the prominence of the horse's hip socket and ends just at the point of buttock. Farther down, he shows well-structured hocks and correct angulation of the hind legs.

The weakest part of his construction is his loins. He shows a medium-length back that is imperfectly coupled and obviously undermuscled. The circumference from loin to groin is small. His owner writes to say that he's "not being starved...you just have to understand, this is a big strong three-year-old, so they are working him hard and not graining him." No, he is not yet at the point of starvation (I don't see

(1) 4-year-old Thoroughbred mare
(2) 3-year-old American Saddlebred gelding
(3) 3-year-old Morgan-Arabian gelding
(4) 26-year-old Appaloosa gelding

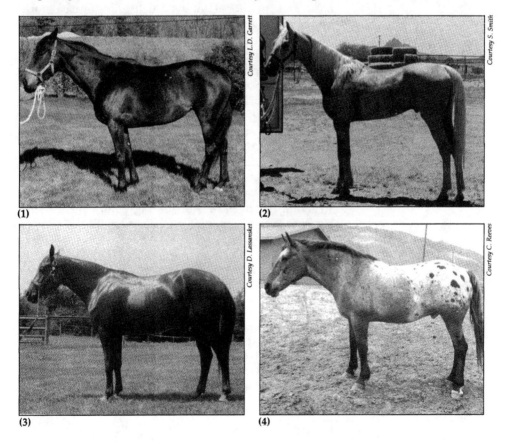

(1)   *Courtesy L.D. Garrett*

(2)   *Courtesy S. Smith*

(3)   *Courtesy D. Lassansket*

(4)   *Courtesy C. Reeves*

ribs), but witholding feed is the wrong way to go about curing this horse's resistances, which stem not from excess strength but a deficit of it, just where it counts most — in his back and belly. He needs grain to build muscles, and he needs a trainer who understands how to use cavalletti, ground driving and stretching the neck down and forward to build the back and belly strength this horse desperately needs.

Horse #3: This gelding shows a neck construction that is in striking contrast to Horse #2, while the structure of his shoulder and arm are exactly the same (compare lengths and angles of both the shoulder blade and the humerus in each). Like Horse #2, the angle at the point of this horse's shoulder is much wider open than 90 degrees. This gelding should be just as pretty and scopey in front as the Saddlebred even though his neck is much shorter.

This gelding's back also contrasts sharply with that of Horse #2. The bone structure of the loin coupling is about the same, as is the total length of the back, but this horse shows much fuller musculature on top and a greater loin-to-groin circumference.

Horse #4: This gelding shows a fault common in stock-type horses: a near-horizontal humerus. The horozontal orientation of this gelding's arm is the result of selection for a long shoulder line, which is a desirable characteristic until the point of shoulder drops too low, as it has in this individual. A shoulder this long and steep would be workable if the angle between it and the arm were maintained at 90 degrees or wider — but as you can see, the angle is less than 90 degrees. As a result, this gelding is more markedly pigeon-breasted than any of the others. His arm construction deprives him of folding ability (he'll hang his knees over jumps) as well as the ability to crouch (as for cutting).

THE FOREQUARTER: LAB EXERCISE 3

Foundation Of The Forelimbs

How the upper arm bones influence the orientation of the lower front legs

Let's now look at the humerus from another angle, for this bone also relates to the structure of the horse's breast and is important in determining the

Figure 34. The "breast box" is visualized from the front and is composed of the left and right points of shoulder (above), and the left and right elbows (below). To locate the elbows, the analyst must "see through" the horse's forearms.

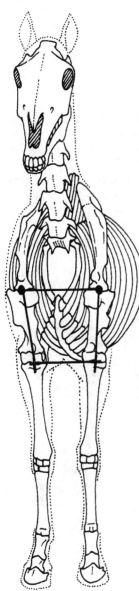

orientation of the front legs. In other words, the crookedness that plagues the equine forelimbs often begins with the structure of the breast.

Seen from the side, the humerus forms a sloping line which connects the point of the shoulder to the point of the elbow. If we move around to the front of the horse, we find that the humerus forms a line that slopes inward from the point of the shoulder (Figure 34). Depending on the amount of inward slope, the elbow may rest close to the rib cage (tight elbows) or farther from it (loose elbows).

To understand how having tight or loose elbows influences the orientation of the lower part of the legs, try mimicking the horse's forelimbs. First, turn your palms down. Then straighten your wrists so that your middle finger is in alignment with your forearm. Now stretch your arms out to the front. This gives you a technically "perfect" set of front legs below the breast. Now, without bending your wrists or fingers, clamp your elbows to your sides. What happens to the orientation of your "hooves"? Do you "toe out" or "toe in"? Now try the opposite movement, turning your elbows out like a bulldog's. Do you toe out or in? The lesson here is that a horse can have perfect front legs below the breast, but if his elbows are too tight he'll toe out; if they're too loose, he'll toe in. It is the "set" of the humerus at the point of the shoulder that determines the orientation of the elbow and of the lower part of the forelimb.

Before reading the analysis, locate the following in each of the four examples:
- the left and right points of the shoulder (marked by dots)
- the left and right elbows (marked by plus signs).

On each horse, form a box by connecting the two points of the shoulder and the two points representing the elbows. A square box is the foundation for a good set of front legs. A box that's wider at the bottom indicates that the horse will toe in. A box that's markedly narrower at the bottom indicates that the horse will toe out, and will plait or "walk the line" when moving. While this conformation is a fault, an asymmetrical box is even worse. If the box leans to the right or left, the horse may not have been "squared up" when photographed. More ominously, he may not be weighting his feet equally due to foot pain, or he may have a curving spine. A box that has a markedly sloping top or bottom reveals that one of the horse's legs is shorter than the other one.

Analysis

Horse #1: This gelding has a very good set of front legs, but because his front hooves weren't quite even or squared up when photographed, he presents a not-quite-square "breast box." The left elbow is drawn up and back, which slightly compresses the left side of the box. This serves to illustrate the importance of squaring the horse before jumping to any conclusions about the animal having foot pain, a curved spine or a short foreleg.

This gelding shows slightly loose elbows, and as a result he toes in slightly when he moves. His square breast box also exemplifies the ideal. Notice how his forelimbs seem to come right off the edges of his chest, which is also of ideal width. Notice, too, how flat his pectoral muscles are; he does not overuse them because he travels in self-carriage.

This gelding is of interest because of his base-narrow stance, which also derives from his loose-elbow construction. Carrying this construction to an extreme (as shown in the next lab exercise) produces undesirable "bulldog" construction. This fellow is, however, a great old horse, still sound and in active

(1) 24-year-old Quarter Horse gelding
(2) 8-year-old Welsh-cross mare
(3) 6-year-old Quarter Horse mare
(4) 10-year-old Quarter Horse gelding

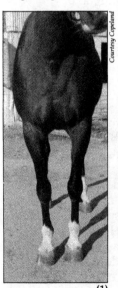
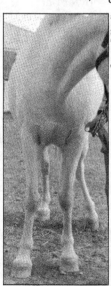

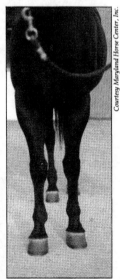

Courtesy Copeland
Courtesy E. Natrelis
Courtesy Maryland Horse Center, Inc.

(1)   (2)   (3)   (4)

service at the age of 24. His one forelimb flaw is a rotation of the right cannon bone under its knee (see
Lab Exercise 5). The gelding toes out on the right not
because he has a tight right elbow, but solely because
of this rotation.

Horse #2: This mare's chest appears very narrow
because she has very tight elbows, each of which is
drawn so close to the chest that the elbows actually lie
under it. The tightness of a horse's elbows begins
with his bone structure but is maintained by stiffness
and tension in the pectoral muscles which span the
gap between the horse's breastbone and humerus
(see Appendix B).

Because its origin lies in the bone structure, this
conformation, to a certain extent, has to be accepted
in horses as inborn. However, tight elbows can be
improved through loosening and stretching of the
pectoral muscles (see "The Gift Of Lightness").
Horses develop tight, hard, short pectoral muscles
when they habitually travel on the forehand. When a
mare spends her life dragging herself forward by
means of her front legs, her pectoral muscles become
short, stiff and overdeveloped and pull the arm bones
in against the body. This effort stabilizes the forelimb
but also causes the horse to travel narrow in front and
the hooves to toe out, as here.

This habit can be changed by altering the horse's
overall state of balance to one of self-carriage, in
which the hind limbs do at least half the locomotory
work. Many horses benefit from having their pectoral
muscles "strummed" through manual massage or the
therapeutic touch (T.E.A.M.®work) developed by
Linda Tellington-Jones. Applied to this horse, these
therapies would likely result in a wider-appearing
chest, more distance between the knees and straight-
er-pointing toes. The outward deviations shown by
both fore cannons here, however, will be unaffected
by these therapies.

Horse #3: This mare has an excellent, wide-open
breast box, similar to Horse #1's, although her chest
is a tad wider. At the same time, she shows less tendency for base-narrowness. Used hard for stock pen-
ning and cutting, this mare is the kind of athlete
which Quarter Horse breeders have always striven to
produce. Her one forelimb flaw is the offset of the
right cannon bone under its knee. Offset or "bench"
knees cause twisting and stress in the joint every time

weight passes over it. Bench knees also predispose to the development of splints. This mare is definitely of breeding quality, but I would look for a stallion with perfect front legs before arranging a mating.

Her feet also need attention: they're trimmed too short and appear "puddled" or "pancake-footed," with the angles of the walls not steep enough. This is not the natural conformation of her hooves; it was caused by trimming her feet too short in her first two years of life. Unfortunately, once established, this foot conformation is very difficult to change.

Horse #4: This horse has a number of torso and limb asymmetries, and it's no accident that he's hard to square up. Notice that both of his front hooves face to the right; at the same time, his left elbow is held farther away from the rib cage than the right one. The breast box is very asymmetrical. An inspection of the horse's back from above reveals a right lateral curvature of the spine. Notice also the uneven development of the pectoral musculature. A big, useful-looking gelding, this fellow competes in low-level eventing but has been known to stop or run out unexpectedly. In light of his "lopsided" bone structure, I'd say the behavior probably has its roots in physical discomfort.

THE FOREQUARTER: LAB EXERCISE 4

When Arms Are Asymmetrical

How every bone and joint of the forelimb affects a horse's stance

There's more to analyzing a horse's front legs than noticing whether his hooves point in or out. Few horses have hooves that point straight forward, either at a standstill or in motion, yet most horses function adequately or better. The reason for this discrepancy is that a horse is a live, three-dimensional, flexible being — not a diagram.

By drawing a picture of the "perfect" forelimb, we necessarily simplify what is naturally more complex.

The horse's *flat* shoulder blade (scapula), which is the uppermost part of his forelimb, must slide over the *rounded* rib cage, resulting in a peculiar outward oscillation. The humerus is oriented and articulated to the scapula in a way that dampens this oscillation effect. This is why, even in horses with "loose" elbows and deep armpits, the humerus still slopes somewhat inward when viewed from the front. With each stride, the humerus moves up and down, in and out, in countercoordination with the movements of both the shoulder blade and the forearm. Should the humerus actually descend straight down or even slope to the outside, abnormal movement, limb damage and unattractive conformation are the result.

The previous exercise discussed how the orientation of the humerus and the relative looseness or tightness of the elbow govern the set of the entire lower forelimb, making it possible for a horse to have perfect limb construction below the breast yet still toe in or out. In these examples, note the location of the points of the shoulder. Do they rest at the same height? Then check the inward slope of the upper arms. Are they the same on both sides of the body? Finally, consider the limbs below the breast. Why does each horse toe out, in or straight forward? The answer usually involves every one of the horse's forelimb bones and joints — not just the hooves.

Analysis

Horse #1: This filly shows markedly asymmetrical development of the shoulder blades and upper arm bones and, as a result, crooked front legs and abnormal hooves.

In the right forelimb, the shoulder blade lies as it should against the body wall, but the upper arm descends straight downward. Thus, the elbow is excessively loose, turning out like a bulldog's. Nature intended for this broad-chested, heavy filly to stand base narrow (with her hooves closer together than her shoulders) and to toe out slightly.

Her right forearm slopes inward as expected for this type of conformation. However, to compensate for the vertically oriented humerus, the cannon bone has twisted under the knee in the course of this filly's development, so that while the forearm and knee face nearly straight forward, the cannon bone is rotated nearly 30 degrees outward.

At the fetlock joint, the pastern bones are twisted inward about 15 degrees, while the hoof toes outward about 15 degrees — exactly the amount that would have been predicted for this filly had her right humerus developed along a normal orientation.

The fact that this developmental compensation isn't perfect, however, is shown by the dished hoof. This hoof profile indicates that with each stride, the filly's foot lands first on the outside wall, then on the inside wall. This lopsided footfall can be attributed directly to her steep humerus, which forces the forelimb to describe a wide, outward arc with each stride — a kind of paddling that originates at the shoulder joint and for which the bones and joints below cannot completely compensate.

In the left forelimb, the lower end of the shoulder blade lies far away from the body wall, and the point of the shoulder is much higher than on the right. For these reasons, the angle of this shoulder (as viewed from the side) is much less than that of the right side. While both elbows lie at the same height, the high placement of the left point of shoulder indicates that the left humerus is longer than the right one. Thus, the filly's left foreleg is longer than her right foreleg above the breast.

A chain of compensations for this asymmetry is

(1) Yearling Belgian filly
(2) 10-year-old Appaloosa mare
(3) 6-year-old Arabian gelding

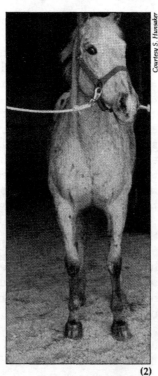

Courtesy A. Gonzales

Courtesy S. Hunsaker

Courtesy the author

(2)   (3)

evident below the breast on the left side. The elbow is held tighter to the rib cage than normal, and as a result, the left forearm faces 30 degrees to the outside. The knee and cannon bone, however, face nearly straight forward, while the left pastern and hoof are actually twisted 15 degrees to the inside. This limb also paddles when the horse moves, but in this case the abnormal swing originates at the knee joint.

Asymmetrical limb length or development is not uncommon in horses. In fact, it is rare to find two front limbs which are exactly alike in any horse. In most cases, the left-to-right differences are minor and have little or no functional impact. This filly was helped by therapeutic shoeing, though the severity of her asymmetries, and the late date at which therapy was begun, will keep her from ever achieving her full athletic potential.

Horse #2: This mare also shows asymmetrical upper arm bones, but the problem here is merely one of orientation. Both her elbows and the points of her shoulders lie level, making her shoulder angles equal and her upper arm bones of comparable length. She toes out on both sides, but more noticeably so on the left. This is because her left humerus slopes inward more than her right one. Her left elbow also lies closer to the rib cage than does the right. Because the elbow is clamped in, the toe points out. There is no significant rotation of either cannon bone below the knees nor of the pasterns below the fetlock joints. The toes of the hooves line up with the front faces of the forearms, cannons and pasterns.

A subtle deviation of the left cannon bone (it tips slightly to the outside below the knee) is this mare's slight compensation for her tight elbow. In fact, her forelimb construction is nearly ideal below the breast. Corrective (actually cosmetic) shoeing or trimming in order to make this mare's *hooves* face straight forward would only harm her *joints*. The objectives of trimming and shoeing are to minimize stress on the limbs, not to make the limb match a graphic or diagrammatic ideal. The mare's well-shaped feet indicate normal breakover, and her joints show no evidence of stress or damage of any kind from the way she now moves.

Horse #3: This mare's front legs are not only normal and symmetrical from left to right, but nearly perfect in construction. The observer gets a slight impression of pigeon toes, even though the grass actually hides her hooves. A straight line cannot quite be dropped from either point of shoulder downward to bisect the limb, because both of this horse's cannon bones are slightly offset to the outside of the knee. However, the mare's big, shield-shaped knees help to compensate for the slightly offset cannons.

Even more indicative of normal functioning is the absence of either splints (bony enlargements often present on the outside of the cannon bone in horses with offset knees) or puffiness in any of the joints. As a result of her strong construction and ability to accomplish her work in a pain-free manner, this mare shows the eye typical of well-conformed horses — large, confident and relaxed.

THE FOREQUARTER: LAB EXERCISE 5

See How They Stand

Charting the factors that influence front-leg alignment

Major support elements of the forequarter lying below the the scapula and the humerus include the forearm (radius-ulna), the knee (carpus), the cannon bone, the long and short pasterns and the coffin bone. Misalignments at any of the joints between these support elements also contribute to forelimb crookedness. Toes that point out or in are not a cause but rather the *result* of the structure and alignment of all the other forelimb bones.

The chart (Figure 35) that accompanies this exercise will help you analyze your horse's forelimbs in front view. After reading the commentary for each of the following three examples, you'll be ready to grab a pencil and a clipboard and head for the stable to practice on your own horse — the most valuable teacher of all.

The first thing to keep in mind is that you will never see two front legs that are exactly alike — not even on the same horse. Therefore, it is necessary to analyze one leg at a time. The second thing to keep in mind is that you will rarely find a perfect equine leg.

There are very few limbs in which the proper front surface of the forearm, knee, cannon bone, fetlock joint, pasterns and the hoof *all* point forward. As

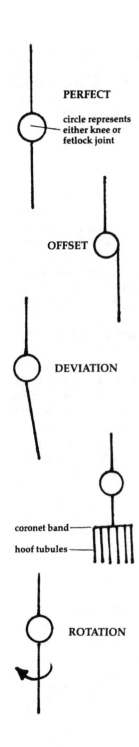

PERFECT

circle represents either knee or fetlock joint

OFFSET

DEVIATION

coronet band

hoof tubules

ROTATION

Figure 38. Charting The Horse's Forelimbs

feature/joint	left forelimb	right forelimb
knee joint: high rotations		

attachment of cannon bone to knee:
   rotations
   deviations
   offsets		

attachment of pasterns to cannons at fetlock joint:
   rotations
   deviations
   offsets		

relationship of hoof tubules and coronary band to pasterns: deviations		

a result, it's best not to stand squarely in front of the crease in the horse's breast when analyzing a limb. If you've decided to begin by analyzing the horse's left foreleg, for example, first walk around the left side of the horse until you're lined up with the front of the knee.

It's easy to walk around to the side if you're working with a live horse, but in a photo the point of view is fixed. Nevertheless, compare the left and right knees of Horse #1. The arrows help to indicate the knee orientation, which is nearly straight forward on the right, but points outward on the left some 15 to 20 degrees. This indicates that the horse holds his left elbow tighter against his body than his right elbow, and this, in turn, indicates either that the horse isn't standing "square" and needs to be repositioned, or that he is habitually bent or "crooked" to the left (such is the case, to some degree, with nearly all ridden horses, including this one).

Now that you're in a position to accurately analyze the left forelimb, let's complete the chart for that leg. First, in the box next to "knee joint: high rotations," record that you had to walk 15 degrees around to the left to line up your eyes with the front surface of the knee. Having done that, three areas of this leg remain to be examined: the attachment of the cannon bone under the knee, the attachment of the pasterns to the cannon bone at the fetlock joint and

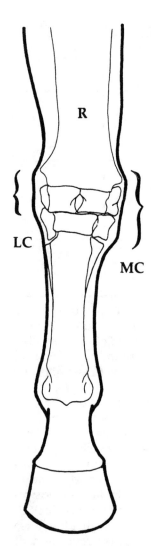

Figure 36. A lateral deviation of the cannon bone at the knee is frequently due to unequal development of the bones comprising the medial and lateral parts of the horse's carpus (knee). Here the bottom of the radius bone (R) and the medial carpal bones (MC) have undergone more growth than those on the lateral side (LC).

the relationship of the hoof tubules and coronary band to the pastern bones.

Misalignment of the limb bones in any of these three areas is classified as a **rotation**, a **deviation** or an **offset**. Refer to Figure 35 for a pictorial definition of these misalignments.

Analysis

Horse #1: Making use of our method, we saw that this gelding's left knee and forearm rotate outward 15 degrees. Additionally, the cannon bone rotates inward 10 degrees. There are no offsets, deviations or rotations at the fetlock joint, although there is a slight outside (lateral) deviation of the hoof tubules at the coronary band. As a result of these spiraling twists of the forelimb bones, the horse toes out about five degrees.

Now take a look at the gelding's right forelimb. From the elbow down, the leg rotates outward about five degrees. There are no other rotations, offsets or deviations. As a result of the nearly ideal carriage of the elbow, the lower part of the limb is nearly perfect — and so, too, are the hoof tubules, the breakover pattern of the foot, and the movement of the limb.

In the box next to "other comments" on the chart, there is room to include comments about pathologies (no physical ailments are present in this case) and blemishes (none). Also note the ideally large, shield-shaped knees, the substantial amount of bone and the general cleanness and lack of puffiness at all visible joints. Though minor flaws are evident (as they always are under intense scrutiny), this field hunter and cross-country horse has excellent legs with few peers among domestic horses.

Horse #2: This crossbred gelding also has excellent front legs and has been a comfortable, reliable and durable school horse for most of his long life. Examining his left foreleg reveals that his knee rotates outward five degrees. The cannon bone rotates inward slightly and is deviated five degrees to the outside as well. The pasterns deviate slightly to the outside while the hoof tubules deviate slightly to the inside. "Other comments" include slightly puffy fetlock joints, exceptionally substantial bone and heavy but rather short pasterns. On the right foreleg, the knee faces straight forward. The cannon bone rotates outward slightly and deviates five degrees to the outside. The pasterns and hoof tubules are straight. Other comments are the same as those noted for the left foreleg, with the addition of some thickening just above the coronary band on the right fore. (This may be investigated by palpation and perhaps X-rays.)

Horse #3: At the top, this mare starts with an excellent breast box and the desirable loose elbows, so that her forearms appear to come right off the sides of her chest. Tracing the line of her forearms downwards, one expects to see absolutely straight legs, but an interruption appears just below the knee joint of both front legs. Here the cannon bones are markedly offset to the outside. This conformation, called "bench knees," causes stress to the knee each time weight is applied to the leg. Since the lower end of the forearm does not line up with the upper end of the cannon bone, vertical shear occurs in the knee. This stresses the knee, and, through the course of development, tends to deform it and to encourage splint formation below it. In this mare, the deformation is most evident in the right knee.

(1) 18-year-old Thoroughbred gelding
(2) 20-year-old Thoroughbred-Tennessee Walking Horse gelding
(3) 10-year-old Thoroughbred mare

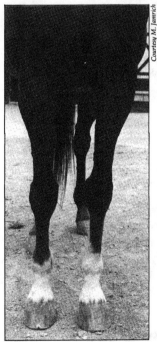
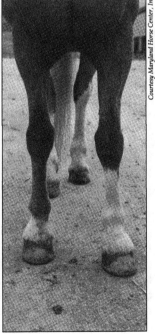
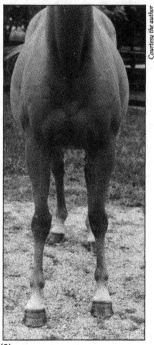

Courtesy M. Jamrich
Courtesy Maryland Horse Center, Inc.
Courtesy the author

(1)   (2)   (3) Bench knees

Figure 37. What horsemen call "the tendons" are continuations of the flexor muscles, which lie above the carpus. The flexor muscles (above the knee) must be properly conditioned to prevent injury to the flexor tendons (below the knee).

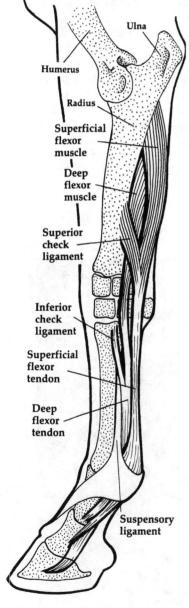

Humerus

Ulna

Radius

Superficial flexor muscle

Deep flexor muscle

Superior check ligament

Inferior check ligament

Superficial flexor tendon

Deep flexor tendon

Suspensory ligament

THE FOREQUARTER: LAB EXERCISE 6

Putting The Knee In Perspective

Viewed from the side, the joint's contours provide telling clues about a horse's potential soundness

If you've practiced analyzing your horse's forelegs by using the chart in the last lab exercise (Figure 35), your eye for their structure, as viewed from the front, is likely to be much sharper. Now it's time to walk around to your horse's side in order to view his front legs from that equally important perspective.

The alignment of the bones and the size and quality of the joints are the first things to observe, just as you did when you viewed the horse from the front. A small "knee" joint (actually the carpus, which is equivalent to the human wrist) that's puffy in front or rounded in back is cause for concern. So is misalignment of the knee with the cannon or with the pastern bones. Ideally, there will be no lumps or sharp angles at the coronary band, the hoof tubules will extend perpendicular from the coronary band and the heel will be slightly more upright than the toe.

Next, examine the muscles originating on or passing over the forearm, as well as their tendons, which extend downward in front of and behind the knee joint. Ideally, the contractile or "fleshy" parts of these muscles, found above the knee, are smooth, sinewy and large without being disproportionate. Be aware, however, that extra fibrous components make these muscles feel harder and tougher than those of the horse's neck and quarters.

The noncontracting, tendinous parts of the flexor muscles, which horsemen simply call "the tendons," lie parallel to the back of the cannon and against the pastern bones (Figure 37).

Good tendons are prominent by virtue of their definition from surrounding tissues and not by size alone. They are easily distinguishable from the suspensory ligament and set well back from the splint bones and cannon bone. Good tendons are hard and tough, yet elastic; when the horse is standing, they feel neither like cement nor like modeling clay but rather like tightly stretched rope. Desirable tendons are not "tied in": the front and back profiles of the

Figure 38. The bones of the horse's forelimb can be aligned in a range of different ways. A, "calf knee," in which the axis of the radius is too vertical. As a result, the carpus and cannon bone tip backward, and the projection of the axis of the radius falls behind the hoof. B, a calf-kneed horse that is also "tied in" below the knee (arrows). This is the worst possible conformation for this body zone. C, "overstraight" knees. The axis of the radius is perfectly vertical. Since the radius is a curving bone, its lower end does not align perfectly with the top of the carpus and cannon bone. The projection of the radial axis falls slightly behind the hoof. D, perfect alignment. The axis of the radius slopes slightly to the front, thus ensuring perfect alignment of the curving radius with the carpus. The projection of the radial axis lies below the hoof but behind the navicular bone; it is directly below the bottom of the cannon bone. E, "buck knees," in which the radial axis tips too much toward the front. The projection of the radial axis falls too far forward; it lies in front of the bottom of the cannon bone, and directly beneath the navicular bone.

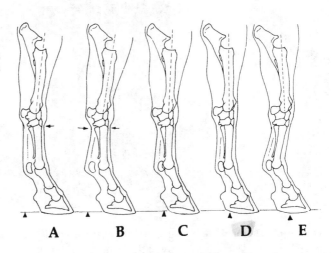

A   B   C   D   E

cannon are parallel and the circumference of the forelimb, taken with a tape measure just below the knee, is equal to the circumference just above the fetlock.

The position and orientation of the forearm bone (the radius-ulna) are also important because the way this bone meets the top of the knee determines whether the horse will have straight forelegs, overstraight forelegs, calf knees or bucked knees (Figure 38).

Analysis

Horse #1: This very attractive mare serves as an example of a horse with straight forelegs. The muscles and tendons have the look (and feel) of excellent quality. Note the diameter of the widest part of the forearm. The fleshy flexor and extensor muscles are large and smooth, yet proportioned to match the bulk of the breast and shoulder. The three major muscles on the outside of the forearm are clearly defined.

As Figure 38 shows, the bone structure inside a straight foreleg isn't actually straight. Rather, the ideal foreleg, as exemplified by this mare, is ever so slightly bucked. Such a configuration helps to produce a shield-shaped knee with well-defined corners; its front profile is nearly (but not quite) flat.

Because of the excellent alignment of this mare's forearm bone and knee, she is the only horse in this

Courtesy the author *Courtesy K. Smith* *Courtesy P. Millott* *Courtesy the author*

(1)   (2)   (3)   (4)

(1) 6-year-old Thoroughbred mare

(2) 4-year-old Anglo-Arabian gelding

(3) 2-year-old Bureau of Land Management feral horse from Oregon

(4) 8-year-old Thoroughbred gelding

group showing no puffiness either at the knee joint or over the tendons, despite having been raced as a two-year-old. The major structural weakness in this mare's forelimbs lies at the fetlock joint: her pasterns are thin and slightly too sloping, and her racing career has predictably produced a pair of puffy ankles which possibly point to osselets.

Horse #2: The overall structure of this very smooth gelding predisposes him to natural self-carriage. His owner intends to maintain his suppleness with dressage exercises while competing him as an endurance horse. Since endurance work tends to make horses stiff-backed, and because posture governs gait quality, stiff-backed endurance horses often become lame. For this horse, then, the endurance/dressage combination is a particularly good idea because his front legs — classic examples of the over-straight type (Figure 38) — are his weakest point.

Although this type of front leg is favored by many American judges, it is actually halfway between the ideal form and the seriously weak calf knee. Several drawbacks of overstraightness are visible in this photograph:

• The muscling on the forearm is thin compared to the muscling on the forearm of Horse #1.

• The knee joints are large but puffy-looking; note how they hang over in front.

• The left hoof has been allowed to get slightly too low in the heel, and as a result, the left foreleg is functionally calf-kneed. Low heels and upright pasterns interact with overstraight structure to increase backward strain on the knee joints.

● The tendons are well-defined but slightly tied in below the knee, diverging from the cannon toward the fetlock. The more calf-kneed the horse, the greater this divergence will be (compare this horse's conformation to Horse #1 and Horse #3).

Luckily, this gelding has excellent pasterns in terms of both length and angle, and first-class hooves in terms of size and probably of horn quality. If his owner keeps his hooves trimmed to the angle shown in the right foreleg, and works him between rides as well as in the off-season to stretch and supple his neck and torso, this gelding should not only be a pleasure to ride, but a winner as well.

Horse #3: There's nothing in the look of the Spanish Barb or even of the Andalusian horse — ancestors of the original "mustangs" of the Great Plains — that would lead an observer to expect the draftiness displayed by this filly purchased from the Bureau of Land Management. Her build is the product of an unfortunate chapter in American history: when native Americans were first confined to reservations, the U.S. government wanted to change them from nomads to farmers. The officials did this by paying bounty hunters to shoot Indian ponies (they got $3 for a pair of ears), and by requiring the Indians to breed draft stallions supplied by the government to their pony and feral mares. For this reason, the Cayuse or Indian pony is now nearly extinct in the United States, and our mustangs are largely crossbreds — nothing like the fleet, compact and agile animals of the nineteenth century.

The owner of this two-year-old assures me that the filly is 14.3 hands, 1,015 pounds and still growing. Although she probably won't top out any taller than 15.1 hands, she'll most likely be quite heavy, perhaps 1,300 pounds as an adult.

If the filly had an excellent set of forelegs, I would recommend her for light draft, utility and trail work. Unfortunately, she also possesses calf knees, which will certainly tend to make her less durable.

Horse #4: This gelding's bucked knees are not an inheritable defect as are the calf knees of Horse #3 and the overstraight front legs of Horse #2. There is such a thing as congenital bucked knees (also called "over at the knee"), but in this individual the bent stance is acquired, either through contracture of the tissues lying on the back of the knee and cannon bones, through strain of the check ligaments during his racing career or a combination of both.

Whether it is acquired or congenital, a buck-kneed stance is an unstable one. Such horses can be ridden, although ultimately I think they are unsafe. In the buck-kneed horse, the axis of the forward-tipped forearm bone (the dashed line in Figure 38) moves the point at which the horse's weight is transferred to the ground abnormally far forward. This is the opposite of the calf-kneed horse, whose weight is borne abnormally far back.

THE FOREQUARTER: LAB EXERCISE 7

The Links Of The Forelimb

How this chain of bones determines the scope and stability of the horse's movements

N ow it's time to expand our horizons a bit by examining the angles and proportions of *all* the forelimb's bony elements.

To assess proportionality in the chain of bones forming the horse's forelimb, you can check three key points:

✔ **the point of the shoulder**. How high is this prominence located? Find this point on a horse and use it to mentally construct the shoulder angle as shown in Figure 33. Is this angle open at least 90 degrees? Generally, the higher the point of the shoulder and the wider open the angle formed by the shoulder blade and the upper arm, the greater the scope and freedom of the horse's forelimb movements.

✔ **the knee**. Pretend that the horse's knee is a little elevator that can slide up and down and stop anywhere between the elbow and the fetlock joint. This helps to illustrate that the proportionality of the forearm and cannon are reciprocal: the higher the knee, the shorter the forearm and the longer the cannon. In general, the lower the knee (and thus, the shorter the cannon bone), the stronger and more structurally stable the horse's forelimb.

✔ **the fetlock joint**. With your eye, measure the length from the fetlock joint to the coronary band on a horse's leg. Now mentally compare this length with that of the cannon bone. The pastern segment is too long if it exceeds three-quarters of the length of the cannon and too short if its length is less than half that of the cannon.

With these considerations in mind, let's analyze each of the following four examples.

Analysis

Horse #1: A fine individual with few flaws worth mentioning, this gelding's pelvis (croup) could be a smidgen longer and his withers could be better defined and carry back a bit farther. Everything else is on the positive side. His back, which is no longer than necessary, is particularly pleasing. The coupling is good. The lump that appears in the profile of the topline over the point of the hip is not a pathology but the bulging gluteus medius muscle. Development of this muscle indicates that the horse possesses vigorous, well-suspended gaits and jumping ability. His muscular stifles and gaskins indicate strong, problem-free folding of all three hind-leg joints. His large, well-structured hocks are clean, revealing that the energetic use of his "drive train" isn't harming its structural components at all.

Correct use of the horse's hindquarters has had its usual effect on the muscular development of the neck and back, too. The shoulder is structurally upright and the neck is thick at the root; if this horse had been ridden badly, the lower portion of his neck would be even thicker. There would also be a dip in the topline just in front of the withers and the neck would not look so arched. Good riding and good movement have produced the best possible habitual posture in this gelding.

With his upright shoulder, the angle formed between the gelding's shoulder blade and upper arm at the point of the shoulder is just 90 degrees. The arm length is slightly more than half the length of the shoulder blade. This is not the construction of an Olympic-caliber open jumper, but one which nevertheless predisposes the gelding to pretty, safe performances over medium-sized obstacles.

The gelding's single best feature is his front legs below the breast: his excellent knees, which are well-structured and placed low, lengthen the forearm and shorten the cannon. The pasterns, too, show ideal length and slope. The hooves are the right size and

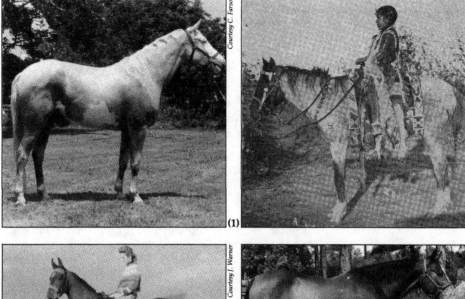

(1)

(2)

(3)

(4)

Courtesy C. Farson

Courtesy the author

Courtesy J. Warner

Courtesy J. Eide

(1) 7-year-old Arabian-cross gelding
(2) Aged Appaloosa gelding
(3) Aged American Saddlebred mare
(4) 13-year-old grade gelding

correctly trimmed.

Horse #2: This photograph, taken prior to 1910 on the Kiowa Indian Reservation in Kansas, shows a real Cayuse or Indian pony — actually a lightweight, agile horse standing not more than 15 hands high.

The young warrior had good reason to be proud of his mount: first for his color, which is a combination of "wolf's head" (dark red roan) and "corn" and "zebra" marks. Secondly, note the size and power inherent in the horse's pelvis and quarters as well as how low the stifle joints and hocks are. The horse is undeniably plain about the neck, shoulder and arm; compare the acute angle (less than 90 degrees) at the point of the shoulder to the wide-open angle of Horse #3.

However, such a set of legs is hardly to be found today. This gelding's large knees are ideally "sprung" (slightly bucked). And look at the size of them and of his hocks! As a foal, this Cayuse must have looked like a knob-kneed puppy. His hooves also approach perfection and, having developed on the hard, limy soil of the prairie, they were surely as tough as flint yet as resilient as a hard rubber hockey puck.

From a historical standpoint, the beautiful, individually meaningful saddle appointments and the rider's costume also bear mentioning, as do the wonderful "double S" sweet-iron cavalry bit and the three-quarter-rigged "Mother Hubbard" saddle.

Finally, let us humbly take note of the young warrior's superior position in the saddle. He is totally natural and relaxed, yet his seat would be the envy of many a prize-winning dressage competitor.

Horse #3: This Saddlebred mare has beautiful forequarters *and* hindquarters. Her long shoulder, wide-open shoulder angles, long neck and low, well-set knees are marred only by her slightly long pasterns. The length of her back is compensated by the great length of pelvis, which is fortuitously highlighted by the sun in the photograph. The depth and power of the mare's thighs and gaskins are complemented by her ideally angulated hocks.

Horse #4: Once again, there is a range of acceptable knee angulations. Horse #2 illustrates as much "buck" as I would like to see, while Horse #3 shows as "straight" a foreleg as is called for. This fellow is unfortunately past "overstraight" and into the weak and potentially damaging calf-kneed construction, in which the carpus is angled behind the ideal straight line of front-leg structure when viewed from the side.

The gelding's shoulder and arm construction are good. The point of the shoulder is high and the angle there is 90 degrees. The arm is nearly three-quarters the length of the shoulder. For these reasons, I expect that he has the ability to deliver a decent performance over a course of hunter-sized fences. However, because of his calf knees and very short pasterns, I would be reluctant to jump him.

Epilogue

The Gift Of Lightness

How an uncooperative riding horse was transformed into a graceful, athletic mount

I would like to share a tale of hope and encouragement to all those whose ambition it is not just to keep, but to improve the horses they own and enjoy.

This is the story of my own mare, Sadie, a 21-year-old Arabian-Quarter Horse cross. Sadie spent the second and third years of her life working as a bareback bronc in a third-rate rodeo somewhere in the Great Plains — and she has a matched set of rowel scars on her shoulders to prove it. After that, she spent time with a heavy-handed amateur barrel racer. Fearful of having her sensitive mouth jerked on yet again, one day Sadie reared up and dumped her rider. After that she was sold, and spent the next five years living in a 40-acre pasture where she learned dietary self-sufficiency and became notoriously hard to catch. When her owner got tired of keeping her as a pasture ornament, Sadie was sold to a teen-age girl who stabled her, rode her lightly, hand fed and petted her a lot, and taught her good ground manners and how to stand up for halter class.

I bought Sadie for 60 cents a pound in 1982, when she was 14 years old. That was really more than she was worth, because the very first time I got on her, she reared — the most dangerous behavior a riding horse can exhibit. I responded by lambasting her with a whip behind my leg — and that was the last time she ever reared under saddle.

One success was behind us, but our difficulties were far from over. I knew that Sadie had taken to rearing because, as dressage theory puts it, she had "lost her impulsion" — the natural desire to go forward. I decided that a program of road riding was a practical solution, but it took an investment of time and patience to see the two of us through what came next.

Our first 20 rides were miserable, because Sadie was very barn sour. I had to use spurs or a whip to get her to trot away from the stable. When we turned back, she'd try to dash toward home. I cured her of that habit by making her circle every single time she tried to go faster than I wanted her to. We made hundreds of circles, and if I rode out for an hour, the return trip would take three. She gave up this anxious behavior after the first month, however, and eventually we went on to place in several competitive trail rides. By this time, Sadie was 17 years old and galloping 16-mile loops as part of her conditioning program.

Forward riding across country had restored her impulsion. But because of her history of rough handling in a curb bit, Sadie was still "afraid of her mouth" and unwilling to accept any kind of steady bit contact. When we moved to the East Coast in 1984, I sought expert help in solving this problem, and received it from several professionals who were willing to work with a horse who, rather than being a dressage competitor, was in need of dressage as physical therapy. Regular longeing in side reins, a temporary switch to a flexible rubber bit, work over cavalletti and exercises to increase her lateral flexibility, as well as improvements in my own riding skills, have been major factors in my mare's continual progress.

At long last, Sadie is able and willing to go softly onto the bit, to carry me comfortably and athletically at a sitting trot, to depart on either canter lead with equal ease, and to jump logs and handle up- and downhill terrain while remaining supple and balanced. The greatest wonder of all is that she has achieved self-carriage; that is, she habitually carries at least half of our combined weight with her hind legs.

Figure 39. Good riding and dressage used as physical therapy have improved Sadie's conformation over the seven years I've owned her. A, Sadie's forelegs in 1986. The plumb line shows that she stood base narrow, with tight elbows and toes that pointed out. Sadie's forelegs in 1988, age 20. Notice how much looser her elbows are and how much squarer her breast box is. C, Sadie in 1983 while we wait our turn for a dressage test. The lower triangle of her neck is hollow, and the rhomboideus and brachiocephalicus muscles are dominant. The complexus muscle is not evident. Her quarters look flat and angular; her groin is high and she shows a "waist." D, Sadie in 1985; the lower triangle of her neck is fuller, and the upper part of the complexus muscle can be seen. The brachiocephalicus is smaller, but the rhomboideus is now much too big. Her quarters are fuller and her groin has dropped; she shows less waist between ribs and hips. E, Sadie in 1989, age 21. The whole posture of her neck has changed; because her scalenus muscle (not visible from the outside) is now strong, the root of her neck is supported internally and thus her neck appears to come off her withers and shoulders much higher than in the "old days" when she was a mere teenager. Her quarters, especially the gluteal area (on top), and the "pants muscle" (on the side of the thigh) are full. Her waist has entirely disappeared. Other pictures of Sadie are shown in Figure 14. At the present time, we're working to improve her lateral work (traverse), and hoping to see piaffe next year.

As a result of her relaxed, rounded and stretched topline, and of her active use of her belly and hind-limb muscles, Sadie has achieved a degree of lightness. This means that there is less weight pressing down onto her forelimbs with each stride. This, in turn, relieves her breast and forearm muscles of the need to stiffen in order to stabilize her forelegs.

Our years of working together have made a noticeable difference in Sadie's conformation, and thus, in her usefulness as a riding horse (Fig. 14). What greater gift can a horse and rider give to one another?

A

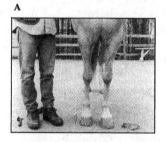

B

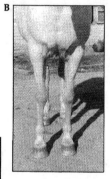

C

D

E

Appendix A

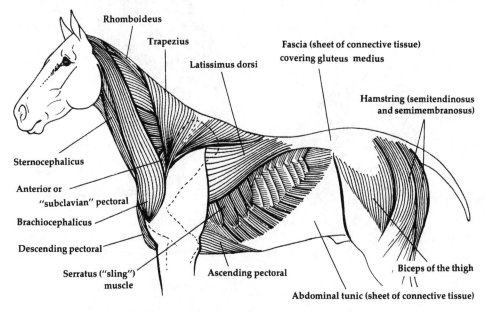

Rhomboideus

Trapezius

Latissimus dorsi

Fascia (sheet of connective tissue) covering gluteus medius

Hamstring (semitendinosus and semimembranosus)

Sternocephalicus

Anterior or "subclavian" pectoral

Brachiocephalicus

Descending pectoral

Serratus ("sling") muscle

Ascending pectoral

Biceps of the thigh

Abdominal tunic (sheet of connective tissue)

Shallow muscular layer of horse's neck and torso

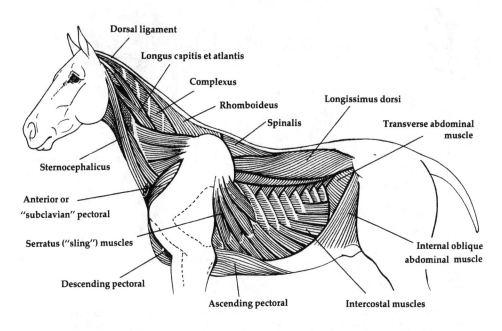

Dorsal ligament

Longus capitis et atlantis

Complexus

Rhomboideus

Spinalis

Longissimus dorsi

Transverse abdominal muscle

Sternocephalicus

Anterior or "subclavian" pectoral

Serratus ("sling") muscles

Descending pectoral

Ascending pectoral

Intercostal muscles

Internal oblique abdominal muscle

Deep layer of torso and neck muscles. For deepest layer of neck muscles, see Fig. 22.

Appendix B

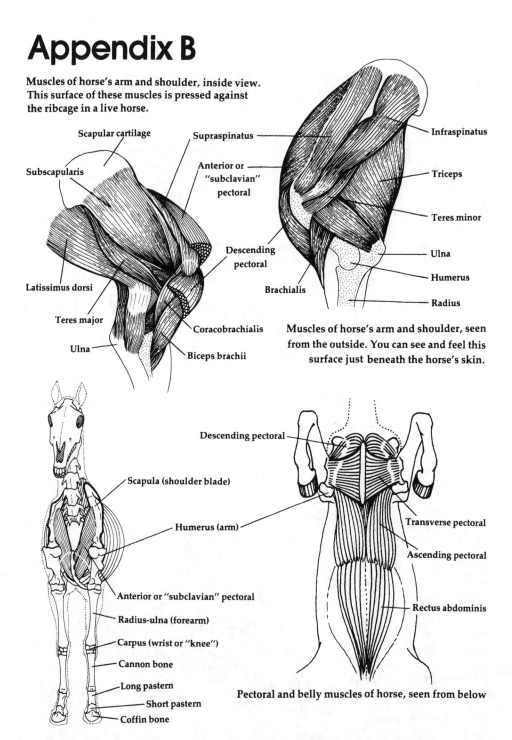

Muscles of horse's arm and shoulder, inside view. This surface of these muscles is pressed against the ribcage in a live horse.

Scapular cartilage
Supraspinatus
Infraspinatus
Subscapularis
Anterior or "subclavian" pectoral
Triceps
Teres minor
Descending pectoral
Ulna
Humerus
Brachialis
Radius
Latissimus dorsi
Teres major
Ulna
Coracobrachialis
Biceps brachii

Muscles of horse's arm and shoulder, seen from the outside. You can see and feel this surface just beneath the horse's skin.

Descending pectoral
Scapula (shoulder blade)
Humerus (arm)
Transverse pectoral
Ascending pectoral
Anterior or "subclavian" pectoral
Radius-ulna (forearm)
Carpus (wrist or "knee")
Cannon bone
Long pastern
Short pastern
Coffin bone
Rectus abdominis

Pectoral and belly muscles of horse, seen from below

Pectoral muscles as seen from the front. The anterior or "subclavian" pectoral muscle is overlain by the descending and transverse pectoral muscles. The white line shows the upper border of the descending part as it appears in front view.

Principles of Conformation Analysis

Volume III

Volume III

Part I

How To Look At A Horse's Hindquarter

Introduction: The Hind Limb Stay System

Although last in a "cook's tour" of the horse's body, in reality the hindquarter stands first in functional importance. The hindquarter, which begins at the lumbosacral joint, continues rearward over the croup to the tip of the tail and extends downward from the croup to the hooves, supplies the power for all of a horse's forward and upward movements. The particular structure of this area also serves to determine how a horse is "geared" — for high revs with a short stroke, as in sprint racing, or for lower revs with a long stroke, as in dressage. To assess the conformation of this body region, it's necessary to look at the horse from the side as well as from the rear.

Over and over again in this series of three booklets on conformation principles, I have emphasized the vital role of the vertebral column in determining a horse's athletic potential, and when it comes to discussing the hindquarters, the importance of the back certainly does not come to an end. The horse's hindquarters are joined to the rest of its body where its loins meet its croup. This point, called the lumbosacral joint, comprises about a six-square-inch

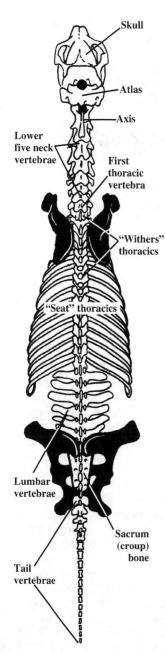

Skull

Atlas

Axis

Lower
five neck
vertebrae

First
thoracic
vertebra

"Withers"
thoracics

"Seat" thoracics

Lumbar
vertebrae

Sacrum
(croup)
bone

Tail
vertebrae

Fig. 1.

surface of attachment. Consider the consequences of such an arrangement:

✔ The whole of the horse's massive hindquarters are attached to its rib cage — and the rest of its body — by a bony surface smaller than the palm of your hand.

✔ All the thrust generated by the horse's hindquarter flows forward through this small junction.

✔ The uppermost joint of the horse's hind limb is not the hip socket, but rather this, the lumbosacral joint.

The uppermost joint of a given limb determines the power associated with the movements which the limb makes. In the case of the horse's hind limbs, which are invested by a specially-designed set of tendons and tendonized muscles called the stay system, this is especially true. The hind limb stay system functions to ensure that the horse's hind joints open and close together, in a coordinated manner safe for high-speed, high-propulsion activity. The tendons and tendonized muscles which compose the stay system act as a tensionally co-adjusted set of cables which parallels the bones of the hind limb. Because of the way the stay system is designed, the horse's hindquarters operate under two laws:

✔ Whatever the stifle does, the hock must do. If the stifle folds, the hock must fold; if the stifle opens, the hock must open.

✔ Whatever the loins do, the stifle must follow. If the loins coil, the stifle must fold; if the loins are flattened and extended, the stifle must open.

The first of these "laws of the equine hind limb" has been widely known and understood for many years, but the second — which is at least as important — is known only to a few. Yet a correct knowledge of anatomy always aids the aspiring horse trainer. Dressage trainers, for example, are always talking about the importance of getting "equal and deep bending" of the horse's hind joints for full and correct collection, but few indeed approach the task with an understanding of where in the horse's body that deep bending actually originates. One great trainer who was aware that bending of the hind joints originates in the loins, not the hip sockets, was the German, Richard Wätjen. Because of his understanding, Wätjen's horses always showed magnificent, even incredible, degrees of collection and were therefore also capable of correct extensions.

Conversely, over the last fifteen years there has been an increased demand from "park" horse trainers in the United States for the veterinary surgical procedure known as stifle

L-S joint in front view

Side view of L-S joint

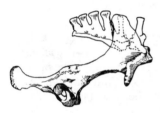

Fig. 2. Front and side views of the bony anatomy of the horse's lumbosacral (LS) joint. Top, horse's head toward the viewer; bottom, horse's head toward the right.

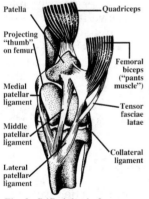

Patella — Quadriceps

Projecting "thumb" on femur

Femoral biceps ("pants muscle")

Medial patellar ligament

Tensor fasciae latae

Middle patellar ligament

Collateral ligament

Lateral patellar ligament

Fig. 3. Stifle joint in front view, showing ligaments which stabilize it. When the stifle "sticks," the medial patellar ligament catches on the projecting lower end of the femur *and remains caught* through too much of a given stride.

cutting. In this procedure, the horse's medial patellar ligaments are severed, which prevents the horse's stifles from "sticking" (the surgery severs the medial patellar ligament and therefore prevents it from catching on a projection of the lower end of the femur). It is worth asking why such operations should be demanded in the first place. The answer from the trainers has been that it is the breeders' fault for producing horses with poor hind limb conformation — horses with naturally wide-open stifle joints (upright or "post-legged" hind limbs) — that are prone to the difficulty.

The apparent outbreak of "sticking stifles" is not, however, the breeders' fault. Instead, stifles that stick or become swollen from repeated partial catching (a condition called gonitis) are very often due to these trainers' own procedures and demands. In this country, it is still generally believed that in order to "balance a horse back" or "set a horse over his hocks," the rider ought to lift the horse's head and pull it back.

Professional trainers communicate to the finished horse that he is to lift his own head and neck and hold it up and back by himself; this is known as "setting the head." We have already seen in Volume I of this series that the whole idea of balancing a horse this way, as if it were a wooden rocking horse, is false. A head set, moreover, inevitably means a shortened and contracted topline, and that means shortening and contracting all the horse's crest and back muscles from his poll to his hocks. It means an "elk neck," a hollow back and flattened and extended loins. And that, in turn, for many horses, even those with perfectly good hind limb conformation, means sticking stifles and eventual permanent damage to the bones and cartilages of the stifle joints.

The stifle cannot bend in proper coordination with the other hind joints if the horse continuously trots with flattened and extended loins. If the horse is forced to bend its stifles while its loins are flattened, something has to give, and what gives first is the stifle ligaments (they become stretched or "micro-torn," and then the stifle joint is said to be "loose"). This sets the horse up for gonitis, or sticking.

How then can we have exhibitions of park riding, and still hope to see sound horses? Those who enjoy park horses put a premium on beautiful head and neck carriage — that means the horse must *carry* his neck, not set it (see p. 41 of Volume II). Park fans also put a premium value on big, beautiful, open and high forelimb action. This means the horse's shoulders must be free, not bound; and that in turn means the horse must be able to lift his entire forequarter *from coiled loins*. This lifting is the state called self-carriage, and it lies at the root of collection.

In order to "balance himself back," the horse does not rock back but instead coils his loins. The rider who sits or leans back over the horse's loins can only hinder the horse's efforts. Even more important, no pulling back or fixing that a rider can do with his hands will ever help to "balance the horse back." Hard hands will only prevent the horse from raising (carrying) the root of its neck and from coiling its loins.

When the rider can elastically follow the horse's motion, by sitting in the stillpoint of the horse's back between his withers and his loins; when the rider's calves become effective in causing the horse to raise its back; and when the rider's hands, through the medium of the bit, can softly rest upon the horse's tongue, following whatever movements it may make, then the horse will be able to coil its loins and raise the root of its neck.

When the horse coils its loins, not only does its back and the root of its neck rise, but its pelvis and hocks become tucked up under the body. This is true engagement of the hindquarters.

When the pelvis rotates downward on the lumbosacral joint, bringing the hocks forward with it, the hind joints bend evenly and deeply. From this bend — and only from this bend — can the horse make powerful forward or upward springing movements. When the trainer allows the horse's lower back, croup, thighs, and hocks to work in this, their natural coordination, even hard work poses no danger to a horse's soundness. At such a moment the meaning of the words of the Greek cavalrymaster Xenophon becomes evident: "no one can take his eyes from a horse when it thus displays its beauty."

A Definition Of Collection

The biomechanical definition of collection calls for three independent motor functions that are all linked together. Collection begins when a horse coils his lumbosacral joint. This coiling, in dressage parlance, is "engagement of the hindquarters," or in Western jargon "sticking his tail into the ground."

Collection continues when relaxation of the muscles of the horse's topline, combined with loin coiling, raises the

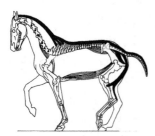

Fig. 4. Skeletal view of a horse performing the trot-in-place movement called piaffe. When the rectus abdominis and iliopsoas muscles of the abdomen and inner loin, respectively, cause the loins to coil, all the hind joints of the horse bend evenly and deeply, shifting his balance to the rear. Loin coiling also stretches the horse's topline; this stretching, combined with effort from the scalenus muscles at the root of the horse's neck, acts to lighten the forehand. This is a synopsis, pictorial and verbal, of how an active "ring of muscles" empowers the horse to achieve full collection.

back. Relaxation and stretching of the topline are always desirable; contraction always undesirable.

Collection is completed when the horse makes a neck-telescoping gesture. When the horse makes this gesture, he "goes onto the bit." Notice that this is something the horse does to the reins, not something the reins do to the horse. See pp. 39-44 in Volume II of this series.

According to the above definition, collection occurs when the horse's "transmission" works properly. The vertical position of the animal's forehead, the extra springiness of his steps and changes in his forward speed all result from the flawless functioning of his loins, back, and neck. The implication? If you can get the horse's back and neck to work better, you will obtain collection, even in a horse with otherwise marginal conformation.

You'll also improve the way the hindquarter functions, just as you improve the efficiency of your car's engine

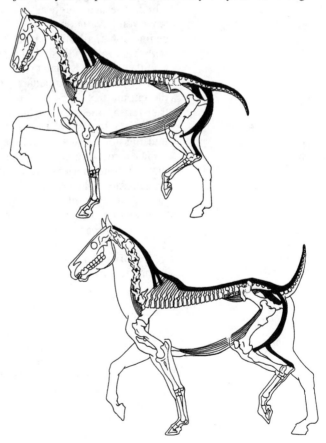

Fig. 5. "Park" and "three-gaited" riding must (like all other forms of equitation) find its definitions of correct form in the horse's inborn mechanism. This mechanism is the same in all horses, no matter what their particular build or breed, and therefore it is easy to find similarities between the "park" horse in good form, above, and the piaffing horse on the preceding page. The hollow-backed and "upside-down" horse, below, is ugly, inharmonious in its movement, and unlikely to remain sound under conditions of work. Training regimes which "break a horse back at the root of the neck," or which cause the horse to tighten and hollow its back, are misguided and damaging.

when you shift gears at just the right rpm's.

The Upper Quarters

Exercise 1: LOIN COILING: MUSCLES AND BONES

Quarter Horses are famous for their large, powerful hindquarters. If we were studying cars rather than horses, we would discover that such hindquarters compare to a Cadillac or Rolls Royce engine — lots of horsepower, not to make a bad pun. And anybody who has ever tinkered around in a garage knows that if you take that 440 horsepower engine and put it in the body of a Mustang, which doesn't weigh as much as a 'Royce or a Caddy, what you have is one mighty hot car. Once you winch the engine down, all that remains is to put the hybrid together with what Johnny Cash, in his song about the Psycho-Billy Cadillac calls an "a-dapter kit," with the accent on the "a."

Well, what are you adapting? In order to do any good, the engine has to be linked with the car's transmission, transferring the power from the engine to the drive train and the wheels. Without the mating of engine and transmission, even a powerful engine is useless.

The same may be said for a horse, once you understand that his hindquarters are his motor and his back is his transmission. The coupling between these two parts — the lumbosacral joint — is where the engine bolts to the transmission. If the horse shows poor or weak structure at that point or anywhere in his back, large hindquarters become useless. In the freespan of the horse's back, length trades off against strength; thus, all other factors being equal, the longer the distance from the withers to the coupling, the weaker the horse's back. A high "waist" as well as narrowness from left to right sides over the coupling also indicates weakness. Structural strain or breakdown is evidenced by lumpiness in this area.

The five examples presented here provide a review of loin conformation and function. Ideally, a horse's loins are high (the topline shows a slightly convex profile all the way from where the back part of the saddle lies to the dip above the hocks); short (having little space between the last rib and the point of hip); wide (as seen from the top); smooth, and muscular. Based on these criteria, which of these five "transmissions" would you buy?

Analysis

Horse #1: This horse is working against a number of structural disadvantages, and from the looks of this photograph, he's not getting much help from his owner. Right off the bat, let's pick up the halter and lead line from under the horse's feet so that he doesn't accidentally tangle one or both front hooves in his unbreakable halter.

The gelding's major problem — a very weak back — is obvious. The weakness in this case is three-dimensional; not only is the back long, it is also narrow across the coupling and shallow from loin to groin. His owner writes that she'd like to see the horse in Western Pleasure competition, but that he seems to have trouble achieving and holding collection. This is not surprising: collection doesn't depend in any way upon the size of the hindquarters or the position of the horse's forehead; it depends on his ability to powerfully coil his lumbosacral joint (see page 8, "A Definition Of Collection").

While the bone structure of this horse's hindquarter is excellent, notice that its muscular development is uneven. Where there should be a bulging mass of gluteal muscle lying on top of the croup, it is flat; and where the hamstring muscles on the back of the thigh should be flat, they bulge. This development is a sure sign that the horse does not thrust with much power (the gluteals are responsible for thrusting the body upward away from the

Courtesy, C. Deal

(1) **Four-year-old Quarter Horse gelding**

HORSE #1

earth), and that he runs forward onto the forehand (the hamstrings are responsible for pushing the body forward like a wheelbarrow).

Similar maldevelopment is evident in the gelding's neck. Structurally, there is nothing wrong with it, and he has a nice shoulder and arm. However, the fact that this horse carries his neck like a lady sheep (ewe) is a sign that the scalenus muscles (see p. 40, Volume II), which lift the root of the neck and which power the neck-telescoping gesture, are too weak.

In addition, he is very thin. What is to be done for him? Besides upgrading his nutrition, correct and systematic exercise on the longe line over cavalletti will produce all the desired results.

Horse #2: This gelding presents a medium-length back which is sufficiently, if not spectacularly, well-coupled. Ideally, in looking at the loin area from the side, the musculature of the hindquarters should appear to carry forward into the back (see examples #3 and #4). While this gelding's loin area shows no breakdowns, strains or pathological changes, as does Horse #2, it is not as high or fully muscled as it could and should be. As a corollary, the gelding's underline is somewhat sagging, indicating only average fitness and athletic ability. His back can be raised and the shape of his underline improved through a systematic program of longeing over cavalletti (see p. 26-27, Volume II).

I like this gelding's hindquarters. The distance from the peak of the croup to the root of the dock is sufficient. Likewise, the distance between the point of hip and the point of buttock is good (length in this dimension is typical of both Quarter Horses and Thoroughbreds). I'm especially pleased with the vertical depth of this gelding's quarters — that is, the triangular area formed by the point of hip, point of buttock and stifle joint.

This gelding has a well-placed (low) stifle joint. This placement, in turn, causes the hamstring muscles, lying along the back of the quarters, to tie on low or carry down well. In addition, a low stifle is usually accompanied by two other desirable features: medium to short gaskins and low hocks, just as seen here.

All told, this gelding appears to be sound and useful. He stands 14:1 hands tall and has a sweet, placid face — a very suitable mount for the teenaged girl who submitted his photo.

(I am prompted to note that it is poor policy to tie a horse up by the reins. If he were to throw his head up, his mouth might be seriously injured. Likewise, what if he put

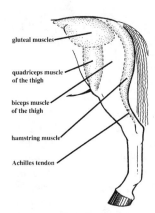

gluteal muscles

quadriceps muscle
of the thigh

biceps muscle
of the thigh

hamstring muscle

Achilles tendon

Fig. 6. This diagram shows the areas of the horse's hind limb in which the four major external muscle groups can be palpated. In an excellent horse, the gluteals are full and firm-feeling and carry foward into the back. The quadriceps are bulky, while the hamstrings feel no firmer than the gluteal mass.

(2) Four-year-old Quarter Horse gelding

(3) 10-year-old Quarter Horse gelding

a foot in the extension ladder?)

Horse #3: This gelding has more muscle bulk on his shoulders and neck than he has on his hindquarters. Such unbalanced development is the signature of a horse that travels on the forehand. Why does he move this way? There are several possible reasons — including rider error — but in this case, the structure of his loins is definitely a factor. His loins are narrow and long. The underline rises toward the sheath, giving him a high, narrow "waist." The topline of the back is concave, stiff, strained, and angular. These signs indicate that the horse does not habitually coil his loins in order to move. Instead, he stiffens his back, flattening and extending the lumbosacral joint.

Collection and self-carriage, and the increased balance and power that result from them, are impossible without loin coiling. Horses that travel in self-carriage develop high, smooth, round gluteal musculature on either side of the croup, whereas in this gelding the gluteal area is hollow.

Likewise, the quadriceps muscle mass, which lies between the stifle and the point of hip, is underdeveloped in this individual. Since the quadriceps is responsible for drawing the hind limb forward with each stride, it is obvious that this gelding also has difficulty in striding up. The only muscle tissue that is well-developed in this gelding are the hamstrings, the only "motor" muscle group that can develop in a horse who moves in a stiff-backed and strung-out manner. Belly-lifts, hind-leg lifts, lateral suppling from the saddle, and systematic work over cavalletti will help to raise his back, deepen his underline and soften and stretch his hamstrings. At the same time, these exercises will also develop both his gluteal and

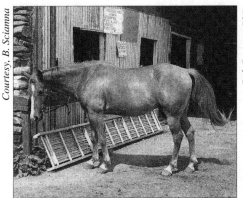

Courtesy, B. Sciamna

HORSE #2

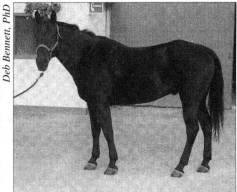

Deb Bennett, PhD

HORSE #3

quadriceps muscle masses.

Horse #4: This young Thoroughbred has by nature an exceptionally high, convex loin area. Such conformation is not due to conditioning, because the horse's underline is still undeveloped: it rises high to the sheath, giving this fellow even more of a waist than horse #2.

Correct bone structure gives rise to correct movement, and the visible musculature provides evidence that this gelding naturally moves correctly. First, his forequarter is less massive than his hindquarter. Second, his gluteal and quadriceps muscles are smoothly bulging. Third, his gluteal mass appears to "carry forward" into his loins. However, horses also posess loin musculature which an observer cannot see, namely, the internal iliopsoas mass. Although it is not visible in a photograph, we may safely assume from the arched profile of this gelding's topline that the iliopsoas is large and strong. Its fitness is the reason the horse's back can be elevated even in the presence of a high waist with no great development (thickening) of the abdominal muscles shaping his underline.

His short, weak neck is another function of his immaturity and will not achieve its adult proportions for a few years. Even then, however, this gelding will always have a straight-out-the-front neck and a very horizontal topline. A horse of this build could have two very profitable careers: as a hunter, or (if he were registered as a Quarter Horse instead of as a Thoroughbred) as a so-called "modern" Western Pleasure mount.

Horse #5: This gelding takes the prize in this group for the best all-around development and the best overall body balance. His high, smooth, short back is flanked, as in #3,

(4) **Three-year-old Thoroughbred gelding**
(5) **Six-year-old Tennessee Walking Horse gelding**

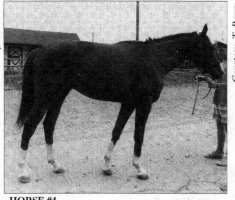

Courtesy, M. Bone

HORSE #4

Courtesy, T. Barry

HORSE #5

by long withers and an excellent loin. While he could be fitter, this gelding's underline is the most robust of the four horses presented here and shows good depth from loin to groin, indicating strong abdominal musculature. The distance from the peak of the croup to the dock could be longer, but the "break" over the top from the peak to the loins is smooth and convex, indicating that the gluteal musculature carries forward into the back.

This gelding's quadriceps and gluteals are full, while his hamstrings are the right size (smooth and no harder to the touch than either his gluteals or his quadriceps). Stiff, hard, stringy hamstrings, as in #2, indicate an individual who travels out of balance — a horse that pushes, rather than carries his weight forward.

Unfortunately, this horse does not carry his neck very well, a habit pointed up by the incorrect development of the neck muscles — all the thickness is on the underside, while the crest is knife-thin and the lower triangle hollow. Less work going straight down the trail, and more work on turns and transitions between the various gaits in an arena will help to correct the posture of his vertebral column (internally) as well as the muscular development of his neck (externally).

Exercise 2: HOW MUCH POWER DOES HE PACK?

S ince the advent of photography in the late nineteenth century, those who breed draft horses and American Quarter Horses have favored posing their animals so that their powerful haunches are highlighted. While in judging conformation it's never a good idea to pay attention to only one part of a horse's anatomy, there are less useful fixations than on powerful haunches, such as to the head, the eye, the set of the tail or the animal's "presence." In the foregoing exercise, we examined the loin coupling; now it's time to look at the next segment back.

The uppermost external surface of the horse's body, located directly behind the loin, is the croup. Internally, the bone which supports the croup is the sacrum. Triangular in top view, the sacrum is a rigid rod formed of five or six naturally fused vertebrae. Its flattened forward surface is the "sacral" part of the lumbosacral joint. Aft, it terminates in a small, circular surface to which the first vertebra of the tail is joined.

The bones of the horse's pelvis surround the sacrum

front "wings" of sacrum, attach to undersurface of pelvis

last lumbar vertebra

upper surface of the pelvis

hip socket

sacrum

first two tail vertebrae

Fig. 7. Top view of pelvis, croup, and first two tail bones. The croup bone or sacrum threads through the curving bones of the pelvis, lying beneath it in front, projecting above it in the rear. The flat, upward-facing surfaces of the "wings" of the sacrum are attached to the undersurfaces of the pelvis in front by a Velcro-like patch of very short ligament fibers. When these fibers are torn, the sacroiliac joint is said to be subluxated, and the horse has "hunter bump."

and help support the upper part of the hindquarters. All the major propulsive muscles of the body are attached to the pelvis. Thus, the pelvis is equivalent to the engine block of a car. The larger the pelvis, the greater the propulsive musculature possible, and the more potential power the horse can pack.

Like any other object in this universe, the horse's pelvis can be expanded in three dimensions: length (size from front to back); breadth (size from side to side); and depth (size from top to bottom). Breadth contributes very little to power, since the muscles of the left side of the body are normally simply reduplicated on the right. Pelvic breadth is desirable, though, because it's an advantage in broodmares and helps in foaling.

Pelvic depth provides space for the ball-shaped gluteus medius muscle, which is responsible for initiating hind-leg thrust in horses. For this reason, having a deep pelvis is especially important in sprint racers and draft horses, who must either get off the starting block quickly, or who spend their working lives in "first gear."

The most important parameter for estimating a horse's overall power is pelvic length. All of the propulsive muscles, including the gluteus medius, are attached along the long dimension of this bone.

The best estimate of horsepower can be obtained when pelvic length is expressed as a fraction of body length. It is the same relationship that explains why a four-cylinder subcompact car has to wheeze and gasp its way up to highway speed when loaded with three commuters, but that same engine makes a big Harley motorcycle fly. In short, you cannot get more power in a horse or a car simply by making the whole machine bigger; you have to make the engine bigger relative to the body.

An old rule of thumb in conformation judging is that the horse's body should be divisible into thirds: the front one-third bounded by the point of shoulder, root of the neck, withers and elbow; another third taken up by the freespan of the back; and the rear third bounded by the point of hip, point of buttock, and stifle. These relationships can be proven to exist by measuring them, and you can greatly improve your "eye" for bodily proportions by sizing up photographs of horses. The object of measuring is to enable you to know immediately when you see a horse that is a little short in the hindquarters, in contrast to one that has a pelvic length constituting more than one-third of his body length.

The breed with the largest hindquarters (relative to body length) is the Thoroughbred, which averages 34 to 35 percent. A ratio between pelvic and body length of over 33 percent is good while one over 35 percent is excellent. At the other end of the scale, the smallest pelvic ratios run in the 26 to 27 percent range: ratios under 29 percent are poor, while those between 29 and 33 percent are average.

Analysis

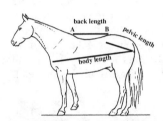

Fig. 8. Horse #1's pelvic length is 38 percent of his body length. His back length (measured from point A to point B) is 42 percent of his body length.

Horse #1: This beautiful and functional animal well typifies his breed. He shows no flaws worth mentioning, but has an outstanding neck (with correct posture and therefore correctly developed muscling) and hindquarter. That much said, let's proceed to a discussion of his body proportions and something about their functional meaning.

The first thing to strike the eye is his hindquarter. The pelvis shows tremendous length, yet the croup and quarters are beautifully shaped. An analytical tracing of this individual reveals that his pelvic length equals 38 percent of his body length. This is as much "motor" as you're ever likely to see in a horse; so much length is a rarity in any breed.

At this point, it is worth asking why this gelding's hindquarters are so big. Is it because the horse's back is short? Or is it because of an extremely short, steep shoulder? Notice that the body-length line includes all three segments of a horse's body, and total body length can be decreased by shortening any or all of these three segments. It is possible through selective breeding to construct an infinite number of different body and pelvic proportions. Since the body-length line represents the divisor in the ratio equation, shortening either a horse's back or his shoulder will enlarge the proportonal size of the pelvis. This is the same as leaving a car's engine the same size while making its body smaller.

The shape of this gelding's hindquarter is typical of nineteenth-century carriage breeding. The desire of breeders at this time was to produce a smoothly coupled, near-level croup with a high tail attachment, yet preserve tremendous length between the peak of the croup and the root of the dock, just as seen here.

Note, too, the gelding's short legs; he stands over a lot of ground, but not a lot of air. This is the European ideal of the "rectangular" horse, an ideal which also derives from nineteenth-century carriage-horse breeding. While the photograph shows the horse bitted and bridled in the style of American "park" or English Pleasure competiton, I would suggest that his owner also try him in hunter hack and dressage, where (like European horses) he should prove his worth through his physical similarity. He could also, of course, succeed in harness.

Horse #2: This is also a nice horse and a useful animal with nearly as good a set of legs as #1, but he just isn't as "punched up" or closely coupled, either at the loin or at the root of the neck. Further, his back is nine percent longer while his pelvis is nine percent shorter. The one point in which this horse is superior to #1 is the angulation of the hind leg, which is just a bit straighter. This makes him a "trotty" Tennessee Walker who can produce all possible gaits: walk, amble (running-walk), trot, canter, and gallop.

Horse #3: This very nice Thoroughbred filly shows the body proportions of the classic-distance racehorse and no flaws worth mentioning. She has a lovely feminine expression and is very refined and breedy about the head,

(1) 13-year-old Morgan gelding
(2) Nine-year-old Tennessee Walking Horse gelding
(3) Two-year-old Thoroughbred filly
(4) Three-year-old Arabian gelding

Courtesy, D. Alspach

HORSE #1

Courtesy, P. Williams

HORSE #2

Courtesy, N. Pongitory

HORSE #3

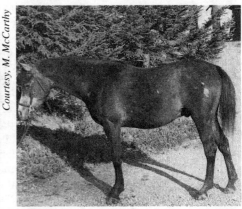

Courtesy, M. McCarthy

HORSE #4

neck, and ears. She epitomizes what Gustav Rau, founder of the modern German school of horse breeding, meant when he called certain Thoroughbred horses "noble."

This filly shows a pelvic length that is 35 percent of her body length. She will continue to grow for the next three to four years, and her pelvis will slowly increase in length over that span of time. Meanwhile, however, her shoulder and back will also expand: she'll have better-defined withers as a six-year-old, and her neck will be longer and not so thin. The last part of a horse to stop growing is the vertebral column, so I expect that at age six she will show a pelvic length of about 34 percent of her overall body length.

Besides a well-coupled, medium-length back, she has the longest and most laid-back shoulder of these four; her withers are located well behind her elbows. The angle between shoulder and arm lines at the point of shoulder is less than 90 degrees. This predisposes her to be an efficient "grass clipper," ideal for racing, but not as good at lateral movements or "folding" over really big fences. She will likely be a winner at the track, but could also make a top-quality show hunter under appropriate tutelage.

Horse #4: Although this gelding and #2 belong to very different breeds, and although they have very different types of heads, the two share almost identical proportions in the torso (the Arabian's back is one percent shorter and his pelvis one percent longer than that of the Walking Horse). Like #2, this fellow is a useful animal. My only complaint with him is that he's somewhat light of bone in front and his knees are just enough too high to bother me (none of the horses presented in this set has quite as low a knee as I would like).

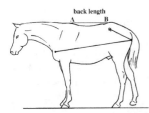

Fig. 9. Horse #4's pelvic length is 30 percent of his body length. His back length is 50 percent of his body length. An Arabian, this individual possesses almost the same bodily proportions as Horse #2, a Tennessee Walking Horse. Their similarity emphasizes that an underpowered "motor" looks the same, no matter in what skin the package may be wrapped.

The Hind Limbs From The Side

Exercise 3: JUDGING HIND LIMB LENGTH

Someone once jestingly asked the sixteenth President, "Abe, how long are your legs?" Lincoln replied, "Long enough to reach the ground."

Unlike people, horses naturally stand with both their knee (stifle) and ankle (hock) joints somewhat bent. The flexible nature of a horse's hind joints can make learning to see the true conformation of his hindquarter a challenge. Depending on what the horse is doing — moving at a

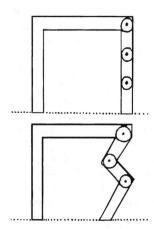

Fig. 10. The top table's legs go straight to the ground and are therefore shorter than the table leg that zigzags on its way to the floor.

collected trot, sleeping standing up, stretching as he awakens or preparing to depart the premises with nose and tail in the air — the hind legs can adopt a wide range of different "natural angulations." Luckily, one aspect of the Abe Lincoln story remains as true for horses as for people: although the angles of a horse's hind joints may change as he moves, the lengths of the individual bones remain the same under all conditions.

Surprising though it may sound at first, you can use the total length of the hind limb bones to find out what kind of "angulation" a horse actually possesses. To make this clear, let's imagine a trip to the furniture store. In the "Early American" department, we'll find tables with legs which go straight down to the floor. If these legs had joints, they would be wide open (see Fig. 10). This is a "post-legged" table. Since a straight line represents the shortest route from the tabletop to the floor, relative to croup height, post legs are short legs.

Now let's go upstairs to see the "modernist" furniture. Here we find tables with zigzag legs. Because the legs zigzag several times between the tabletop and the floor, the total length of these zigzagged or angulated legs is greater than that of post legs.

No horse has hind limbs as straight (or as short) as an Early American table, yet in the horse species there is still a wide range of natural angulations — and thus of hind limb lengths relative to the distance of the hindquarter from the ground. The purpose of measuring the total length of the hind limb is to compare that total to the height of the horse either at the withers or at the croup (the tabletop).

I encourage students of conformation to do the following exercise on paper a few times. After that, your eye will probably be sharp enough to detect and classify hind limbs that are normal, overangulated or crooked, and those that are post-legged or overstraight.

Start with an 8 X 10 side photo of your horse. Tape the photo to a table and then tape a sheet of tracing paper over the photo. With a sharp pencil, trace your horse's outline. Then locate the points representing the lumbosacral, hip, stifle, hock, and fetlock joints. Connect the points with lines representing the iliac part of the pelvis, the femur, gaskin, hind cannon and hind pastern bones (see Fig. 11). Using a millimeter ruler, measure the lengths of these five bones, write them down and then total them. Now, measure the horse's height either from the peak of the croup (if he is not posed in a stretched posture) or from the peak of the withers (if he is stretched). Finally, plug the

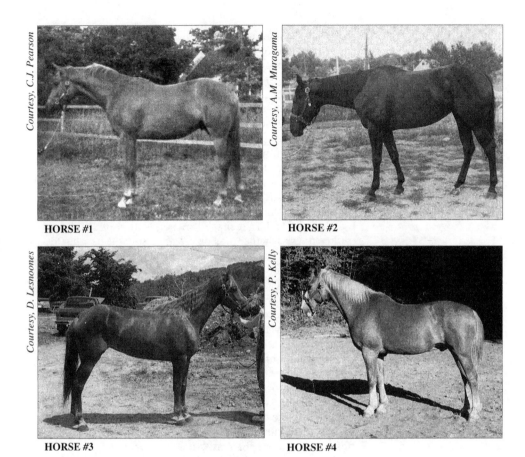

Courtesy, C.J. Pearson

Courtesy, A.M. Muragama

Courtesy, D. Lesnoones

Courtesy, P. Kelly

HORSE #1   **HORSE #2**

HORSE #3   **HORSE #4**

(1) **Two-year-old Anglo-Trakehner gelding**
(2) **Four-year-old Quarter Horse-Thoroughbred mare**
(3) **Five-year-old Tennessee Walking Horse mare**
(4) **24-year-old grade Morgan gelding**

numbers into this formula:

Total Hind Limb Length X 100 ÷ Croup (or Withers) Height = Proportional Length of Hind Limb.

Of the four horses pictured here, which has the shortest (straightest) hind limbs? Which has the longest (most crooked)? Does the stretched pose of #4 make analysis easier or harder? To which other horse is #4 actually most similar?

Analysis

Horse #1: This nicely balanced two-year-old is going to mature into a handsome, easy-to-train horse. I can't find anything about him to criticize. I include him here because of his open hind joints — he's not post-legged, but he certainly is on the short end of the normal range.

Open hind joints make for biomechanical efficiency — little of the energy with which the horse thrusts himself forward is lost at the joint angles but instead travels straight down the bone columns. Horses built like this make the best hunters, steeplechasers, jumpers and racers. Dressage horses, on the other hand, typically have somewhat longer and more angulated hind limbs, but should this horse's owner wish him to specialize in dressage instead of jumping, his straighter limbs will not prevent him so long as he coils his loins (and his back undulates elastically) at the trot. His long femur (low stifle) will also help him in that discipline.

Horse #2: The teenaged owner of this quality mare writes to ask whether the horse will be suitable as a hunter-jumper or for low-level combined training. I certainly like her thin-skinned, breedy look, the wide-open angle between her shoulder and arm, her magnificent heart girth and the size of her pelvis, although its angle is as steep as I would like to see it. Her legs are, however, another matter.

Her somewhat crooked hind limbs act to push her rump up in the air with every stride she takes. Her femurs are fairly long; this is an advantage in either dressage or jumping, but at the same time, her hocks are too high, creating a tendency for excessive or "poppy" hock action. This will make it hard for her to get her hocks up under her body when she engages her hindquarters. In addition, body balance that runs downhill to the front is not an adaptive feature in a jumper or a cross-country horse.

Despite these drawbacks, however, she should do acceptably well at dressage, be a safe ride across country over novice-sized obstacles and stay sound through training and competition.

She has the bone structure on which to build a much nicer neck and topline. As pictured, however, she's a classic example of a horse whose epaxial musculature (the muscles which wrap around the bones of her neck and back) are stiff and weak. Her loin coupling, likewise, is long and weak. She needs two years of steady work by a good rider to build strength in her underline and to stretch the muscles of her topline.

Horse #3: This gelding exemplifies the hind limb conformation known as "cat-hammed," which is seen when a "goose rump" or very steep pelvic angle is combined with markedly long, crooked hind legs such as this fellow has. Such conformation is a strong indication that the animal possessing it will prefer to amble or gait (fox trot, running-walk or even pace) rather than trot.

Those who favor gaited horses, however, should be aware that this combination is just as faulty in a gaited horse as in a trotter. The reason? All gaited horses of whatever breed, at some phase of their training or during certain activities, must also trot or canter for correct muscular development. Just as it is a fallacy to believe that you train a jumping horse by only jumping him, it is also a fallacy to believe that you dare not let your gaited horse trot (or canter). A horse that can do nothing but gait is inferior.

One gaited tradition which has kept this knowledge very much alive is that of the Paso horses. In addition, since stiffness of the torso is an occupational hazard of gaited horses, correct Paso training emphasizes bending the horse in both directions through the systematic riding of figures, much as in dressage. As a result, a correctly trained Paso may not only do one or more lateral gaits, but can also trot a fence line or gallop to allow its vaquero rider to rope or pen cattle.

Horse #4: This photo of an equine senior citizen highlights two special circumstances in which knowing how to measure the total length of a horse's hind limb is advantageous. First, the horse is posed with the hind limbs

Fig. 11. Analytical drawings of the four horses under examination in Lab Exercise 3.

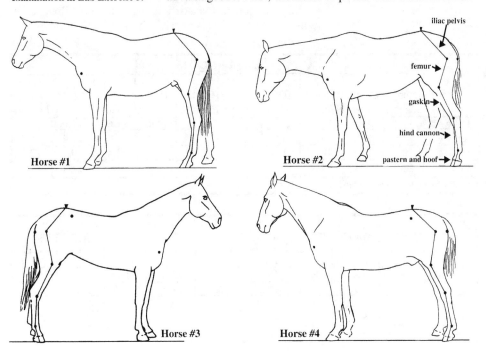

Horse #1

Horse #2

iliac pelvis

femur

gaskin

hind cannon

pastern and hoof

Horse #3

Horse #4

stretched out behind; and second, he's posed with his hind feet in a bit of a hole. The pose and the hole make him look post-legged. Is he?

The Body-Part Proportions table reveals that the total length of his hind limb from the hip socket down (column 2) is the second highest, his femur the second longest (columns 5 and 6) and his hind cannon the longest (columns 8 and 9) in this group. (It should be noticed that columns 1 and 3 are meaningless for this horse, since stretching artificially lowers the croup height). Happily, his gaskin is fairly short (column 7); if it were not, his hind-limb total might exceed that of #3. Thus, if this horse were posed on level ground without being stretched, he might keep the same hind-limb angles but stand rump-high, or he might stand level with a hind-limb angulaton about like that of #2.

His excellent loin coupling, deep groin and substantial bone are pleasing. I believe he actually has more natural angulation to his hind legs than is evident in this photo. Considering their stoutness and his fairly long femur and short gaskin, he would probably have made a pretty fair dressage or English Pleasure prospect and might also have been fun to take reining. A long hind limb from the hip socket down (columns 1 or 2) helps to confer an overstriding walk. Compared to horses #1 and #2, this gelding's major flaw is a deficit of length in the iliac pelvis (columns 3 and 4). This deprives him of some of the power

Body-Part Lengths

	Body Length	Croup Height	Withers Height	Iliac Pelvis	Femur Length	Gaskin Length	Hind Cannon	Hind Pastern & Hoof	Total Hind Limb #1	Total Hind Limb #2
Horse #1	13.2	13.4	13.4	3.6	3.5	2.9	3.0	1.6	11.0	14.6
Horse #2	13.5	13.4	13.3	3.9	3.0	3.5	3.2	1.6	11.4	15.2
Horse #3	10.9	11.1	10.8	2.5	2.8	3.0	2.5	1.4	9.7	12.2
Horse #4	13.9	13.0*	13.3	3.3	3.4	3.2	3.3	1.5	11.4	14.7

*This figure is too low because the horse is stretched.

Body-Part Proportions (given as percentages)

	THL #1/ Croup Height	THL #1/ Withers Height	THL #2/ Croup Height	THL #2/ Withers Height	Femur/ THL #1	Femur/ THL #2	Gaskin/ Femur	Hind Cannon/ THL #1	Hind Cannon/ THL #2
Horse #1	82.0	82.0	108.9	108.9	32.4	24.4	80.6	27.0	20.4
Horse #2	85.0	83.8	113.4	114.3	26.3	19.7	116.7	28.1	21.0
Horse #3	87.4	89.8	109.9	113.0	28.9	22.9	107.1	25.8	20.5
Horse #4	*	85.7	*	110.5	29.8	23.1	94.1	29.0	22.5

*Figures in these columns are meaningless, due to stretched pose of horse.

Exercise 4: THE LONG AND SHORT OF HIND-LIMB CONSTRUCTION

Since the idea of measuring a horse's hind limb bones is a relatively new one in conformation study, more photos are presented here to enable you to get a little more practice with the technique, while at the same time helping you to become more aware of the factors that influence the appearance of a horse's hind legs.

As the last exercise illustrated, the angles of a horse's hind joints change with his every movement, and it is therefore a fruitless and frustrating task to measure the angles themselves. However, if croup height is held constant, the lengths of the five bony segments which make up a horse's hind limb can be measured and compared with croup height. Since the lengths of limb bones do not change as the horse moves, the ratio between the total hind-limb length, or THL (iliac pelvis + femur + gaskin + hind cannon + hind pastern and hoof = THL), and the height of the croup reveals how much hind limb a given horse packs. This ratio in turn is a good predictor of performance aptitude.

Since everything in biomechanical study must be regarded in terms of functional trade-offs, there is no one perfect hind-limb length. A basic rule is this: the shorter and straighter a hind limb is, the more efficiently it can deliver thrust, generated by the muscles of the horse's rump, downward to the ground. It is not surprising, therefore, to find that among racehorses and jumpers, straight hind limbs are common. The downside of this construction is that if the hind limb is too straight at the stifle joint, it may "stick" or "lock," a condition technically known as chronic partial subluxation of the patella. If it is too straight at the hock, occult arthritis, more commonly referred to as "blind jack," is the usual outcome.

The opposite construction is the horse with long bones and crooked (or Z-shaped) hind limbs. Up to a point, the longer a horse's hind limb relative to his croup height, the easier it is for him to bring his hocks and hind hooves forward with each stride ("stride up" or "track up"). This proclivity is especially noticeable in non-suspended gaits such as the walk, running walk, paso, and rack. It is not surprising, therefore, to find that among dressage stars, as well as among gaited champions, long and angulated hind limbs are common. The downside of this construction is that if the hind limb is too crooked — especially at the hock joint — curbs and spavins are likely, and engagement of the hindquarter becomes difficult for the horse.

Before deciding that a horse is post-legged or crooked, however, it is necessary to consider whether he's built level. A rump-high horse may appear to be post-legged, but is that the way he functions? In a well-moving horse, the hind joints fold and flex elastically; at the moment of thrust, the croup should carry no higher than the withers. If the croup is carried high in movement, the horse will be a rough, uncomfortable ride. This type of movement is usually produced by individuals with markedly crooked hind legs, whose excessive length cannot help but push the croup upward with every thrust.

In this exercise, first we'll give every horse the benefit of the doubt, assuming that he can move with withers and croup on one level. Mathematically, this means that we'll apply a correction to the THL/croup height ratio by adding the amount that the horse is rump-high to his total hind-limb length.

As you scan this set of photos, look for open or closed angles at stifle, hock and fetlock joints, and notice which horses stand rump-high. How does a stretched pose alter croup height and hind-limb angulation?

Analysis

Horse #1: This gelding is truly post-legged, as is evident not only by his low THL, but also by the angles of his limbs. The post-legged horse typically has wide-open angles at stifle and hock and also tends to be "coon-footed" — having too horizontal a hind pastern — when the limb is bearing weight.

(1) Seven-year-old Welsh-
 Quarter Horse gelding
(2) Aged Quarter Horse mare

Courtesy, M. Dausend

Courtesy, B.K. Steingraber

HORSE #1

HORSE #2

Body-Part Lengths

Measure-ment	Body Length	Withers Height	Croup Height	Pelvis Length	Iliac Length	Femur Length	Gaskin Length	Hind Cannon	Hind Pastern & Hoof	THL
Horse #1	12.8	12.6	12.9	4.3	3.5	3.3	3.8	2.3	1.5	14.4
Horse #2	15.6	13.5	14.2	4.8	3.6	3.7	4.0	2.6	1.8	15.7
Horse #3	11.7	10.6	10.6	3.7	3.2	2.9	2.4	2.4	1.2	12.1
Horse #4	12.0	11.6	11.9	4.1	3.1	3.0	3.2	2.6	1.5	13.4

Body-Part Proportions (given as percentages)

Ratio	Croup Height: Withers Height	Pelvis: Body Length	THL: Withers Height	THL: Croup Height	THL: Croup Height Corr.	Femur: THL	Gaskin: Femur	Hind Cannon: THL
Horse #1	102.4	33.6	114.3	111.6	114.0	22.9	115.1	16.0
Horse #2	105.2	30.7	110.6	110.6	115.8	23.6	108.1	16.6
Horse #3	100.0	31.6	114.1	114.1	114.1	24.0	82.8	19.8
Horse #4	102.6*	34.2	115.5	112.6	115.2	22.4	106.7	19.4

*Figure is meaningless due to stretched pose of horse

This gelding's short hind limbs combine with a short femur to yield the particular angulation of his stifles and hocks. Notice that his gaskin is a lot longer than his femur. Except in a sprinter or drafter, the gaskin and femur should be about equal in length. It makes considerable difference in stifle and hock angulation to have long femurs. While this gelding and horse #3 have nearly identical hind-limb lengths, #3 has excellent angulation while this gelding does not.

With regard to other parts of his body, I like the wide-open angle at the point of shoulder, another feature besides straight hind legs that tells me this fellow can jump. His short, broad, strong back and big, well-angled pelvis also deserve lauds, and he gets high marks for substantial bone and well-articulated limbs with big, clean knee and hock joints. I don't mind the short pasterns, since their angle is correct, any more than I mind his long ears: they function just fine. Despite his cobby body type, this gelding is built to run and jump.

Horse #2: In our search for the post-legged horse, this mare looks like a good candidate. However, when we consider that she is quite rump-high, and apply a more than five percent correction to her total hind-limb length, she is revealed as a horse that, to move correctly, would have to fold up the hind limbs even more than #4. Actually, I doubt that any training program could produce

Courtesy, J. Davison

HORSE #3

Courtesy, M. McKee

HORSE #4

(3) **Six-year-old Quarter Horse mare**
(4) **Two-year-old Paint filly**

sufficient coiling of the loin and bending of the hind limb joints in this mare. I call her functionally post-legged, just as likely to have stifle trouble as horse #1.

Horse #3: This crackerjack little horse, who has excellent hind-limb angulation and an ideal gear ratio between femur and gaskin, also shows an excellent back and loin coupling. A one to five percent increase in pelvic length would be ideal, but I like the shape and angle of what she has. Her withers carry the topline of her neck far back behind her elbows, a factor which greatly aids stability and "scope." Her head is pleasant, and the eye tells me she's self-sufficient and self-confident.

Horse #4: This Paint filly — posed in a stretched posture — is the "fooler" in this group. Stretching has two effects: it lowers the horse's croup, and it straightens out the angles of the hind limb. As the accompanying illustration shows, measuring the hind-limb bones reveals a much longer hind limb than the picture seems to show. Fig. 12 shows alternative views of this mare, as she might appear without stretching: in reality, she's either mighty rump-high or has fairly crooked hind limbs.

This mare's torso is well put together. I like her short, strong back, which is well coupled to the hindquarter. Her pelvic length is very good — the longest in this group. Unlike #2, the strength of this mare's loin tells me she can and will coil her loins, engaging her hindquarters for athletic movement. Built as she is, eliciting this response from her is a necessity. If, however, she is allowed to move in a lazy, disengaged manner, she is going to be a rough, bouncy ride.

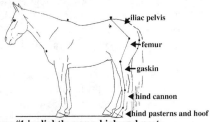

Horse #1 is slightly rump-high and post-legged. His gaskin is longer than his femur.

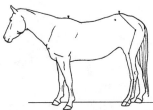

Horse #2 is both rump-high and post-legged.

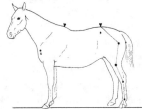

Horse #3 is built level and has excellent hind-limb angulation. Her femur is longer than her gaskin.

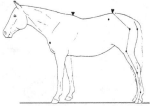

Horse #4 appears to have a level body balance and open angles at stifle and hock when stretched.

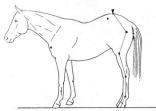

This is how Horse #4 appears if she is reposed without being stretched. In this view, she becomes rump-high because the hind angles have been kept open.

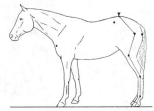

In this view of Horse #4, the topline has been kept level and therefore, the hind limb appears crooked. This view is probably closest to the mare's actual working posture.

Fig. 12. Analytical drawings of horses pertaining to Lab Exercise 4.

Exercise 5: THE PERILS OF CROOKED HIND LEGS

There are several points to be derived from this next set of photos: first, that horses' hind legs can be very long indeed compared to their height at withers or croup. The foregoing lab exercises have focused on horses with shorter hind limbs; now, we learn how to identify hind limbs near the upper limits of length.

As previously mentioned, the longer a horse's hind limbs, the more crooked, camped-out, sickle-hocked or over-angulated he's likely to be. These four terms are actually all the same thing — if a crooked-legged horse is posed with hind cannons vertical, people are inclined to call him "camped out"; if posed with hind limbs up under the body, the same horse would be labeled "sickle-hocked."

This group of photos offers a real opportunity to assess harmonious proportions both within a horse's hind limb and with respect to the whole body. One of the horses pictured is an outstanding example of symmetrical build, overall body balance and athletic potential. Which one is it? How much do you think pose and photographic angle affect your ability to identify this individual? Is there another harmonious horse in this group whose picture simply doesn't flatter him, or are all the other animals unbalanced and rump-high?

Finally, three of the horses pictured belong to a single breed. Can you identify it? As we have previously noted, hind-limb length, in combination with back length and pelvic angle, is a good predictor of whether a horse will be laterally gaited. Horses with long backs, and hind limbs that fall between 112 and 115 percent of their croup height, are likely to be able to "swing both ways" — that is, they are likely to be able to produce an outstanding flat walk, a good trot and a good to excellent canter as well as a paso, rack, or running walk.

Analysis

Horse #1: As posed, this Arabian gelding is only slightly rump-high, but he has remarkably long, crooked hind legs that definitely make him camped out. If he were to step forward, it is possible that he would straighten out the joints of his hind limbs; in that case, he would be markedly rump-high.

Since he is only two, he is still growing upward, and we can hope that growth will be concentrated in the withers, shoulder and arm, raising his forehand. However, since the 32 growth plates (physes) of the horse's neck and back mature last (between the ages of five and eight years), most of this gelding's growth will be fore-aft, serving only to increase his body length. Since his neck looks less mature to me than his rib cage and back, I expect this gelding will follow the normal equine growth pattern, in which the neck matures last of all. In short, there isn't much hope that growth will correct either his over-long hind legs or his rump-high stance.

I like his smooth loin coupling, but how is this gelding going to move? First, even though his back isn't long and his pelvis isn't steep, I predict he'll be inclined to produce a fox-trot or a rack anytime he stiffens his back. There have been a number of purebred Arabs in the U.S. during the last 50 years who were trained and exhibited as five-gaited horses, so there is no use saying that Arabians (or horses of any other breed) "aren't supposed to be gaited." Any horse with this conformation can be gaited if his owner desires to enhance the tendency with appropriate training.

Concerning the quality of the traditional three gaits, this horse will stride up or overtrack at the walk without any difficulty. How could he not, given such long hind limbs? If, in addition, his training has been such as to allow and induce him to coil the loin and engage the hindquarters with each step, the quality of his walk will be excellent. If the back is not much involved in his walk or if the horse stiffens his back, he will justly be branded a "leg mover."

In the suspended gaits, everything depends on whether this horse is able to stretch his topline and coil his loins. With stride-by-stride engagement, his canter will be of good quality and easy to ride. With its opposite, a stiff back and flattened loins, the horse will either pronk (make a two-beat canter in which he hops from two hind legs to two front legs like a rabbit) or pace (make a two-beat

Body-Part Lengths

	Iliac Pelvis	Pelvic Length	Femur Length	Gaskin Length	Hind Cannon	Hind Pastern & Hoof	Total Hind Limb	Body Length	Withers Height	Croup Height
Horse #1	3.1	4.2	3.3	4.1	3.0	1.5	15.0	12.8	13.1	12.7
Horse #2	3.4	4.1	2.8	2.8	2.3	1.6	12.9	11.4	11.4	11.5
Horse #3	3.1	3.9	3.1	3.5	2.9	1.5	14.1	12.1	12.2	12.1
Horse #4	3.9	4.7	3.1	4.0	2.9	1.5	15.4	13.1	13.4	13.1

Body-Part Proportions

	Pelvic Length: Body Length	Total Hind Limb: Withers Height	Total Hind Limb: Croup Height	Gaskin:Femur	Femur:Body Length
Horse #1	32.8%	118.1%	114.5%	124.2%	25.8%
Horse #2	36.0%	112.2%	113.3%	100.0%	24.6%
Horse #3	32.2%	116.5%	115.6%	112.9%	25.6%
Horse #4	35.9%	117.6%	114.5%	129.0%	23.7%

canter in which the two left legs strike nearly simultaneously, followed by the two right legs).

In a horse of this build, the trot is the hardest gait to improve. It is very difficult for a camped-out horse with such long hind legs to find space for them under the croup with each trot stride. Rather than coil their loins, an action which pulls the hocks up under the body, most horses with long hind legs trail them out behind, producing a flat and suspensionless trot. Cavalletti are highly recommended to produce the strength in the ring of muscles necessary to enable this gelding to coil his loins at the trot.

Horse #2: This Tennessee Walking Horse stallion is a gorgeous horse with beautifully formed and symmetrically constructed hind limbs (see table, "Body Part Sizes"). He has excellent pelvic length and his total hind-limb length is ideal for any type of saddle use except sprint or classic-distance racing.

(1) **Two-year-old gelding**
(2) **Aged stallion**
(3) **10-year-old gelding**
(4) **Three-year-old stallion**

Courtesy, S. Punch

Deb Bennett, PhD

HORSE #1

HORSE #2

Courtesy, D. Allen

Courtesy, L. Crumbley

HORSE #3

HORSE #4

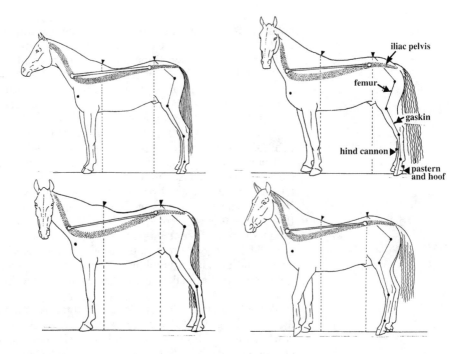

Fig. 13. Analytical drawings of horses pertaining to Lab Exercise 5. Stipple indicates the trace of the row of vertebral centra; see Fig. 38 for further discussion of body balance.

The canon of symmetry begun in the hind limb extends in this individual to all parts of the body. The relatively long back, typical of gaited breeds, is well-coupled with a deep groin, indicating that the horse uses himself well when he moves, coiling his loins and possessing a good, suspended trot besides his running-walk.

Does he pass the test for overall balance? Yes! He goes uphill along the topline, uphill from stifle to elbow, slightly downhill from hock to knee, and nearly level from the loin coupling to the base of the neck. With his excellent pelvic length and smooth, strong loin, I expect this stallion, the classic choice of the North American cavalry officer, to achieve lightness and self-carriage with ease.

His one flaw is insubstantial fore and hind cannons, tied in below the knees and overstraight, verging on calf knees in front, and cut out under the hock behind. Because of the calf knees, it is best for him to maintain quite a bit of heel height, with a fairly steep hoof angle. Don't let a horse of this build get low in the heels of the forefeet.

Horse #3: In this Tennessee Walking Horse we find a longer back which is smoothly and strongly coupled, a pelvic slope nearly identical to horse #2 (though this horse's pelvis is somewhat shorter in length), and a similar construction in shoulder and arm. Other parts of this gelding's structure, however, contribute to significant differences in function. First and most importantly, his total hind limb length is greater than that of #2. If he had been posed like #1, rather than slightly stretched behind, you would see a hind limb nearly as crooked. Even stretched, this gelding is noticeably rump-high. While the stretched pose and his high withers help his topline to go uphill, in reality his overall body balance is downhill.

Temperamentally, this gelding is the archetypal gaited pleasure horse. He has a pleasant, sweet face and ears that tell me he's curious and perky but not overly inventive. He's guaranteed to possess the running-walk and he'll trot flat (if he trots at all), providing a smooth ride. He'll have a pleasant and correct canter, so long as his owner periodically spends time suppling his back and neck by gently and gradually doubling his neck at a halt and by riding him at a flat walk or jog trot on circular figures in an arena.

While he is similar to horse #2 in the torso as well as in the neck (long, but triangular in shape), he must also be criticized for insubstantial cannon bones. He shows a lack of substance and muscling in the forearm and he has small, round knee joints.

Horse #4: This three-year-old Tennessee Walking Horse stallion gets high marks on several points, especially for his bone substance, which is characteristic of the breed and one of its strongest features. His knee, hock and fetlock joints are also outstanding. In gaited competition, a horse that has small, round joints or insubstantial forelegs is as good as lame.

The one area where this colt disappoints me is in total hind-limb length, which indicates that he is nearly as crooked as horse #1, and which pushes this colt's rump unattractively high and tips his body balance down to the front. However, I certainly like the colt's pelvic length. He's destined to have as much back length as #2 and he's about as well-coupled. However, he's not as deep from loin to groin as the mature stallion, a situation that will improve with time.

The heart girth does not equal that of #2, although this colt's rib cage will also enlarge somewhat over the next three years. This colt's shoulder is much more upright than the three other horses shown, indicating that he'll have more natural knee action than they do. However, since the angle at the point of shoulder is still fixed at 90 degrees, the raising of his shoulder angle means that his humerus —

the arm bone stretching between the point of shoulder and elbow — lies too close to the horizontal. The colt will thus tend to work up underneath himself; if he were a hunter, he'd hang his knees.

Please bring this colt some mares sired by #2 — then we'll be on track with solid, substantial horses that are easy to ride, easy to train, and that can "do it all."

Exercise 6: GETTING INTO GEAR

Between the pedals and the rear wheel of a 10-speed bicycle sit two important components: the drive chain, which physically transfers the pedaler's efforts to the rear wheel, and the sprockets, toothed metal wheels of various sizes which act as the bicycle's gear box, determining how fast and how powerfully the rear wheel actually turns. In order for the bicycle to function well, the drive chain needs to be strong and whole. It's also necessary for the cyclist to be able to select the appropriate gear.

In a horse, the same components exist but they don't function in quite the same manner. Each of a horse's two hind legs acts as a separate rear wheel. In a bicycle, the drive chain is multijointed and flexible; in a horse, it possesses five major mobile joints, including, from top to bottom, the lumbosacral (loin), coxofemoral (hip socket), stifle (true knee), hock (true ankle) and fetlock joints. The lengths of the bones separating these joints — the iliac part of the pelvis, the femur, gaskin, hind cannon, the pastern and hoof — determine the gear ratio of each horse. Unlike a 10-speed bike, each horse possesses but one gear ratio.

Just as the intelligent cyclist selects the appropriate gear for road conditions, speed and terrain, it's important for the prospective horse buyer to select an animal with the best "gear ratio" for the tasks at hand. This can be accomplished by assessing the proportions that exist within the hind limbs.

As you begin your analysis, turn your attention to the horse's femur, which plays a critical role in the way the hind limb functions. Consider, for example, that the bones of a horse's hind limb form a series or chain of rodlike links. If you were to remove the horse's relaxed hind limb, pin the upper end of the femur to a horizontal rod and set it swinging, it would act like a special type of pendulum called a chain pendulum. The physical properties of a chain pendulum dictate that whatever the uppermost, governing link in the chain does, the rest of the links must reflect it.

Anyone who has seen a cuckoo clock or a grandfather clock has seen a pendulum in action. The short pendulum of the cuckoo clock swings rapidly back and forth. If longer links were attached below the upper short link, their arc of swing would be a multiple of the rapid swing of the uppermost link. The long, slow swing of the grandfather clock pendulum is likewise simply the result of its length, and even if short links are attached to hang below it, they will also swing slowly.

For a horse, short upper links "fix" him in first gear. They are a desirable feature for a horse involved in speed events or sprint racing (any race under two miles in length). A short femur enables a horse to leap out of the starting gate and continue taking short, rapid strides to the finish line. Draft horses, too, perform best in the equine version of first gear, grinding along in "granny low" through a day of plowing or hauling.

If you're interested in any other sort of equestrian pursuit — and that includes the gamut of activities from cutting and reining through three- or five-gaited riding to three-day eventing, polo, hunter-jumper and dressage — then you need the "third gear" capabilities conferred by a long femur.

After you've looked at the femur, you'll also find it helpful to scrutinize the gaskin. While virtually everyone agrees that the horse whose hocks are placed low is superior to his higher-hocked companion, it's important to realize that there is more than one way to achieve low hocks. Unless you're in sprint racing or drafting, the only beneficial way to lower the hocks is to lower the stifle without lengthening the gaskin. Sprinters with high stifles can have low hocks only if they also have long gaskins.

Long gaskins are always disadvantageous, first, because as in the case of the cannon bones, the longer they are, the thinner and less well-articulated they tend to be. Where stringent selection has operated to keep the gaskin and its articulation to the hock substantial, as in many warmbloods, it's still very likely that the horse with a long gaskin will be cow-hocked or bowlegged, and that the hock joints will bend to the outside like elbows when weight passes over them in movement. These problems are the occupational hazards of sprinters, but there's no reason to buy them in horses intended for other purposes.

In this set of photos, look especially at femur length, gaskin length, and hock placement before you decide which horse you'd buy.

Analysis

Horse #1: This three-year-old is still three years away from full maturity and therefore, it is necessary to forgive him a certain amount of disproportionate gawkiness. The significant faults in this horse all reside in the rear, starting with a grade-B coupling over a slightly weak-looking loin (his owner says she's already riding him, but my advice would be to wait at least a year before doing anything more than saddling this one and sitting on him).

Behind the coupling follows a pelvis that is not long enough to balance out this fellow's shoulder and midbody. Whereas his pelvis measures just 30 percent of his body length, it ought to be above 33 percent, especially in a dressage horse or jumper. Below that, we find a

(1) **Three-year-old Anglo-Hanoverian gelding**
(2) **Aged American Saddlebred gelding**
(3) **Aged Thoroughbred gelding**
(4) **Six-year-old American Quarter Horse mare**

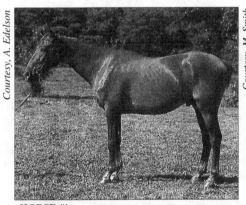

HORSE #1

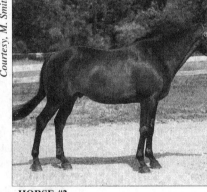

HORSE #2

HORSE #3

HORSE #4

remarkably short thigh (the stifle appears to be above the sheath and the femur has the lowest ratio to total hind-limb length of any horse in this set).

Yes, the hocks are low, but that in and of itself is not going to prevent this gelding from wanting to take short, rapid hind strides — the result of his built-in gear ratio. In training this horse, regulating his rhythm and encouraging him to reach forward and spring off each hind leg is going to be important.

Because his stifles are high and his hocks low, this fellow has long gaskins. Predictably, he's cow-hocked and sickle-hocked and his total hind-limb length is high relative to his croup height. This means his hind limbs are fairly crooked or angulated. In other words, he's compressing a lot of hind limb under his croup. Luckily, he does have substantial hock joints. Lateral work, which strengthens the adductor and abductor musculature lying along the inner and outer surfaces of the thigh and gaskin, can be used to stabilize hocks like these, which bend outward with every stride.

In front, he shows some very nice features, including good bone and withers that carry well back into the free-span of his back and peak well behind his elbows. His neck is well-shaped and of the right length, but is flat and undermuscled as expected in a young horse. As his neck develops, his head will stop looking so disproportionately long and heavy. His shoulder is deep and well-angled, but his humerus (the bone spanning the point of shoulder to the elbow) could be longer. Overall, it will be useful to compare this warmblood with example #1 from the foregoing Lab Exercise 3 (page 23).

Horse #2: Here's the opposite extreme: this horse's hocks are too high. Notice, however, that the femur is longer than in horse #1. The combination of long femur and very long hind cannons produces a remarkably short gaskin. In this gelding, the gaskin is more than 25 percent shorter than the femur, while in #1 the gaskin is longer than the femur.

While extremely high hocks do not promote hind-limb unsoundness, they do predispose to excessive or "poppy" hock action. When the hocks are much higher than the horse's knees, there is also some tendency for the animal to move or balance himself downhill, and to have trouble getting his hocks up "underneath himself." In this case, the hocks are not markedly higher than the knees, but that's only because the horse's knees are also too high. In this case, two wrongs make a right...sort of.

With a rounded, sloping croup (he has the classic "apple butt" spoken of by Thoroughbred breeders) and excellent coupling, short loins and long rib cage, this fellow is going to be easy to collect or make round. Likewise, the fact that his femur is longer than his gaskin will help to confer the slow rhythm preferred in dressage.

However, this horse lacks the substance of #1. What, then, are we to do with this fellow? His lower limbs will always be a problem, at least in terms of an aesthetic distraction. If someone raises him to upper-level performance, where his torso capablities will shine, judges may be willing to forgive somewhat the excess activity going on below the elbows and stifles. Despite his high knees and hocks and somewhat insubstantial limbs, I don't expect training to make him unsound.

Horse #3: The chestnut horse in this photo is presented specifically to contrast with horse #1. He is an absolutely gorgeous animal without a notable structural flaw. His musculature has developed in a perfectly correct, harmonious manner. Of special interest are a perfect loin

Body-Part Lengths

Measure-ment	Body Length	Croup Height	Pelvic Length	Ilium Length	Femur Length	Gaskin Length	Hind Cannon	Hind Pastern & Hoof	[#1] Total Hind Limb (5+6+7+8)	[#2] Total Hind Limb (4+5+6+7+8)
Horse #1	13.80	13.60	4.15	3.45	3.45	3.55	3.40	1.60	12.00	15.45
Horse #2	9.85	10.00	3.15	2.45	2.65	2.10	2.65	1.40	8.75	11.20
Horse #3	10.30	9.70*	3.40	2.60	2.60*	2.40*	2.00*	1.35*	8.35*	10.95*
Horse #4	10.30	10.30	3.75	2.90	2.65	2.50	2.35	1.25	8.75	11.65

Body-Part Proportions

Ratio	(1) Pelvis: Body Length	(2) THL #1: Croup Height	(3) THL #2: Croup Height	(4) Femur: THL #1	(5) Femur: THL #2	(6) Gaskin: Femur	(7) Hind Cannon: THL #1	(8) Hind Cannon: THL#2
Horse #1	30.0%	88.2%	113.6%	28.7%	22.3%	102.9%	28.3%	22.0%
Horse #2	32.0%	87.5%	112.0%	30.3%	23.7%	75.5%	30.3%	23.7%
Horse #3	33.0%	86.1%	112.9%	31.1%	23.7%	92.3%#	23.9%*	18.3%*
Horse #4	36.0%	84.9%	113.1%	30.3%	22.7%	94.3%	26.8%	20.2%

° ratio value smaller than actual value because numerator foreshortened by camera angle
ratio value larger than actual value because denominator foreshortened by camera angle
THL: Total hind limb

coupling; long femurs, on which the thigh and hamstring musculature "carries down" to "tie on low" to the gaskin; gaskins that are shorter than the femurs and of adequate substance; well-shaped, well-articulated, dry hocks; short, substantal hind cannon bones which act to lower the hocks; and large, dry hind fetlock joints.

I also like the gelding's slight uphill overall body balance, his substantial, well-angulated, springy hind pasterns and his long humerus articulating in a wide-open angle at the point of shoulder. This horse is eminently dressable — displaying not only beauty but power, scope, suppleness, and excellent innate rhythm.

Horse #4: This Quarter Horse mare is presented specifically to contrast with #2. She also is an absolutely gorgeous animal with one evident flaw — slightly high knees. Her pelvis is proportionally the largest of the four, although it resembles that of #2 in depth and angulation. Her hind limbs do not appear as crooked as those of #2 for two

Fig. 14. Analytical drawings of horses pertaining to Lab Exercise 6.

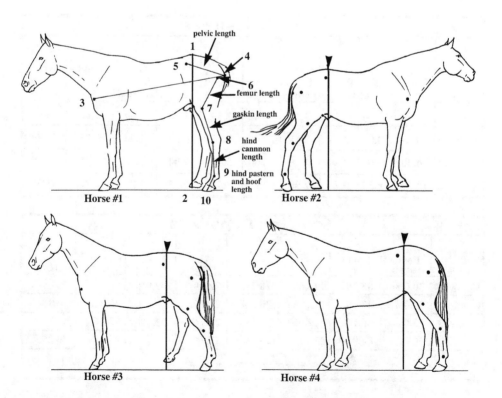

reasons: first, because her hind limb below the pelvis is shorter; that in turn is because her hind cannon is much shorter. Her femur, unusual for a Quarter Horse, is as long as that of the Thoroughbred #2; that's why the hamstring and biceps muscles of her thigh appear to "carry down" so well.

Also praiseworthy are: a good loin coupling, whose functioning is improved by the length and slope of the pelvis; substantial gaskins which, like those of #3, are between five and 10 percent shorter than the femur; well-shaped, well-articulated, dry hocks; and large, dry fetlock joints.

A super ranch cutting horse, she could also rein with the best. It is a delight to highlight not only the similarities in the hind limb of two excellent horses of different breeds, but also to point out their similar shoulder and arm construction — the angle at the point of shoulder is wide open in each. All equine athletes need a good drive train and gear ratio behind, just as they also need elastic, scopey movement in front.

Exercise 7: STIFLING DIFFERENCES

This group of photographs offers the opportunity to practice several principles. We can compare hind-limb length; overall body balance; the construction of the hock and knee; the size and substance of the cannon bones, pasterns, and hooves; the quality of the loin coupling; and the shape and length of the torso and neck. In addition, I've provided a table which lists the angles measured at hip socket, stifle and hock.

As I prepare this segment, I'm looking out over the local Fourth of July celebration, a particularly appropriate backdrop to study the breed to which all four of these horses belong. Which breed is it?

Analysis

Horse #1: This registered American Quarter Horse gelding is discussed first because he represents in extreme form some of the conformational ideals for which Quarter Horse breeders have been striving. For us, this constitutes a lesson, namely, that there can be too much of a good thing.

The Quarter Horse originated in colonial days as a sprint racer, a function that continued to be valued after the Civil War, when the breed was fostered in Texas and other parts of the American West. Ideally, a good sprinter possesses the following conformational features: (1) a noticeably downhill body balance, with the base of the neck much lower than the loins; (2) a relatively long back; (3) an excellent coupling; (4) a very deep heart girth; (5) large, muscular hindquarters; (6) short femurs; (7) substantial hocks; (8) rather upright or straight hind legs with wide-open angles at stifle and hock; (9) substantial forelimbs with muscular forearms, large, square knees and short, stout cannons; and (10) tough, wide-open front hooves sized to match the cannon bones.

This fellow amply displays almost all these features. If we wanted to nitpick, we could lower his knees, thereby

Hind Limb Angles

	Iliac Pelvis-Femur (hip socket)	Femure-Gaskin (stifle joint)	Gaskin-Hind Cannon (hock joint)
Horse #1	115	144	156
Horse #2	111	145	157
Horse #3	110	144	160
Horse #4	119*	135	160

*About three degrees wider open than actual

Body-Part Proportions

	Pelvic Length: Body Length	Iliac Pelvis: Pelvic Length	Iliac Pelvis: Body Length	Femur: Pelvic Length	Gaskin: Femur	Total Hind Limb: Croup Height	Total Hind Limb: Withers Height	Forearm: Body Length	Fore Cannon: Body Length	Heart-girth: Body Length
Horse #1	32.7	109.6	35.8	67.3	117.1	106.7	112.0	22.0	13.8	47.2
Horse #2	31.4	77.6	24.3	71.4	105.7	112.4	112.4	23.0	15.4	44.9
Horse #3	32.6	82.6	26.9	71.7	112.1	112.9	113.8	25.5	18.4	43.3
Horse #4	34.2	70.4	24.0	61.1	86.8	115.1	116.8	20.9	14.6	45.0

Body-Part Lengths

	Pelvic Length	Iliac Pelvis	Femur	Gaskin	Hind Cannon	Hind Pastern & Hoof	Total Hind Limb Length	Croup Height	Withers Height	Forearm Length	Fore Cannon Length	Body Length	Vertical Depth at Heart-girth
Horse #1	5.2	3.7	3.5	4.1	3.4	1.2	15.9	14.9	14.2	3.5	2.2	15.9	7.5
Horse #2	4.9	3.8	3.5	3.7	3.6	1.7	16.3	14.5	14.5	3.6	2.4	15.6	7.0
Horse #3	4.6	3.7	3.3	3.7	3.3	1.7	15.7	13.9	13.8	3.6	2.6	14.1	6.1
Horse #4	5.4	3.8	3.4	3.9	3.9	1.7	16.7	14.5	14.3	3.3	2.3	15.8	7.1

shortening the front cannon bones while at the same time
lengthening the forearm; and we would want the pelvis
even longer, up in the 35 percent range. I am delighted
with his smooth coupling and the way the topline carries,
in a continuously convex curve, from just behind the
withers to the point where the hamstring muscles "tie on"
to the Achilles tendon. More serious criticisms of this
horse as a sprint racer concern the fact that the hamstring
muscles, though bulging, tie on too high — ideally, they
should carry down further, so that the notch in the profile
from buttocks to hocks is not so deeply indented.

Another reason for including this fellow in this group is
to mention that his hind limbs appear to be crooked and
sickle-hocked. This is a serious drawback for a sprinter,
because it means that thrust generated by the rump
muscles cannot be efficiently delivered to the ground.
Instead, it "leaks out" at the highly angled joints in
crooked hind legs, causing strain and wobble.

This gelding also shows a defect in hind limb
construction which is common in Quarter Horses but
which most owners find hard to detect. The defect is that
the stifle angle is open enough to fit a straight-legged horse
like #3, but the hock angle is much more closed than that.
Notice also the disparity between the horse's sickle-
hocked appearance (an indication of long, overangulated
hind limbs), and the low percentage totaled by his hind
limb in the Body Part Proportions chart (which indicates,
on the contrary, that he's post-legged). This mismatched
combination occurs when the angles of a horse's hind
limbs are nonconcordant, that is, when the horse is post-
legged in the stifle above but sickle-hocked below.

Luckily, this gelding has substantial hocks which act to
protect him, to some degree, from strain arising from the
"sickle" hock. However, in the Quarter Horse the stifle
angle is harder to see, covered as it is by so much bulging
muscle.

The combination of open stifle and closed hock is a
conformation I call "kicked-back stifle," since the stifles of
horses possessing this construction do not come as far
forward as they should. (Ideally, *when the hind cannon
bone is vertical*, the horse's stifle lies directly beneath the
point of hip. If it doesn't, the horse is post-legged above
even if the hock appears to be sickle). It's important for
owners to detect this fault, for such horses are just as prone
to "locking," "sticking," or subluxation of the stifle joint as
are the obviously post-legged ones such as #3.

Notice that this gelding's total hind-limb length,

compared to his croup height, is similar to the percentages shown by #2 and #3. Finally, consider whether this gelding's conformation, suitable as it is for sprint racing, is also suitable for pleasure riding. The answer is no. As a pleasure horse, this guy's heavy chest and downhill body build are faults that are difficult to overcome.

His owner can, of course, try him out in Western Pleasure, where little engagement or physical effort of any kind is required, but although he's typey in a certain sense and he has a good enough head, the appearance of his short neck is probably going to be a disadvantage in this division, which is largely about appearances. My advice is to see if he has any "cow" in him. In cutting, neither his downhill build nor his crooked hocks will handicap him greatly, and his excellent topline will help him.

Horse #2: This filly also shows some extremes of ideals sought by Quarter Horse breeders. A three-year-old, she has all the breediness and refinement a person could want, but let's take the heavy saddle blanket and the

(1) **Eight-year-old Quarter Horse gelding**
(2) **Three-year-old Quarter Horse filly**
(3) **Nine-year-old Quarter Horse gelding**
(4) **Four-year-old Quarter Horse mare**

Courtesy, L. Ferreira

HORSE #1

Deb Bennett, PhD

HORSE #2

Courtesy, K. Youngwirth

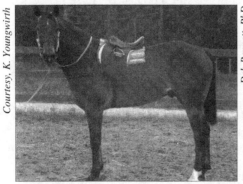

HORSE #3

Deb Bennett, PhD

HORSE #4

mummifying leg wraps off and see what lies beneath. Here we find extremes, indeed — wispy, insubstantial front cannon bones and tiny feet made tinier by cosmetic farriery that causes the foot to contract, pinching the bones and vital circulatory tissues inside.

I think this filly has good withers, but her loin is long and weak and she's really still too structurally immature for hard riding. This can be seen in the way the rider's weight, transferred back through the saddle bars, acts to press the filly's back down and deform her topline, changing it from slightly convex to concave with a telltale peak over the lumbosacral joint.

I like what I can see of the filly's neck, shoulder and heart girth, and I especially appreciate the way her hamstring muscles flow downward to tie on low to the Achilles tendon (contrast with #1). Likewise, this filly has excellent balance from back to front — she's certainly a saddle horse, not a sprinter. She could be longer through the pelvis — she's a bit below the acceptable minimum of 33 percent. Like #1, although to a slightly lesser degree, this filly also shows a kicked-back stifle: she's post-legged above but sickle-hocked below and needs to be treated accordingly.

Horse #3: This fellow possesses an overall body balance halfway between that shown by #1 and #2, but stands so much higher on his legs that the casual observer might mistake him for a Thoroughbred, that is, for a racehorse bred to carry speed over distance. I'm pleased to see him tacked up this way, for here's a fellow well-built to shine in a discipline most people don't associate with the Quarter Horse: jumping (did you know that five Quarter Horses have been members of the U.S. Olympic Equestrian Team since 1940?).

His hocks are really impressive, for they show width and substance both fore-aft and side to side. His hind cannons, pasterns, and hooves are structured to match. Just below the left hock, he shows a scar from a cut or possibly a lump from a rap, but it's too low to be a functional defect. While his stifles are as wide open as those of #2, the angle at his hocks is also appreciably wider — in short, this horse has straight hind legs all the way down.

Like #1 and #2, this gelding is long-bodied, but is coupled better than #2 (not quite as well as #1). The somewhat angular look of his topline — particularly the lumps and hollows between the lumbosacral joint and the dock, the bulges at the top of the hamstring muscles where they flank the dock and the subtle bulge in the left hamstring just above the point where it ties on to the Achilles tendon — tells me that this fellow is doing too much jumping and not enough suppling work. He's probably "ham-bound," a common problem in jumpers in which the hamstring muscles are stiff and tight. Although he's surely talented and probably eager, I recommend that his owner incorporate a 30-second stretch for each hind leg as a normal part of tacking up.

His neck is somewhat thicker from crest to base than ideal and is somewhat slabby-looking, which also indicates stiffness. I wonder if he is supple enough to reach around on either side to take a treat offered at the point of hip. If not, it would be beneficial to begin feeding him treats every day from as far behind him as he can reach, as well as a program of riding on the flat that emphasizes lateral flexions, 30 to 45 minutes three days a week.

As a jumper, this gelding's problems lie in the forelimbs. His long, laid-back shoulder does not predispose him to raise his forearms above level. Neither

Fig. 15. Analytical drawings of horses pertaining to Lab Exercise 7. Open circles and bar connect the centra of the 5th-6th cervical vertebrae and the L-S joint; see Fig. 38 for further discussion of body balance.

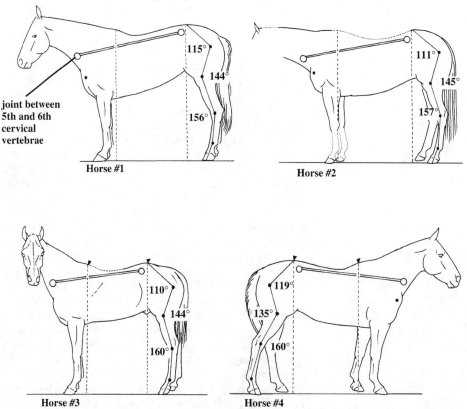

does the angle between the shoulder blade and the arm bone, which is less than 90 degrees. His forearm is the longest in this group, which is a good thing, but his fore cannon is also the longest, which is not. He has big, open feet and a well-angled left front pastern, but could use more substance in the forelimb from the elbow down. His left fetlock joint looks a bit puffy.

Incidentally, the saddle is too far forward: the panels cover and restrict the horse's shoulders. If his rider finds that the saddle slides back, then the proper position for this saddle indeed lies farther back, or perhaps the saddle just doesn't fit properly.

Horse #4: This mare, not quite four years old when photographed, to me represents a near-perfect example of a stock horse. In her we do not have to speak of extremes, but only of the realization of ideals. She is what the old time Quarter Horse breeders were trying to produce.

I can't say enough good things about this mare's hindquarter. She has a big, well-angled, well-muscled pelvis. Her hind limb is ideally angled, with concordant stifle and hock angles; she's neither sickle-hocked nor kicked back in the stifle. Her stifle is exceptionally muscular and her buttocks and hams are wide. To nitpick, her hamstrings could tie on a bit lower, and the hocks could be a bit lower, too.

She possesses all of the structural features which a horse used to work cattle ought to have — starting with substance, foursquare balance and sheer power, so that when you rope off of her, the steers cannot jerk her off balance. Yet as you examine the photo, you can see that this mare can, in no sense, be considered coarse. She has beautifully formed joints, muscular forearms and gaskins, substantial cannon bones and clean, well-defined tendons that are probably as hard as iron.

The only flaw in her limbs is the trim on her hooves, which is so short that she's standing on her soles. On the front feet, she's got too long a toe and too little heel, so that the angles are way too low. The whole foot needs to be grown out and the angle adjusted.

Her withers, which top an absolutely gorgeous shoulder and arm, carry well back. It's instructive to note exactly why this mare's body doesn't slope downhill to the front as much as either #1's or #3's. She gets no demerits for having a shallow heart girth — hers is second only to that of #1. Nor are her forearms long (short forearms are a characteristic of Quarter Horses); nor are her forecannons long.

How then can the base of her neck sit so high relative to her rump? The secret is to breed a horse with a deep chest and a good shoulder like this one, yet keep the point of shoulder high. That construction guarantees that the angle formed between the shoulder blade and the arm bone is wide open, and that, in turn, not only prevents the horse from being too low in front but preserves the scope and mobility of the forearms necessary in cutting, reining, and general stock work.

The posture of her neck — and therefore the muscular development of her neck and crest line — could be improved, but only if we can convince her owners to think of riding her not to work her but to supple her. Here is where having a goal like winning at reining becomes "real" — a real spur to the owner to improve his horse.

The Hind Limbs From The Rear

Exercise 8: BRINGING UP THE REAR

In rear view, we look for the same merits in the hind legs that we pointed out with regard to front legs in Volume II. First, we'll focus on the overall width of the animal; the most useful rule is to look high before looking low. In rear view, the hocks are the most visible joints, but keep in mind that the hind limb starts far above the hocks. Just as in the case of the forelimbs, the "set" of the hocks and the other joints farther down is largely the product of the conformation of the pelvis, croup, hip sockets, and stifles above. We'll scan all of the visible joints for size and "dryness," and finally we'll check the alignment of the long bones which surround the joints.

Initially, it's important to position the horse in such a way that it's possible to accurately evaluate the conformation of his hind limbs. Make certain that the horse isn't standing with one hind hoof ahead of the other; his hind hooves must be even or "square." Likewise, stand himwith his two hind feet bearing about the same amountof weight, rather than with a hoof cocked or hipshot. Ensure that the horse isn't stretched — both hind cannons need to be vertical.

Once the horse is correctly positioned, three body zones

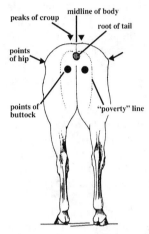

peaks of croup

midline of body

root of tail

points
of hip

points of
buttock

"poverty" line

Fig. 16.

can be assessed: croup and pelvis; stifle joints and "britches"; and finally the hock, fetlock, and hoof. In this set of photos, the croup and pelvis are the major focus.

In rear view, this uppermost body zone displays the following prominences: the peaks of the croup, the points of the hips, the points of the buttocks and the root of the tail. Ideally, none of them is unduly prominent, knobby, hot or swollen, and there is absolute symmetry from left to right.

Notice that the prominences of the left side are exactly on the same level as their mates of the right side. If the horse is well squared up on smooth, level footing and you still feel that his pelvis tips, look next at the croup and dock. Note whether the tail is hanging freely, straight down, in the middle between the buttocks, and if the entire croup bone, from the lumbar region to the dock, exactly bisects the hips. If the tail is cocked to one side or hangs closer to one buttock all the time — or especially if the croup bone seems to angle off to one side — use an elevated vantage point to look again at the horse's croup and back (see pp. 8-11, Volume II).

Absolute symmetry in this body zone is critical because one of the cardinal tenets of horse training is making the horse straight, that is, aligning his vertebral column when he is being worked under saddle. For this to be possible, the horse's "motor" (rump) and "drive train" (hind legs) need to be in perfect alignment with his "transmission" (back). A horse with structural twists or displacements here, including one version of the common condition called "hunter's bump," cannot be made straight and is not a suitable candidate for such sports as dressage or reining.

I define hunter's bump (sometimes called "racking bump") strictly — it isn't just a bump. Rather, it's the result of tearing the sacroiliac joint, the junction between the croup bone and the pelvis. As the accompanying illustration shows, the sacroiliac joint and the lumbosacral joint — where the spine joins the croup — are different joints, though they lie close together.

A rough-coupled horse, no matter how strained his lumbar region may look, stays symmetrical in lower back, croup and pelvic structure. Such a horse has either a poorly conformed, slack or strained lumbosacral joint. But since rough coupling does not involve the misalignment of any vertebrae, it does not prevent the horse from carrying himself straight.

The horse with hunter's bump, on the other hand, has a

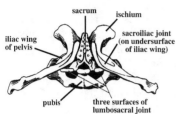

sacrum

ischium

iliac wing of pelvis

sacroiliac joint (on undersurface of iliac wing)

pubis

three surfaces of lumbosacral joint

Fig. 17. View of pelvis and sacrum from above and in front. A "hunter bump" or "racking bump" results when the sacrum is torn from its attachment to the iliac "wings" of the pelvis, and then heals, reattaching to the pelvis as an enlarged joint which is often twisted or rotated.

misalignment of the croup (sacrum bone) with both the pelvis and the lumbar vertebrae. If the misalignment is lateral, one of the horse's hips is always in advance of the other and the croup as seen from the rear slants off to one side. Or an equally serious misalignment may be produced through twisting of the pelvis relative to the croup.

In the latter case, one of the horse's hips is carried further from the ground than the other, causing one of his hind legs to exhibit more open angles (i.e., "be longer") while the other leg is carried with more closed angles ("be shorter"). However, as the accompanying photo illustrates, the pain of a sacroiliac injury may very well cause a horse to strain the muscles covering his loins in compensation. Thus, many horses with hunter's bump also appear to be rough coupled.

Besides checking for hunter's bump, which shows up only at the two uppermost corners of the pelvis (the tubera sacralae or peaks of croup), look out for the other common pelvic injury, bruising (enlargement) of one or the other point of hip. A "knocked-down" hip occurs when one point of hip is crushed, for example as when a horse rushes through a door and smashes his hip against the jamb. In this case, the affected point of hip will appear sunken in instead of prominent.

As you study this set of examples, make sure you're looking at a horse that is standing still. If the horse is moving, you'll have to judge how much swing of the hips you feel could well go along with a free-striding gait.

Analysis

Horse #1: This gelding is presented first for two reasons: first, because Arabian horses are often accused of being cow-hocked, which this fellow decidedly is not; and secondly, because he's posed nearly perfectly, making the job of assessing his conformation a bit easier. And yes, Dorothy, Arabians do come in shades of yellow (he's not buckskin, for there is no dorsal stripe). South of the border, in Spanish-speaking lands, this color is called *doradillo*, meaning golden. This gelding also, by the way, carries the gene for gray, but it's very, very slow-acting in his case.

The equine pelvis, seen from the rear, comes in all shapes from round ("apple-butted") to rectangular to A-shaped to T-shaped ("rafter-hipped"). This gelding is halfway between round and rectangular, with plenty of width from his left to right point of hip, and plenty also from his left to right point of buttock. Ideally, a horse's stifles span a greater distance than his hip sockets, since the stifles must clear the rib cage for good movement. This arrangement is especially important when the horse is as short-coupled and round-barrelled as this one.

There are no misalignments or deformities in this gelding's croup or pelvis, and none, I might add, where the hocks, fetlocks or hind hooves are concerned. A good horse, as Xenophon noted some 2,400 years ago, is structured wide in back like this, so as to permit space for the development of thick muscles in the "britches," the inner buttocks and thighs. This gelding could have more in that department, as well as along the inner gaskins — he needs more lateral work and a greater degree of self-carriage, which are the kinds of exercises that put that muscle in there. I fear no evil to his hocks, and am always delighted to see such substance in any horse. A military officer of Xenophon's day would have paid a king's ransom for a sturdy, useful, lively horse like this.

Horse #2: This gelding falls more into the A-shaped or subrectangular category of rump shapes. His croup is structured to lie higher relative to the points of hip than the croup of Horse #1. This is a shape quite typical of Thoroughbreds, although this fellow's Quarter Horse breeding shows up in the widespread points of hip. Did you notice that the left point of hip is enlarged? This may be due to uneven development of the tensor fasciae latae muscle or may be the result of bruising. Perhaps he bumped the hip on something as he was getting into or coming out of the trailer on the way to the endurance competition where I snapped this photo.

At the end of the long ride, this gelding stands like a tired horse, without the mischievous expression of #1. Despite fatigue, however, this gelding is structured to stand with his hind legs closer together than #1. So long as the hocks never touch, either at rest or in motion, however, the closeness makes little difference. If a horse's hind limbs from the stifle down are correctly structured — no twists or misalignments, as in this fellow's — the distance between the hocks is simply a function of the distance between the horse's hip sockets.

Note that the pelvis narrows perceptibly from front to back; the points of hip are much wider apart than the points of buttock. This cone-shaped pelvis is typical of male horses, while broodmares ideally have rear ends like horse #1, which do not taper much toward the rear.

Horse #3: This horse isn't standing, but walking. The inner

(1) **14-year-old Arabian gelding**
(2) **Aged Quarter Horse gelding**
(3) **Five-year-old Quarter Horse gelding**
(4) **Five-year-old Thoroughbred mare**
(5) **Aged American Saddlebred gelding**

half of the left hock is obscured by a tail bag, but you can see that the camera snapped just as the right hind was about to leave the ground, and while the left forefoot was swinging through the air toward the front. Notice that as I took this photo, I stood directly behind the horse — you can't see either of his knees. Does this horse "paddle" with his forelimbs when he walks? You bet — he's been caught in the act.

Look at the handy marker provided by this claybank dun's dorsal stripe. Notice the rider is sitting all upon his left buttock, twisting around in the saddle to call to some of his friends. His abrupt movement has shifted the saddle to the right. Does this cause the tip in the dorsal stripe and the height difference between the left side of the pelvis and the right? No, although the horse may be looking left to see what his rider is paying so much attention to (notice the animal's left ear). At the same time, notice the right side of his rib cage bulging out beyond the hipbones on the right. These things simply reveal normal movement — the horse's torso arcs first right, then left, as he strides along in a swinging walk.

At the moment this photo was taken, the horse's right legs were as far apart as they will get in this gait. At the same time, the left legs were maximally close together. A horse's torso naturally bends in coordination with the opening and closing of his legs, and the more supple the bend, the better the quality of the horse's walk. This is a motion that the rider must go along with not only at the walk but also at the trot and, with a bias toward the side of the lead, at the canter.

Courtesy, S. Cranston

Deb Bennett, PhD

Deb Bennett, PhD

HORSE #1   **HORSE #2**   **HORSE #3**

Deb Bennett, PhD

HORSE #4   **HORSE #5**

Fig. 18. From the front, Horse #4's hunter's bump is evident on only one side.

Fig. 19. In side view, a sacro-iliac subluxation, which is known as "hunter bump" or "racking bump," is not always very prominent.

This is a round-rumped gelding, perfectly symmetrical and wide enough from one hip socket to the other. Like #1 he's a pleasure horse and would benefit from some lateral work to put more muscle between the hind legs.

Horse #4: This mare has a true hunter's bump. The picture taken in front view shows the asymmetrical appearance of the injury even better than does the picture taken in rear view. The photo in side view shows that the hunter's bump need not be very prominent. It is often followed by the development of the undulating lump-hollow-lump profile in the loin region, several inches in front of the peaks of the croup, which is characteristic of loin strain.

Horse #5: This gelding models a very large and prominent "racking bump," acquired after repeatedly being trotted hard uphill and downhill while his rider held his head up and back in a misguided attempt to strengthen his back. He not only tore the ligaments of his sacroiliac joint, but subsequently strained his back muscles as well, producing the characteristic lump-hollow-lump of strained loins (see pp.14-16, 25-30 of Volume I).

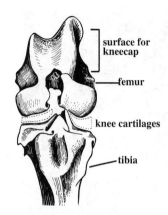

surface for kneecap

femur

knee cartilages

tibia

oblique grooves

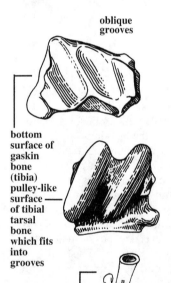

bottom surface of gaskin bone (tibia) pulley-like surface of tibial tarsal bone which fits into grooves

hock

tibia

tibial tarsal

cannon

Fig. 20. In the horse, none of the bones forming the stifle or hock joints forms a level plane. All the joint surfaces are oblique to accommodate the normal out-in-out structure of the equine hind limb.

Exercise 9: THE SPIRAL HIND LIMB

Now that we've looked at the structure of the upper part of the horse's hind limb — the sacrum (croup) and pelvis (rump) — we can now begin the journey down the hind limb from hip socket to stifle and from stifle to hock.

The structure of the bones which come together to form these joints is responsible for the horse's really very peculiar way of getting up and lying down. While the femur bone (above, within the thigh) and the tibia bone (below, within the gaskin) have straight shafts, neither end of either of these bones is "squared" to its shaft. Rather, the bottom of the femur and the top of the tibia form broad surfaces, the plane of each of which is oblique — neither perpendicular nor parallel to the bone shaft.

In short, the ends of the bones tip. This makes it impossible to fold the bones up parallel to the midline of the body. Within the hock joint, the bottom end of the tibia carries two grooves which align with the prominent ridges of the tibial tarsal bone. This bone is shaped like a pulley, but a pulley that has been "squashed" from side to side, so that its ridges tip. This shape is primitive — that is, it is shared by most mammals, including yourself.

You can see the effect of this squashed pulley in your own ankle. Put one foot out in front of you and flex your ankle, bringing your toes nearer your shin. You'll notice that as you fold your foot upward, the sole of your shoe doesn't remain perpendicular to the floor; instead, the side near the little toe rises higher. Your foot is not hung squarely off the end of your leg. Next, try flexing your foot upward, keeping the sole of your shoe square to the shaft of your calf. Uncomfortable, isn't it?

The oblique construction of the hock is also, more subtly, evident in the construction of the stifle joint and hip socket. The ball-shaped head of the femur does not fit squarely into the hip socket. It is designed so that the thigh bone angles outward as it goes down. This orientation guarantees that the stifle clears the horse's broad belly when he brings his hind limb forward.

For this reason, in evaluating the hind limbs from the back, one of the most important things to look for is width from stifle to stifle. In rear view, you should not be able to see the horse's belly; ideally, it will be blocked by the horse's "pants muscles" (femoral biceps) which lie above and behind the stifles. If the belly is visible, the horse is either pregnant or "sprung" too much in the rear ribs

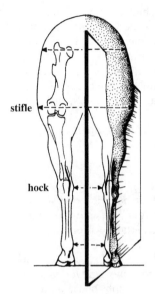

Fig. 21. The *normal and desirable* stifles-out, hocks-in stance of horses. In the ideal equine hind limb, it is a two-dimensional plane (not, as most manuals indicate, a one-dimensional line) which should bisect the thigh, gaskin, hock, hind cannon, bulbs of heel and the toe of the hoof.

(indicating a low back and weak belly), or the distance between the stifles is too narrow.

Too-narrow stifles mean one of two things: either the horse's pelvis is narrow, or the thighbones themselves do not diverge as much from the hips downward as they should. If the pelvis is narrow, as it is in many male horses, the thighs may diverge, but the hocks will nevertheless lie close together.

Having the hocks lie far apart is not as important as having the stifles angled well outward. Ideally, the stifles will be placed so that if you installed a little flashlight on the face of each stifle-cap (patella), the beams of light emitted would clear both the horse's belly and his shoulders.

The conformation of the hip and stifle joints above is reflected in the hock joint below: if the stifles face out, the hocks will point in. The hind cannon bone, when it is perfectly attached to the hock, carries the hock's orientation downward. Likewise, the hind pastern, if perfectly attached to the lower end of the cannon bone, will reflect the same oblique orientation, as will the toe of the hind hoof. All will face outward to the front.

From a position directly behind the horse, the angled orientations of the thigh and gaskin bones yield a zigzag out-in appearance. Looking at the horse's hind limbs directly from the rear, you should see:

✓ a pelvis in which the hip sockets are set wide apart, especially in a prospective broodmare

✓ thighs that angle *out* as they go downward from hip socket to stifle

✓ gaskins that angle *in* as they go downward from stifle to hock

✓ hind cannons that go straight downward

✓ hocks that are directed inward to the same degree as the stifles face outward

✓ hooves oriented in exactly the same direction as the stifle.

It's best, however, not to draw all conclusions from behind the horse's tail. Taking the right limb first, sidestep to your left as far as necessary until you are directly behind the point of the right hock. Then ask: can I imagine a plane — like a sheet of glass — extending upward through the hind cannon and hock so as to bisect the thigh? Can I extend it downward to bisect the hind pasterns and hoof?

From this view, all the bones of the hind limb should lie *in a single plane, which is not parallel to the midline of the horse's body*. The rounder and wider a given horse's rib cage, and the shorter his loins, the more oblique this plane will be.

Because the horse's hind limbs are hung from the hips at divergent angles, they are not meant to work like folding ladders. The bones and joints form a zigzag, spiraling structure — a spring. As a result, any trimming or shoeing regimen that aims at forcing a horse's hind toes to point forward will injure the interdigital, fetlock, hock, stifle and hip joints. Forcing the toes to point forward is like straightening out a spring — it loses its "springiness."

Analysis

Horse #1: This quality gelding has the cone-shaped pelvis — narrower toward the rear — typical of male horses. His pelvis is, however, certainly broad enough from left to right hip socket to assure that his hocks do not interfere as they swing forward and back in movement. Since the left and right legs are almost never exactly identical, it's best to analyze the hind limbs one at a time.

In studying this gelding's right hind limb from directly behind the point of hock, we find that an imaginary plane can indeed be extended up to bisect the stifle and downward to bisect the pasterns and bulbs of heel. The same result occurs when we examine the left hind limb from directly behind its point of hock. The only difference between the two limbs is the total amount that the stifles and toes turn outward: the right turns out more than the left. Asymmetry in the hind-limb stance is frequently related to the horse's "handedness" or preference in turning; the hind limb that turns out more shows the direction in which the horse finds it easier to bend. In this case, the right hind limb turns out more, so this horse probably turns right and canters upon the right lead more easily.

The degree of difference seen here is normal; one of the primary goals of training is to systematically exercise the horse on both bends to cause him to move straight. Over time, with appropriate training, the difference between left and right stance can be diminished. The accompanying photo shows the normal forward swing (protraction) of this gelding's right hind limb.

Horse #2: This drafter, standing some 17 hands and possessing massive muscle and bone, is nevertheless a bit narrower from left to right hip socket than is ideal. Her hocks lie close at standstill and are likely to interfere when in motion. Neither are her stifles wide enough apart; it

Fig. 22. Horse #1 takes a forward step with his right hind leg. As the femur bone swings forward, the stifle clears the belly. Below, the hock lines up perfectly with the stifle, as does the fetlock and hind toe still farther down. The horse swings his hind feet forward in shallow arcs, but this does not mean that he steps wide behind. The arc starts at the point behind the horse where the foot leaves the ground. As the hoof is brought forward, it swings inward, but is then set down at a point directly in front of where it started.

Fig. 23. A foal, its young body still very flexible, can do a "splits" that no normal adult horse can do. An adult horse in this position would have serious injuries, but thanks to stretchy ligaments at the hip and stifle joints, the very young foal can still lie down like a dog or cow.

(1) Nine-year-old Thoroughbred gelding
(2) Eight-year-old Clydesdale mare

would be better if her thighbones angled out more, so that the pants muscles (at the level of the rider's toes) bulge farther outward than the horse's hip sockets. Here the flashlights of the stifles point more or less forwardly, while the hind toes point strongly outward; the bones of each hind limb do not lie in a single plane and thus the mare is moderately cow-hocked.

However, she shows a commendable degree of symmetry between left and right hind turnout; the right turns out only slightly more than the left.

Horse #3: This mare shows the square pelvis typical of female horses with plenty of capacity for easy foal delivery. Ideally, a broodmare's pelvis has plenty of width from left to right hip socket, and is not cone-shaped.

Notice that this mare's stance is a little narrower at the fetlocks than it is at the hocks. Such a vase-shaped stance indicates that she is slightly bowlegged behind. While her stifles point well enough outward, a plane passed upward through the center of her hock does not bisect the fleshy thigh. Instead, the plane passes to the outside of the stifle. She is helped by her very substantial, wide, angular-looking hocks — the best set of hocks of these four.

The accompanying photo shows how her hind leg folds; the stifle turns sufficiently outward, but the hock goes a bit farther to the outside than it should. Even a slight outward displacement of the hock is enough to bring the fetlock and hoof inward. This mare could strike the opposite cannon or

Courtesy, C. Engel

HORSE #1

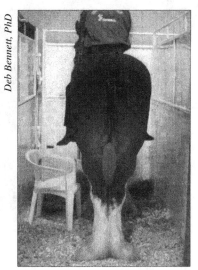

Deb Bennett, PhD

HORSE #2

Fig. 24. Western riding is truly a pleasure on this beautifully conformed gelding. Because of the oblique grooves present in his hock joints, in this horse as in all other normal equines, the stifles face out, the hocks point in, and the cannon bones descend straight down from the hocks, parallel to one another. This gelding is not cow-hocked.

fetlock with her hoof as she trots.

Horse #4: This gelding, though narrower through the rib cage and longer-coupled than #1, nonetheless has pretty good hind limbs. Because he's longer-coupled and more slab-sided, his stifles can point straighter forward and still clear his rib cage. Likewise, his hocks can and should point straighter rearward.

He has the cone-shaped pelvis typical of male horses, but plenty of width separates the left and right hip sockets. The pants muscle on the left hind blocks our view of the rib cage and stands wider than the hip socket, and I presume it does likewise on the right. The left hind leg turns outward to a greater degree than the right leg, indicating a left-handed horse.

The hind toes point outward slightly more than the stifles. A plane passed upward from the rear face of either hock would bisect the fleshy thigh, but the same plane passed downward cuts to the inside of the center of the toes, very slightly on the right, but more noticeably on the left. This and the puffiness and lack of definition on the hocks as well as the fetlock joints indicates that the hocks probably wobble in and out as weight passes over them, and the hind pasterns and cannons are slightly twisted under the hocks as the subtly curving lines of the hind tendons show. Thus, this gelding is structurally a little cow-hocked. Given that he weighs 1,200 pounds, hocks as narrow as these are insufficient even though the orientation

HORSE #3　　　　　　　　　**HORSE #4**

Fig. 25. Horse #3 picks up her hind foot. Since she is a bit bowlegged, the hock carries outward a little too much, while the hind toe is brought inward. She may interfere by kicking herself in the hind ankle or cannon when she moves.

(3) 12-year-old Thoroughbred gelding
(4) Nine-year-old Quarter Horse gelding

of the different hind-limb elements is pretty good.

Exercise 10. COW HOCKS: NOT JUST FOR COWS

A ssessing hind-limb conformation can be a matter of subtlety, as you may have discovered in working with the last lab exercise. In this exercise, however, the differences are about as plain as they ever get. In general terms, there are only three possibilities for the hind limbs in rear view: the animal is either cow-hocked or he's bow-legged or he's okay.

A cow-hocked specimen has stifles that face straight forward, hocks that point in toward each other, and toes that face out. This gives his muscular quarters a narrow, "pinched" look; a line connecting left and right stifle is too short. The cow-hocked horse will carry his weight on the inside edges of his hind hooves.

A bow-legged specimen, on the other hand, has stifle-caps facing out, hocks that point straight back and toes that face straight forward or even inward. His muscular quarters will often be full, but the animal will carry his weight on the outside edges of his hind hooves. When he moves, his hocks usually bow outward like elbows as weight passes over the hind leg.

A horse with well-oriented hind limbs has stifle-caps that face out, hocks that point in and toes that face out to the same degree as the stifle-caps. Ideally, he'll have broad, full muscular quarters with a goodly distance from left to right stifle; below, he'll have substantial, clean hocks. He'll stand with his weight square in the middle of his hind hooves; when he picks up a hoof at the end of a stride, he'll "break over" slightly to the inside of the toe.

Analysis

Horse #1: This gelding merits praise for a very well-conformed rear end, starting at the top, with a wide, full-muscled pelvis and attractive tail set. Notice how broad his thighs are. There are several hand spans of muscle between the midline of the body and the swell overlying the stifle. The meaty "pants muscle" is evident thanks to good conditioning and feeding, but that bulging set of adductor muscles — the ones that fill up the inner surfaces of the hind legs — develop most easily only in well-conformed

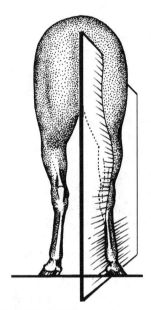
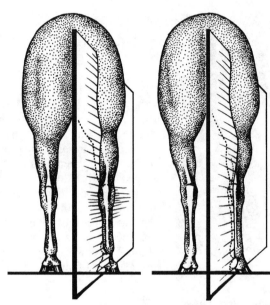

COW HOCKED
Hock lies inside plane; fetlock
joint and hoof lie outside it

BOWLEGGED
Hock lies outside plane; most or
all of hoof lies inside it

CORRECT HIND LIMB
Plane bisects stifle, hock, fetlock
joint and hoof

**Fig. 26. Two conditions must
be met for a horse's hind limb
to be correctly conformed in
rear view. (1) Stifle, hock, and
fetlock joints must all lie in a
single plane; (2) that plane
must be sufficiently oblique to
the midline of the body to
permit the stifles to clear the
belly when the hind limb
swings forward. If the horse is
round-barreled and short-
coupled, the plane must be
quite oblique, whereas if the
horse is flat-ribbed and long-
coupled, it can be nearly
parallel to the midline of the
body.**

horses who not only have good legs but also good backs.
It's especially desirable when the inner thigh muscling
carries right down onto the inner side of the gaskin. Many
Quarter Horses show even more development there than
this gelding, but this amount is good.

Below his gaskins is a handsome and clean set of wide,
substantial hocks, which drop straight down into equally
substantial cannon bones, pasterns and heels. The camera
caught this gelding in the act of taking a step. Note that
since the left hind leg has swung forward, the joints have
bent, bunching up the left stifle and flexing the hock.
Despite the folding of this leg, what would you see if you
stood straight behind the point of the left hock? You would
see all the joints in a single plane — a plane oblique to the
midline of the body. Note that the right hind leg is
stretched back. Even so, the toe points outward to the same
degree as the stifle. What would you see if you stood
straight behind the point of the right hock? Once again, all
the joints are in a single plane — the correct alignment.

Thanks to the alignment of the bones in his hind limbs,
there's no puffiness about his hocks or ankles. And there's
one last test: the gelding's weight presses down squarely in
the middle of each hind hoof, despite the fact that he's

Courtesy, K. Gambrill

HORSE #1

stepping up toward his handler. Paradoxically, this would not be the case if all the elements of his hind limbs did not have a spiral construction. If this still isn't clear, read on!

Horse #2: This gelding possesses a classic set of cow hocks. There is nothing at all wrong with the big, wide, flat hips shaped like a Chinese parasol (what American judges call "rafter hips"). However, the great distance from the left to the right point of hip really serves to highlight the narrowness between the left and right stifles. Notice that his stifle-caps face straight forward, while his hind toes face strongly outward. The orientation of stifles and toes doesn't match!

The tendency of the cow-hocked horse

(1) **Eight-year-old Arabian-Quarter Horse gelding**
(2) **Five-year-old American Saddlebred gelding**
(3) **Eight-year-old Tennessee Walker-Quarter Horse gelding**

Courtesy, M. Kernen

HORSE #2

Deb Bennett, PhD

HORSE #3

to bear weight on the inner edges of the hind hooves is obvious in this photo.

The thighs carry down well to gaskins that are muscular on the outside but thin on the inside. There is, however, bone structure where adductor musculature could be built. Lateral work (leg-yielding, half-passes, turns on the forehand and hindquarters) will significantly help a horse built like this.

Like many Saddlebreds, this fellow has plenty of substance, low-set hocks and sturdy hind cannons, but because of the severe misalignment of the hind limbs, he has been lame behind on one side or the other all of his life. Though the picture does not show it well, the hocks have large curbs. The last time I had occasion to ride this horse, now 15 years old (he has a lovely temperament and is a great trail horse, which is why his owner has kept him since foalhood), he could easily execute a 20-meter circle at a trot or canter to the right, but could only manage a 30-meter circle at a trot and a 60-meter circle at a canter to the left because (we suspect) of pain in his left hock.

Horse #3: This gelding scores highest in this group for power, for there's no lack of meat on the upper and outer surface of his croup and thighs. Likewise, there's plenty of distance between his left and right stifles.

The first time I ever saw this horse work, I was riding my mare behind him on a Kansas trail ride — which means, on a white-lime gravel road. (Too bad farriers so rarely have an opportunity to view their clients from this perspective). The level road surface made it easy to see how this horse's hind hooves struck the ground and where and how they took the weight on each stride. What I saw appalled me: each foot, as it landed, would strike on the back of the outside heel, and then with a rolling, twisting action like a dying Frisbee, the weight would pass around the toe and finally to the inner quarter. The inner heel never carried weight. Along with this went an amazing movement of the hocks: they were forced in and out with each stride like the flapping wings of a chicken.

I suspected that this debilitating hind-limb wobble had more to do with the gelding's shoes than with his conformation: he was wearing shoes with trailers, extensions which project out behind the outside heel. Even in this day and age, some owners order (or allow) trailers to be put on their horses in the mistaken belief that the animal's hind toes "should" point straight forward. But what this owner had not considered was the fact that, though trailers do point the feet prettily forward when a horse is standing still, they can cripple him as he moves.

After explaining this to the owner, she agreed to have the hind shoes pulled. I took this photo the same day the shoes came off: you can see that the gelding is still standing bowlegged, as the trailers trained him to stand.

It took about six weeks and a couple of balanced trims for his joints, ligaments and tendons to readjust. After that, the gelding showed a normal hind-limb alignment with only a very slight tendency for bowlegs. He also turned into a really magnificent mover — not the shuffler that the trailers forced him to be.

Exercise 11: THE SEARCH FOR THE PERFECT HIND LEG

Every breed of horse has some defining structural characteristics, and very often an individual's breed affiliation is quite apparent to the observer. In other words, Arabians often "look like" Arabians, Quarter Horses like Quarter Horses and so on. The word "often," however, is wise to cite, because within any breed there is a large amount of variation in physical structure. As a result, a "typey" look in and of itself confers neither uniformity nor excellence, as some typey individuals will still fall short of an acceptable structural minimum, while others no more typey will far exceed it.

The goal in all intelligently managed breeding programs is to produce foals that are superior to their own sires and dams. This concept becomes important against the backdrop of absolute values in conformation. There is, in short, such a thing as an ideal set of front legs, an ideal coupling, an ideally formed and carried neck, ideal bone structure surrounding the eye and an ideal set of hind legs. Conformation analysts of all times and nationalities have agreed that no matter what you intend to do with a horse, from the least physically demanding pleasure riding to the strenuous efforts required for warfare, you can do it only if your horse is composed of perfectly formed and articulated parts and has energy and temperament to go with his excellent structure.

By establishing political boundaries such as nations and breed registries, we artificially partition the domestic population of horses. Across such boundaries, horse breeding is restricted; there are stallions and mares which, even if you could afford them, you can't include in your breeding program.

No matter what breed or bloodline you may be involved with, however, the objective is still to produce foals that are better than their ancestors; in terms of structure, everybody wants and needs the perfect horse. Thanks to the restricted gene flow we have just spoken of, within a given breed, great hind legs, for example, may be a rarity, while in another breed, conformational problems may be centered on the back, neck, front legs or some other body region. Just as with individuals, there is no perfect breed.

In this last hind limb exercise, we examine individuals belonging to three different breeds exemplifying three sets of great hind legs — among the best you can expect to find within their respective breeds. Of the three, however, one is particularly close to the ideal of absolute perfection. This perfect structure involves:

✓ hocks that are broad and angular, with the rear surface below the point of hock equally broad and square

✓ clean joints, with no signs of puffiness anywhere

✓ hind cannon bones that are attached exactly in the center below the hock

✓ a broad pelvis, with no chance of one hind leg striking the other

✓ muscular thighs with the stifle-caps pointing well outward

✓ muscular gaskins, both inside and out

✓ stifle, gaskin, hock, fetlock joint and hind toe that all lie in a single plane when the leg is viewed from directly behind the point of hock.

Analysis

Horse #1: Thanks to his overall bulk, this drafter certainly exemplifies a broad pelvis. He has much better thighs than the draft horse shown in Lab Exercise 9: these are more muscular and spread out as they go downward so that the "pants muscles" appear even wider than the pelvis. His gaskins, too, are well-muscled both inside and out.

His hocks are also excellent, being wide enough to match and support the bulk of his upper body. The points of hock are particularly wide and the rest of the hock structure appears as it should in rear view: clean and angular.

The "feathered" hind cannons are sufficiently substantial and are centered beneath the hocks, but angle outward slightly from the ideal; this horse is thus cow-hocked. Although he is standing a bit funny, his structure is really vase-shaped, narrower below than above.

Compare to mare #3, Lab Exercise 9.

Draft-horse breeders sometimes say they like to breed for this close convergence of the hind limbs, so as to make it easier for the horse to work in traces, but I think if this slight crookedness were taken out of this gelding's hind limbs, he would be a world-beater both on the line and in harness. If you've ever watched a pulling contest, it's easy to see that the hocks endure a tremendous strain at peak effort. Any crookedness there can only subtract from a horse's ability, willingness and potential soundness.

Below the feathers, this gelding once again pleases for his beautifully healthy, symmetrical and open heels. The bars and walls of the hooves are not crushed or deformed, and the feet are not flat. Such strong feet deserve high marks in any draft horse, for modern draft horses, which weigh 1,800 pounds and up, are twice as heavy as the average riding horse and more than twice as heavy as any wild form of equine.

Horse #2: This mare is registered as a Paint on a technicality, because her stockings rise higher than her knees and hocks. Conformationally, she's all Quarter Horse. Her muscularity is extreme. When her photo is

(1) **Eight-year-old Percheron gelding**
(2) **12-year-old Paint mare**

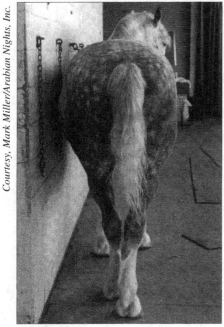

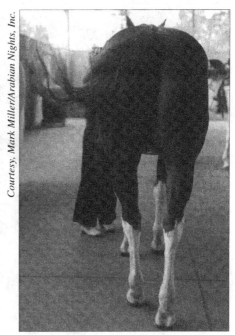

Courtesy, Mark Miller/Arabian Nights, Inc.

HORSE #1

HORSE #2

printed at the same croup height as that of the draft horse, her pelvis appears equally broad, though a little flatter in shape across the top.

Like those of #1, the mare's thighs diverge outward as they go down; her pants muscles appear to be even thicker, though her gaskins are slightly less so.

Her hocks are exemplary for her breed. Rarely do I see a Paint or Quarter Horse with such breadth and sculpturing in the bony hock. The hind cannons have sufficient substance, though they're not quite centered beneath the hock. Her hocks are not set quite as low as those of either of the other horses shown this month.

The most serious flaw concerns the orientation of her hocks and hind toes compared to that of her stifles. She is slightly bowlegged: while her stifles point out to a proper degree, the points of her hocks face nearly straight backward, while the toes point nearly straight forward. In use, this inward rotation strains the outer elements of the hock and fetlock and can lead to the development of hard or "jack" spavins. Below, her heels are less widely open than they should be — verging on contracted — and her feet are a bit too small.

(3) **12-year-old Lipizzan stallion (View 1)**
(4) **12-year-old Lipizzan stallion (View 2)**

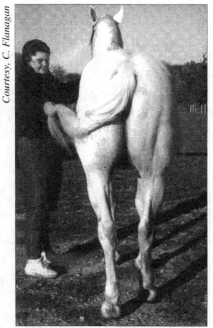
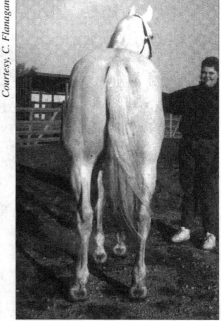

Courtesy, C. Flanagan

Courtesy, C. Flanagan

HORSE #3

HORSE #4

It is not rare to hear those who breed stock-type horses praise this form of hind limb. Insofar as they might be comparing this particular hind limb with that shown by other horses within their breeds, they are right to do so. However, very often I suspect that conformation manuals, which teach students to prefer "plumb-line" hind limbs, have caused a confusion between this type of bowleggedness and the ideal structure shown by the next example. It is hind limbs like those of horse #3 that I encourage stock-horse breeders to shoot for if they are interested in producing sound, athletic horses for reining, racing, and ranch work.

Horse #3: I took two pictures of this stallion to demonstrate what can happen to the look of a hind limb when the horse adopts different stances. In the first photo, he's standing as "close" as he ever stands, with the right hind leg fairly far forward under his belly. In the second picture, he's standing spraddled.

This stallion does not have as broad or flat-topped a pelvis as either of the other two horses, and his tail is set lower. He is not as muscular as either of the other two, although he is still well-endowed through the pants muscles and gaskins. He has better muscling, however, on the inner surfaces of the hind legs than do the other horses.

His hocks are sculptured, clean and wide in proportion to his weight (1,200 pounds). The hind cannons are short, stout and exactly centered beneath the hocks. The pasterns are longer than those of #2, and the bulbs of the heels are wide open and symmetrical over strong, well-formed hooves.

In the first picture, the alignment of the elements of this horse's hind limbs meets the standard that I presented in previous rear-view analyses: a single plane bisects the thigh, stifle, hock, hind cannon, pastern and hoof in either hind limb. The planes of the hind limbs converge behind the horse and open to the front of the horse, following the direction of the points of hock and stifles, respectively.

How has this stallion changed his stance between the first picture and the second? He has pushed against the ground with his left hind leg and moved his right hind leg to the right, thus spreading his hocks wider apart. He has also rotated the head of the right femur in its pelvic socket, bringing his right stifle closer to his belly than before. As the stifle swings inward, the hock must swing outward to the same degree. Thus, higher up you see less bulge on the right pants muscle than before. At the same time, the rear surface of the right hock points straight backwards, while the right toe points straight forward.

Even though the horse has shifted, the plane of the left hind leg still widens to the front and converges to the rear, but the plane of the right hind leg has now swung into a direct fore-aft orientation, parallel to the horse's spine. Notice that no matter how the horse may rotate his hind limbs, the elements remain in a single plane and the stallion's weight is always carried squarely in the center of each hind hoof. What would happen to the right hock of horse #2 if she were to rotate her stifle inward in the same manner as this stallion has done? Would she still carry her wieght evenly on the two sides of her hind hooves? Because she is bowlegged, inward rotation of her stifle would carry her hock too far to the outside, and her weight would rest much more heavily on the outer edge of her hind hoof.

Learning the difference between these two kinds of hind limbs is of vital importance in American horse breeding. Horse #3 exemplifies what experts of the last century were trying to express when they diagrammed a plumb line passing down the hind limb. Horse #2, however, represents a faulty approach to that ideal.

Part II

How To Look At A Horse's Head

Introduction: A Matter Of Bone Structure

First though it may often be in the eye of the beholder, I have waited until last in this series of three booklets to discuss the equine head. What's in a dished face — or one that's nobly arched — is, like everything else, a matter of bone structure.

In the annals of equestrian history, the word "type" originally described the sort of work a horse performed. A hackney-type horse, for instance, was a road trotter, while a hunter was a cross-country galloper. A palfrey was an easy-gaited traveller, and a drafter or dray was a weight-puller. Today, however, type has come to mean all of the physical characteristics which identify the breeding (or closest relatives) of a horse. The principles of conformation analysis teach us that a horse's function does indeed predict, to a considerable degree, how he will look.

If we use the word type in its original sense, four basic types of horse currently exist in the world: draft horses, carriage horses, race horses and riding horses. Each of these has a characteristic body build which suits it to its work and is defined by factors such as the animal's weight, his limb substance and construction, his muscle mass and definition, his hoof quality and overall body balance. Yet, when applying the word "type" in its original sense, there is no mention of the horse's head. So long as it is

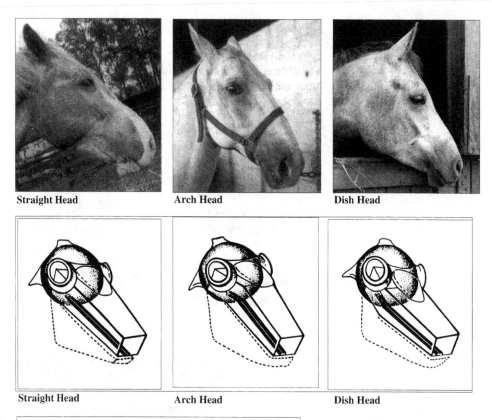

Fig. 27. Head shape is determined deep within by the direction and amount of "bend" in the parasphenoid rod. These horses also sport other features—an undulating nasal profile, a bulging forehead, a large, attractive eye — but they are surface embellishments.

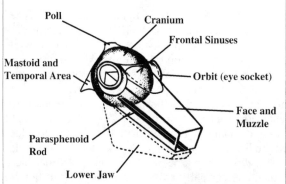

Fig. 28. Structural parts of a horse's skull.

functional, the particular shape of a horse's head is largely a matter of taste — an embellishment or a blemish, depending on your point of view.

Over time, points of view have changed greatly and so have peoples' preferences for the shape of a horse's head. It is possible, through the process of selective breeding, to "blueprint" many different kinds of heads, all of which can be considered good.

Specifically, a good head is a functional head and that means, first of all, that it's equine and not asinine. Horses and asses (as well as three kinds of zebras and three kinds of onagers) are classified together in a single genus, *Equus*. Both have skulls which are composed of two basic elements, the cranium (from the eye sockets to the poll) and the face (from the eye sockets to the tip of the muzzle). It is handy to visualize these two parts as a ball and a shoe box (see illustration). Attached as smaller appendages to these two parts are the frontal sinuses, the eye sockets, the cheekbones and the lower jaw.

To pinpoint the differences between equine and asinine heads, let's first consider the ball. From every angle, the ball in a donkey's skull is smaller than that in a horse's skull. The donkey's poll is less wide than the horse's and in side view, the donkey's skull (specifically, the mastoid and temporal area) is compressed while the side of the horse's skull is large and expansive. The mastoid process of the donkey, like the rear surface of the skull, angles forward, whereas that of the horse angles straight down or

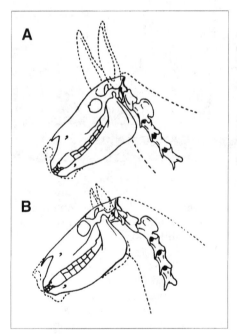

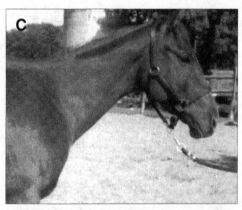

Fig. 29. Because the ass' skull will not balance, its neck bones are forced to approach the ears from below (A, D). In well-conformed horses (B), the neck bones approach the ears from behind. In a ewe-necked and hammer-headed horse (C), the back of the skull is formed like that of the donkey.

Fig. 30. A horse's skull (C) will balance when set upright on a table. The fossil *Dinohippus* (A) has a skull resembling that of the living ass and the living Russian kulan (B). Skull D, an Abyssinian zebra, has a more advanced construction but still will not balance when set upright.

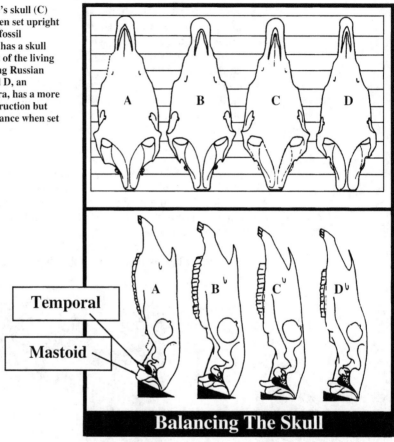

even rearward, again providing a larger cranial ball.

Thanks to this latter feature, you can almost always tell a horse skull from a donkey skull by a very simple test. Just sit the skull snout-up on a table so that it rests on its rear surface. A donkey's will fall forward, while a horse's skull will usually balance.

Thus a good head for a horse first has a wide poll, so that the ears appear to be rooted far apart, and secondly, a wide-open throatlatch. The latter feature in a live horse indicates that his skull would balance when set snout-up on a table. A horse whose skull would fall forward has a narrow throatlatch, and that, in turn, means that the upper two neck bones have to join the skull more or less below the ears instead of from behind them. If these upper vertebrae meet the back of the skull from below, the horse will appear hammer-headed or "muley-headed." He'll probably also be ewe-necked, like most donkeys.

Correctly visualizing the horse's cranial ball is not, however, enough to ensure that he has a good head. The next step is to learn to see how the ball is attached to the shoe box. In the horse, the two elements are connected by a rod of bone called the parasphenoid, which extends forward from the bottom of the ball along the bottom of the shoe box. This rod may bend either up or down, and it is this bend between the basic structural elements of a horse's skull which renders the animal either straight-headed, arch-headed, or dish-headed.

These differences in head shape go back to a very early time. Before horses were domesticated some 6,000 years ago, different populations characteristically sported different arrangements of the "ball on box" structure. For example, the fossil record shows that the most primitive equine population still in existence, the central European warmbloods, have always had a tendency for an arch-headed construction, whereas the Oriental group has tended toward a dish-headed construction. In contrast, the draft, Tarpan and Przewalski populations usually show a straight construction.

The overall shape and proportions of the shoe box can be, and often are, modified through selective breeding. The most common modification has been to shorten the shoe box. American breeders, in particular, like a horse with a short face. This preference is fine, although short-faced horses tend to have short bars — the open spaces on the jaws between the incisors and cheek teeth — and if that is the case, the individual can be more difficult to fit for a double, or even single bridle than a horse with a longer mouth.

Fig. 31. A "teacup" muzzle (left) does not provide enough space for air intake or for the proper rooting of the teeth. The Arabian (right) has thin skin and excellent bone structure.

Horses are also bred so that the shoe box tapers abruptly toward the snout. This practice originated from a saying about well-bred Arabian horses, that their muzzles were "so fine they could drink from a teacup." The saying, however, was never meant to imply that the horse could jam the end of his snout into the teacup; instead, the Arab's admiration was meant for the horse's fine skin and lips, which enabled him to sip. In shrinking the diameter of a horse's muzzle and jaws, a breeder also shrinks:

✓ the bony nares through which the horse must breathe;

✓ the maxilla bone, in which the upper teeth take root;

✓ the lower end of the mandible, in which the lower incisor teeth take root.

None of these changes confers any functional benefit and such a snout should be considered no more beautiful than a rabbit-faced human. There's nowhere in such a person's receding chin and too-small jaws for teeth to properly take root, leading to crowding and crookedness. In horses as in people, overbites, underbites, and other dental misalignments and malocclusions often accompany this type of skull construction.

Good construction in the bones which support the upper and lower batteries of grinding teeth is also important since the shape of the head is dictated by the work of chewing. In side view, a horse's grinding teeth lie along a line starting below the upper corner of his eye and ending about an inch above the corner of his mouth. Ideally, the bone structure supporting this part of the skull is broad and substantial, and one of the indications that this is the case is the width of the horse's cheekbones. Plenty of width between left and right points of cheek continues the broad-polled structure begun above. Ideally, the individual cheekbones are clean, prominent, and sculptured.

Fig. 32. This gelding acquired the "dish" in his face not from his parents, but from a weanling halter carelessly left on his growing skull too long.

You'll notice that the shape of the nasal bones has not yet been mentioned. They form only the upper surface of the shoe box and their basic orientation is merely a product of how the ball and shoe box are put together by the parasphenoid bone. Once this orientation has been set, however, a horse can be bred for certain modifications in the shape of the nasal bones.

One common, heritable form is nasal bones that arch. An arch which is truly in the nasal bones always occurs low down, toward the snout, and gives the individual's face the undulating profile that is common in the South American Criollo, as well as in many breeds derived from the old west-European draft population.

Another modification in the shape of the nasal bones is

seen only in districts where weanlings are commonly turned out to pasture with halters on, then left until the farm manager rounds up the young stock for veterinary attention or branding as yearlings or two-year-olds. The young horse's skull is very plastic and grows an enormous amount during the first two years of life. It is not rare for it to become so large as to completely fill the loose halter originally placed on the weanling. As the noseband of the halter becomes tight, it restricts the growth of the nasal bones, deforming them into a notched shape.

After considering the construction and shape of the horse's cranium and snout, the next most important embellishment is the eye sockets. Think of the eye sockets as goggles covering the junction between the ball and the box and which can be adjusted to occupy several different positions (higher or lower) on the side of the head. Like goggles, the bony orbits surround the eyeballs. In determining whether a horse has a structurally "good" eye, it is not the eyeball, but the bony orbit which is most important.

The orbit should be well-sculpted and stand well off the side of the head. In other words, there should be a goodly

Fig. 33. Good bone structure supports vital organs in all three of these dish-headed horses. The Thoroughbred (left) shows inflated frontal sinuses and "full" forehead, while the Quarter Horses (right) show the elevated orbits and "wisdom bumps" of the ancient ox-headed breeds.

width between the outer corners of the goggles. This will especially be the case when the ball of the cranium is already large; the perfect head has both a broad poll and a broad forehead.

If you look at the head directly from the side in most horses, the upper edge of the eye socket is about level with the plane of the forehead; if you were to lay a ruler across the forehead from eye socket to eye socket, its edge would touch the horse's skin all the way across.

There are three basic variations on this normal theme. One is found in horses who are a bit small-eyed — here the orbit may lie below the plane of the forehead, yet the plane of the forehead will be straight. The other two variations represent historically very early advances in selective breeding. The first advance was made by the ancient Hittites of Anatolia (modern Turkey) who bred their horses to have heads that honored the Great Mother, one of the Hittites' two chief dieties.

The Great Mother (Isis to the Egyptians, Astarte to the Greeks, Ishtar to the Assyrians and Babylonians) was deeply concerned with fertlity and the raising of crops and livestock. As a result, it was natural for her worshippers to value horses whose heads most resembled those of her favorite animal, the cow. Seven centuries later, we find Alexander praising his famous black horse Bucephalus, whose name in Greek means "ox-head."

Thus, to be ox-headed was never intended as an insult, and even today those breeds which descend from this ancient mid-Eastern stock often bear the single most characteristic feature of an ox's head: the goggles of the eye sockets placed not only wide apart (as in well-bred cattle), but high up, so that the upper edge of the orbit lies distinctly higher than the plane of the forehead. A ruler laid from orbit to orbit in such a horse spans the hair of the forehead without touching it.

The north African Barb, as well as its descendants the Paso and Criollo horses of the Americas, are the prime repositories today of the old ox-headed bloodlines. The Morgan and the American Quarter Horse are also descendants of the old ox-heads, via the English and Irish hobby. Welsh and Connemara ponies, as well as many Iberian, Kazakhstani, Afghani, Chinese and Iranian breeds, also spring from this font.

Ox-headed horses characteristically show what Quarter Horse fanciers call "worry" or "wisdom" bumps. These oblique ridges of muscle appear prominent on the ox-head because the eye sockets themselves are so substantial and placed so high on the ball of the horse's cranium that they tend to carry the musculature upward with them. In rare instances, not only is the musculature carried upward, but the tops of the bony orbits themselves overgrow into bony "dragon points."

The temporal muscles forming the ridges in this type of head also seem prominent because the frontal sinuses are of only modest size. These sinuses — actually pockets in the frontal bone — lie between the eyes and extend forward into the upper part of the nasal bones. The pockets interconnect with each other and with the equally large sinuses in the part of the maxillary bones which form the horse's cheekbones. All of them, in turn, connect directly or indirectly with the rear part of the nasal cavity.

Mucus-lined in living horses, the function of the sinuses is to warm and moisten incoming air and to provide a light, hollow framework that is nonetheless extensive and strong enough to withstand the huge crushing forces involved in chewing. It is, therefore, no surprise to find that many species of animals living in arid climates have very large frontal sinuses and bulging foreheads — the jackrabbit, gerbil, and donkey are three familiar examples.

The most familiar breed of horse sporting the distinctive bulge of extra-large frontal sinuses is, of course, the Arabian, but the same type of forehead can be found with almost equal frequency in two related breeds, the Akhal-Teke and the Caspian, both of which descend from the same old Iranian and Afghani bloodstock which gave rise to the Arabian. Since both the Arabian and the Akhal-Teke (which used to be called the "Turk" in England) contributed to the origin of the Thoroughbred, it is not surprising that this facial structure sometimes also appears in individuals of that breed.

Likewise, since both the Arabian and the Thoroughbred have for several hundred years been in widespread use as "improvers" of other breeds, an Arabian-like head can also be found, for example, in registered Quarter Horses, Appaloosas, Lipizzans, Welsh riding ponies and POA's (Pony of the Americas).

So what's in a dish? Several things, by design. Most importantly, the shoe box snout must be flexed upward upon the cranial ball to form the basic dish-headed construction. Both ox — and Arab — heads are dished, but the Arab possesses one thing more: expanded frontal sinuses filling up the space between the high and well-constructed orbits. Though the facial profile of a drafter or a Criollo may undulate and the head of a Quarter Horse may possess a bulging jaw under a flexed cranium, only the Arabian and its sister breeds of the Orient possess the "full dish," with the deepest downward slope below the eyes, not between them. This is the head most widely preferred in North America today — appealing, perhaps, because of its look of intelligence or childlike innocence.

Yet it is important to remember that no matter what the shape, all well-constructed heads are good. Neither the noble head of arch-headed breeds such as the Tennessee Walker or the Lipizzan, nor the quality evident in a good ox-headed Paso or Quarter Horse should be scorned or passed over out of prejudice; rather, such heads deserve to be fostered and valued for what they are: functionally excellent and fitting the history of the breeds to which they pertain.

Exercise 1: THE EYES HAVE IT

Most older books on conformation, as well as the literature of many breed organizations, advise the buyer to look for a horse with "good eyes." Unfortunately, where the eyes are concerned, horsemen's lingo is fraught with colloquialisms, and thus it's necessary to define exactly what is meant by such frequently used terms as "large," "dark," "prominent," "soft," and "liquid." Such phraseology can be downright confusing, or can harden into the root of a prejudice, such as the one against horses with blue eyes or "human" eyes (eyeballs in which the white sclera shows all the time). At the same time, excessive focus on the literal meaning of the words can lead to disastrous consequences. Is "prominent" really supposed to mean "bulging"?

Art teachers say that the eyes are one of the most difficult parts of the body to learn to draw. In sketching humans, the urge of the beginner is to make a Raggedy Ann face — two eyes and a scarecrow nose set on the front of a circle. We do this because of our left-brain-induced urge to diagram, rather than observe and sketch what we actually see.

When we draw (or imagine) ideal horses' faces, we tend to the same error: the cartoonist puts Barney Google's eyes on the front of the horse's skull, where horse's eyes never occur in nature. In reality, the horse's eyes lie on the sides of its skull, and the left and right pupils, formed as horizontal rectangles, take in two largely separate, panoramic views.

It would be a fool's game to pretend that the Raggedy

Ann image has not influenced the course of horse breeding. More than one little girl who played with *My Little Pony* has grown up to insist that real horses — what we believe to be the noblest species in all of Creation — have the same over-cutesiefied heads and exaggeratedly big eyes they loved in their childhood.

Anyone who doubts that horse owners may carry destructive fantasies of this kind into adulthood has only to check the records from the 1988 U.S. Arabian nationals, where two exhibitors were caught and reprimanded for applying makeup, complete with mascara, to optically enhance the size of their horses' eyes. Yet these two unhappy women represent only the tip of an iceberg, since the practice of shaving the hair around halter horses' eyes, and even the cruel practice of shaving off their eyelashes, is still widely practiced and goes unpunished.

Every book I own on conformation mentions the desirability of being able to see the horses' eyes from in front. But I believe that the emphasis humans place on this point stems from the misguided mindset to make horses look like ourselves.

Good eyes begin with the supporting bone structure. The hard, bony rims surrounding the eyeballs should be well-sculpted: the goggles shaped by these bones should stand well off the *sides* of the skull. This construction correlates with two other desired features: eyes that are prominent in the intended sense of the term, and a broad forehead.

The eyeballs should never bulge out farther than the upper bony rim. If they do, the horse is "bug-eyed" — sometimes a symptom of a hormone imbalance. Breeders who fail to distinguish between bug-eyes and well-structured bony orbits can, and have, raised the incidence of inherited endocrine disorders in certain American bloodlines.

The term "soft" as it is used by horsemen refers to the degree of muscular tension to be observed in the eyelids and eyebrows. Although horses have less mobile faces than people or dogs, much can be inferred concerning their state of mind and emotions from the lips, eyelids, and brows.

For example, a frightened or surprised horse opens its eyes wide, just as you might; an angry one frowns or grimaces, and a tense one shows a fixed expression. Submission and acceptance are shown when the horse smacks or licks its lips and relaxes its eyelids and brows. When the eyelids are soft, the upper eyelid and brow folds into many small wrinkles. At the same time, in a sense exactly paralleling the way riding instructor Sally Swift uses the term "soft eyes" to speak of her human pupils, the horse's gaze widens to take in a broad visual field. This gives the eye a "liquid" appearance.

The next six photos illustrate a range from broad to narrow-headed. Notice that a horse's forehead can be broad even if the poll is not (the ideal skull is broad both at the poll and across the forehead). Some of the muzzles are long; others are short. To some extent, the photos show different types of eyeballs and expressions, although expression is best studied in the live animal. Four of these heads fall in the range considered good to excellent; two are average to poor. See if you can pick out a good head in front view.

Analysis

Horse #1: This photo of an outstandingly well-conformed pony shows the extent to which it is naturally possible to see the eyes from the front. Yet look again, please: the eyes are actually aimed mostly to the sides.

Notice, too, how the bony orbital rims, the upper eyelids, the brows, and the eyelashes all overhang the globe of the eye. The wrinkled eyelids speak to me of a mixture of submissiveness and curiosity.

More importantly, this pony's entire skull shows excellent structure. The muzzle is broad, allowing plenty of space for air intake and well-rooted teeth; the forehead is even broader, with evident sculpturing about the cheekbones as well as the orbits. To top it off, the pony has a marvelously broad poll. In a horse, the brains don't lie under the forehead; they lie higher up, under the poll. If it's brains and trainability you're after in a horse, this is a likely candidate.

Horse #2: Whereas the pony discussed above belongs to the dish-headed group, the skull of this Lipizzan stallion is of the opposite, arch-headed variety. Regal, masculine, and massive, it possesses in its width dimensions the same advantages as #1. Here again, the poll is very broad, the distance between the bony orbits even broader, and the muzzle substantial. The sculpturing about the orbits and on the cheekbones continues upon the nasal bones. Notice, too, how the jowls stand away from the neck, providing an enormous space for air flow between the branches of the jaws. While the bone structure is substantial, the skin covering it is fine; many blood vessels are evident, and the edges of the nostrils are thin and flaring. The expression is calm, intelligent, and submissive.

Horse #3: This gelding has the most prominent eyeballs

(1) **Aged Connemara-cross gelding**
(2) **14-year-old Lipizzan stallion**
(3) **10-year-old Quarter Horse gelding**
(4) **23-year-old Arabian-Quarter Horse mare**
(5) **Eight-year-old Thoroughbred gelding**
(6) **12-year-old Appaloosa gelding**

permissible; they stand out just to the edge of the upper bony rim of the orbit. As in the previous two horses, his forehead and muzzle are broad, and, meeting the American fashion, the distance from the cheekbones to the tip of the muzzle is quite short. His cheekbones are exceptionally wide and as a whole he has a very attractive head.

His poll, however, is less broad than either of the first two, which, in combination with his short muzzle, gives this gelding a "classic" diamond-shaped head. I am not inclined to fault him too severely for having only an average poll width: he's certainly a sweet, cooperative fellow, pleasant to work with and very trainable. Besides,

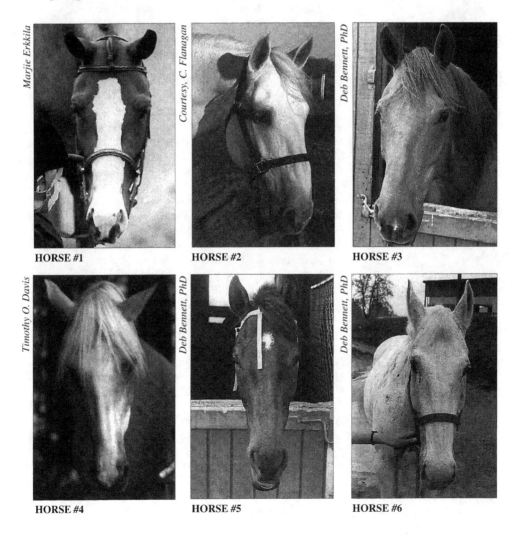

HORSE #1   HORSE #2   HORSE #3

HORSE #4   HORSE #5   HORSE #6

not everyone enjoys having a horse that picks locks, opens gates, and invents things to spook at, which can be characteristic of the brainier members of the equine species.

Horse #4: This mare also has a nice head. It's narrower throughout than any of the others so far presented, and is as long in the muzzle as the Lipizzan's, but is exceptionally well-formed about the bony orbits. Like horse #3, this mare has a diamond-shaped skull; and like #2, the skin covering it is fine, revealing many details of muscle, nerve, tendon and bone. A wise old thing, she's shown accepting a food treat from my hand (she's smelling it and her left ear is "looking" at it). The many small wrinkles on her brow show surprise and interest.

Horse #5: Well, being caught in the middle of a yawn never made anybody's head prettier, so we must forgive this gelding's funny expression. Perhaps yawning and other fine things that do not depend upon breadth of head, are what endears this horse to his owner. Across the poll, he's about as broad as either horse #3 or #4, and his muzzle resembles that of #4 both in width and in length, although he lacks her breadth across the forehead. Unlike mare #4, this gelding's orbits do not stand off from the side of the skull, and that puts his head into the average category. There's nothing wrong with his eyeballs.

Interestingly enough, this gelding is quite aggressive and independent. Hard to catch, he also bosses around horse #3, with whom he is pastured. That's what the yawn is actually about: in male horses, it's often a passive-aggressive emotional mixture which says: "you're just too boring to mess with right now."

Horse #6: This aged gelding is almost blind in both eyes. The cause of the blindness has not been certainly diagnosed, though there's a good chance it is congenital. Whatever its cause, it has nothing to do with blue color (both of his eyes have always been dark brown) or being an Appaloosa or having visible white sclera (this gelding has the same dark-appearing globes considered ideal in other breeds).

His eyeballs have not deteriorated in the course of the blindness (they are unwrinkled and spherical), but there is little or no fat behind them and the nervous tissue that normally underlies the globes has probably degenerated, giving his eyeballs a sunken appearance. Before purchasing any horse, the buyer should always request an eye examination by a veterinarian, for there is no way to tell from appearances alone that a horse is blind.

In terms of bone structure, this horse's head is very plain. He has the classic shoebox head, one which is about the same width at all three critical points — across the poll, across the forehead, and across the muzzle. I like a substantial muzzle and this guy's cheekbones aren't bad, but his orbits lie closer together than do his cheekbones.

Surprisingly, this fellow once served as a school horse. Ridden only by responsible adults who would not purposely crash him into things, he was tractable and trusting to a touching degree. His eyelids and eyebrows are relaxed and wrinkled, but I find his expression hard to interpret; it's asymmetrical. Perhaps — I hope — it reflects a kind of cheerful resignation.

Exercise 2: IN SEARCH OF ANCIENT FACES

Whether a skull has an arched or a dished construction depends upon the bend in the parasphenoid rod. But the parasphenoid rod lies deep within the skull, above the horse's palate, and is not visible from the outside. We can draw diagrams, but how can the observer tell from the outside whether a skull is truly arched, or just has curving nasal bones? How can the observer identify the skull with dished internal construction, not just an externally dished shape?

You can find a bend in the parasphenoid rod by comparing two lines on the outside of the horse's skull. The first is traced by the edge of the horse's cheekbone; the second is the line formed by the bony prominences which extend back from the horse's orbit toward the base of his ear. If these two lines are nearly parallel, the horse's parasphenoid has little or no bend and his skull has a straight construction. If the crest of the cheekbone points down relative to the eye-ear line, the horse has an arch-headed construction. If, instead, the crest of the cheekbone points up relative to the eye-ear line, the horse has a true dish construction.

The skull construction, determined by the bend in the parasphenoid rod, determines the basic category into which a horse's head may be classified. However, it is possible for a horse in any of these three categories to have any style of frontal sinuses (inflated or flat), nasal bones (straight, arched, or damaged), or orbital bones (high, medium, or low). Some combinations are rare (an arched construction combined with inflated frontal sinuses, for example) but all are possible.

In the following set of photos, first classify each head as basically arched, dished, or straight. Then note the condition of the frontal sinuses, and finally the shape of the nasal bones. Only one of these combinations is rare; all are quite interesting.

Analysis

Horse #1: This one is easy — I hope you were able to immediately identify his skull as arched. In overall shape, because this gelding's skull is somewhat shallow as well as strongly arched, he presents what Lipizzan breeders are fond of referring to as a "banana head." However, I am more than ready to forgive him for it; its only flaw is its shallowness. He has a superb eye, and I value arched skulls for their antique and noble appearance.

Courtesy, Mark Miller/Arabian Nights, Inc.

HORSE #1

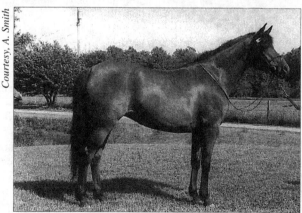

Courtesy, A. Smith

HORSE #2

(1) Aged Lipizzan gelding
(2) Seven-year-old Morgan-Arabian mare
(3) Four-year-old Quarter Horse gelding
(4) Six-year-old Thoroughbred gelding

Deb Bennett, PhD

HORSE #3

Courtesy, S. Burk

HORSE #4

I include a picture of the whole horse because this animal is really gorgeous. Especially handsome are the large, muscular hindquarters, set off by perfect joint angulations, an attractive tail-set and "Rock-of-Ages" hocks. His neck and throatlatch are also very attractive. To nitpick, we might lay his shoulder back a bit more and lengthen the pasterns a bit. His back is as long as I care to see, but not too long; the horse is very well-suited for his discipline, dressage.

Horse #2: In the matter of basic skull construction, here we find the exact opposite: a head as dished as horse #1's is arched. Because a shadow hides the eye-to-ear line in this mare, analytical drawings point up the lines to be compared.

This mare is particularly useful to our study because she takes after her Morgan rather than her Arabian ancestors in lacking inflated frontal sinuses. Morgans, along with Barbs, Pasos, and Criollos, derive from the very ancient ox-headed lineage in which the basic skull construction is dished but lacking inflated frontal sinuses. Without bulging frontal sinuses, the deepest part of the dish in an ox-head appears to fall between the eyes, not below them.

Whereas the nasal bones of gelding #1 are ruler-straight (the tip of his muzzle appears rounded because his nasal cartilages have dessicated and shrunk somewhat with age), the mare's arch upward somewhat toward the tip. In this characteristic, the mare harks back to that part of her Morgan ancestry which came from Dutch drafters imported to the New York area before the Revolutionary War.

Horse #3: This fellow represents a straight basic skull construction, in which the crest of the cheekbone and the

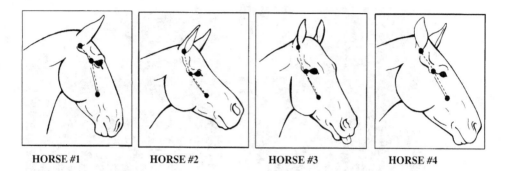

HORSE #1   HORSE #2   HORSE #3   HORSE #4

Fig. 34. The equine head is built in two major blocks, which are joined at the eye.

eye-to-ear line are nearly parallel. There is no inflation of the frontal sinuses, but the "goggles" of the orbits are nevertheless set quite high on the skull. A ruler laid across from eyebrow to eyebrow will span the forehead without touching it. Thus, despite a straight construction, this gelding, like mare #2, is in the ox-headed group.

His head is distinguished not only by a broad forehead, well-shaped and well-set ears, but also a lovely eye (too bad the owner can't find something nicer than a piece of twine to use for a bit-lifter).

Horse #4: This gelding represents something of a rarity among Thoroughbreds — a slightly arched basic skull construction. Like the last horse, this fellow also has a nice eye, possessing the right size and degree of prominence and well-supported within a bony orbit as well. This fellow's orbital goggles, however, are placed very low on the sides of the skull, in contrast to either horse #3 or horse #1, which only goes to show that all combinations are, indeed, possible.

Exercise 3: WILL THE REAL DISH PLEASE STAND UP?

As we have already seen, horses' heads come in all shapes, from broad to narrow, lovely to plain, arched to dished, all by the skull's internal design. In this exercise, you'll have more opportunities to review and practice the basic principles discussed above.

No matter what their breed affiliation, a lot of Americans nowadays seem to be looking for an "Arabian head," as if that were the only good form of head there is. This is an uninformed attitude. Any head showing good bone structure and good organ function is a good head.

Historically speaking, ox-heads, with their characteristically elevated orbits, belong on Lipizzans, Morgans, Quarter Horses, Criollos, Pasos, Moyle horses, Bashkir Curlies and Barbs. Some breeds typically have an arched skull construction, notably the Lipizzan, Appaloosa, Andalusian, Kladruber, and most warmblood strains. Others, such as the Arabian, Barb, and Morgan have a dished basic skull construction, while still others, such as the Quarter Horse, Tennessee Walker, American Saddlebred, Thoroughbred, and most draft breeds, have a straight basic construction.

The combination of straight, dished or arched construction with such variables as elevated orbits, arched nasal bones, or inflated frontal sinuses is what distinguishes each different breed. Someone recently wrote to me praising her Tennessee Walking Horse, but criticizing him for his one fault, which in her eyes was that the animal did not have an Arabian-like head. It is, I had to tell her, misguided and historically insensitive to wish an Arabian head on a Walker.

A secondary problem is to correctly identify the Arabian-type head, whether or not that type of head is the appropriate choice for the breed at hand. The Arabian head possesses not only the dished basic construction and high-lying orbits characteristic of the ox-heads, but one thing more: inflated frontal sinuses, which cause the whole forehead to bulge. The facial profile thus undulates, with a bulge between the eyes and a dish below them.

From their heads, can you correctly identify the breed of each of the horses below? Warning: some of the merchandise that you're looking at is damaged, while one animal in particular may prove surprisingly difficult to identify.

(1) **Five-year-old gelding**
(2) **Aged gelding**

Courtesy, L. Darnell

HORSE #1

Courtesy, P. Haney

HORSE #2

Analysis

Horse #1: Well, if you didn't get the right answer from the bulging forehead and straight nasal profile, the grin on this gelding's face and the quizzical look about the eyes and ears ought to have tipped you off that this is an Arabian. He deserves praise for his deep muzzle, providing plenty of space for air intake and the rooting of both upper and lower incisor teeth. He's also quite deep and muscular about the jaws (not so much as in a Quarter Horse, yet big and deep enough to support well-structured teeth).

The fine skin about the nostrils and over the face shows the blood vessels below his sculpted cheekbones. Though his face is short from cheekbones to muzzle, his mouth is surprisingly long, making him easy to bit. His well-shaped head attaches beautifully to a nicely-arched neck.

Horse #2: The skull of this Thoroughbred is built upon a straight parasphenoid rod — there is no bend in its basic construction, either up (dish) or down (arch). Nor is there a bulge in the forehead between the eyes. Yet there is a bulge below the eye. In this case, it's a bony overgrowth left from surgery to drain an infected sinus. Lesson: any old bump an Arabian doth not make.

Shallower in the jowl than #1, this gelding nevertheless shows a good deep muzzle and substantial lower jaws. He has thin skin (especially thin lips), prominent cheekbones, and a big, intelligent-looking eye. The face is slightly longer than the Arabian's.

Horse #3: This Thoroughbred was the victim of a too-tight halter, left on too long when he was a weanling. His

(3) Aged gelding
(4) Eight-year-old gelding
(5) Aged gelding

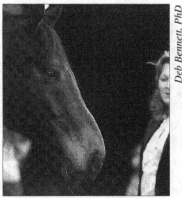

HORSE #3

Deb Bennett, PhD

HORSE #4

Courtesy, G. Hoff-Carmona/Los Alamos Dressage Center

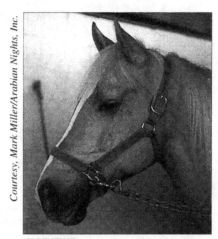

Courtesy, Mark Miller/Arabian Nights, Inc.

HORSE #5

young plastic skull gradually grew to fill the loose halter. As the noseband of the halter became tight, it restricted the growth of his nasal bones, deforming them into the notched shape evident in the lower part of this horse's facial profile.

This gelding also shows another peculiarity, probably not related to haltering. Near the center of his forehead, just below the eyes, a pair of bumps emerges. Often referred to as "stubborn bumps," these merely represent extra-sturdy growth at the junction between the nasal and frontal bones. Despite their name, their presence (or absence) is not a reliable guide to temperament; this fellow is a champion working hunter.

While he is longer in the face than any of the other horses of this group, this gelding nevertheless shows a fairly short mouth. He's rounder over the snout than any of the others, too, but this simply indicates that his nasal cartilages have dessicated and shrunk a bit, a common sign of age. With fine skin and prominent cheekbones, he shows a patient, somewhat resigned eye — it's been a long day, with a lot of classes.

Horse #4: Did you guess this horse is a Warmblood? (He was imported from Sweden.) In recent years, in response to an enormous American market, Europeans have made a great effort to "improve" the heads of their horses to meet American tastes. While this head is not bad, it reflects nothing of the proud history of European horsebreeding, either.

In all fairness, however, we must mention that a head

like this comes from very discriminating selection. That means, it comes from Europeans' choices of sire and dam, and not a few of those, even in warmblood breeding, have been Arabians. There is no doubt that the purebred Arabian appears in this fellow's pedigree — a few generations back perhaps — but still exerting its influence on the construction of the head.

Therefore, we can catalog a long list of similarities between this gelding's head and that of Horse #1: dished basic skull construction, orbits placed high on the skull, bulging frontal sinuses, prominent cheekbones, thin skin, and a very short face. Only the nasal bones, which stand in relatively high relief, and the lips and nostrils, which are thicker than in the typical Arabian or Thoroughbred, hark back to this horse's ancient central European heritage. The eye, large and liquid, is very appealing; it speaks of a sweet-tempered horse perhaps a little worried by many new experiences.

Horse #5: This registered Quarter Horse is blind in his other eye. With his remaining organ of vision, this wise old trooper sizes me up, wondering what I'm up to in pointing a bit of equipment (the camera) at him. One can almost hear him saying "humpff."

Compare his head to that of #1 and you will find many similarities, this time because of the desire of some Quarter Horse breeders to produce Arabian-like heads. Here indeed is the deep and muscular jowl characteristic of the Quarter Horse, but combined with a face just as short as the Arabian's. The basic skull construction of both Quarter Horse and Arabian is dished, but here instead of the ox-head's flat forehead with wisdom bumps, we find a bulging forehead supported internally by enlarged frontal sinuses. This horse demonstrates the true dish, just as if he were in fact an Arabian.

He comes by the construction in the same manner as #4: by having a plethora of Arabian and Thoroughbred ancestors. Lesson: even the "right" bump doth not an Arabian make!

Part III

Extremities And The Center

Hoof, Tail And Body Balance

Before finishing our study of equine conformation, at least a few words must be addressed to the horse's body periphery (tail and hooves) and how they relate to his center — the vertebral column. Last but not least is the most important of all — his overall body balance.

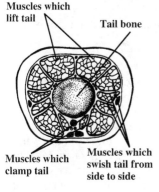

Muscles which lift tail

Tail bone

Muscles which clamp tail

Muscles which swish tail from side to side

Fig. 35. Cross section of tail of horse.

The Tail

The Mexicans refer to the steer's tail as "that dangerous appendage," because the vaqueros of that country can catch hold of it and use it to unbalance and throw down even a very large and powerful bull. In both the horse and the cow, the tail is the only segment of the vertebral column in which top, sides, and underside are all exposed.

Like other parts of the spinal column, the horse's fleshy tail consists internally of a chain of vertebrae wrapped in layers of muscle. The diameter of the root of the horse's tail is a good indicator of the substance in the rest of the vertebral column. A large and apparently powerful horse with a small, whiplike tail probably has relatively small, "weedy" vertebrae within and weaker epaxial musculature than would be expected by his external appearance.

Epaxial musculature wraps around not only the vertebrae of the tail, but all the other vertebrae from poll to dock. This is how a snake is constructed, and internally, the horse's vertebral column can indeed be thought of as a sort of snake. Strength in these "snake muscles" is necessary for good posture in riding horses, including such attributes and abilities as good carriage of the base of the neck, loin coiling, raising the back, engagement of the hindquarters, collection, and self-carriage. A thin tail suggests that a horse may have difficulty acquiring one or all of these. A "rubbery" tail or a tail with abnormally low resting tonus suggests the same.

While the diameter of the horse's tail can be discovered simply by gently grasping it at the root, its tonus can only be found by pulling on it. To safely do this, gently but firmly announce your intentions to the horse by grasping the tail high up and then sliding your hands about halfway down the tail. Then, firmly holding the tail (and keeping an eye out for flattened ears or a cocked hind leg) slowly lean backward until your full weight rests on the tail. At some point during this gradual increase in rearward drag, most horses will correspondingly lean forward. As they do so, they will coil their loins and tuck their quarters, assuming almost the same posture as for urination.

The normal horse responds this way because tail-pulling stimulates the internal loin-coiling muscle, the iliopsoas, to contract. In the horse with a "rubber" tail, however, the loins will not fill and rise nor the quarters dip, and the tail itself will stretch like a big rubber band. Poor posture due to insubstantial, weak or rubbery epaxial musculature can, as has repeatedly been mentioned, be improved by the systematic use of cavalletti, lateral flexions, and transitions.

The Hoof

Any substantive discussion of the horse's hooves would require a volume of its own. It must suffice to mention here that every horse owner ought to know the shape and characteristics of the normal fore and hind hoof. Owners ought to demand — and be willing to pay for — farriery that preserves normal hoof shape and functional characteristics. Both owners and prospective buyers ought to be appropriately alarmed about hoofs which deviate from the functional norm. In particular, hoofs with flares, dished surfaces, pushed-up sections of wall, founder rings, and contracted or asymmetrical

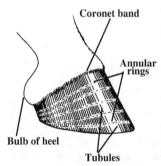

Coronet band

Annular rings

Bulb of heel

Tubules

Fig. 36. Side view of a normal fore hoof. The normal hoof shows annular rings and tubules. The coronet band is healthy, smooth, and evenly fringed with hair. The angle of the toe is adjusted so that (to the best estimate of eye and ear), the hoof strikes the ground with toe, walls, and heel simultaneously, making one sound. The angle of the tubules of the heel is slightly more upright than the angle of the tubules of the toe. There are no cracks, splits, lumps or dishes in the normal hoof. The hoof should have a surface patina and a feel similar to a hard rubber hockey puck.

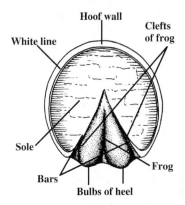

Hoof wall

Clefts of frog

White line

Sole

Bars

Frog

Bulbs of heel

Fig. 37. Sole view of a normal fore hoof. The fore hoof is larger and rounder than the hind hoof, but otherwise similar. The hoof wall is thick and not flaky. The bars are thick and healthy, and should never be cut out of the foot. The white line is visible and the same width everywhere. The sole is off-white in color when freshly trimmed, is evenly and slightly concave, and is slightly resilient under firm thumb pressure. The bulbs of heel are equal in size, soft and dry to the touch, and wide open. The frog is full and resilient to the touch. The clefts of the frog are deep but widely open; no foul smells eminate from the clefts. The hoof should be trimmed so that (to the best estimate of eye and ear), the hoof strikes the ground with toe, walls, and heel simultaneously making one sound.

bulbs of heel should immediately cause concern.

The Greek cavalrymaster Xenophon said 2,400 years ago that, like a house, the horse is built upward from its hoofs and both of these entities are useless if built upon a weak foundation. While most books on conformation have agreed with Xenophon and have begun their discussions with the hoof, I have not handled this series that way. While it is not pleasant to drive a car with flat tires or bent rims, it is at least possible to do so. On the other hand, a car that is too stiff to steer, or one with a bent frame, or one lacking brakes or motor or transmission or functional joints between these parts can hardly be driven at all.

Our ideal is a horse with all parts well conformed and in good working order. However, I believe that in normal equine movement vertebral column function governs limb function. It is only when the horse feels pain in foot or limb that the reverse becomes true. In training the normal horse, the rider should therefore think first of the neck, back, croup, and tail; when their strength, suppleness, posture, and movement are correct, correct limb movements will inevitably follow. He who can think only of the limbs will, on the other hand, eventually make his horse lame.

Conformational Balance

Overall body balance has often been mentioned in these volumes as a side issue. Yet body balance is a crucial characteristic of a good riding horse; no amount of excellence in the individual parts can make up for its lack.

Body balance is best assessed by first finding the widest point at the base of the horse's neck. To find this point, place the palms of your hands against the sides of your horse's neck and slide them downward until you find the widest point. Mark this point, which externally indicates the junction between the fifth and sixth cervical vertebrae, on your horse's skin.

Now walk toward the horse's croup on the same side. As directed on pp. 11-17 of Volume II, find the lumbosacral joint. Whereas the palpable bulge in the cervical vertebrae overlies the centra of the vertebrae, the lumbosacral joint is actually about 4" lower than the peak of the croup. Therefore, drop down about 4" from the "hollow spot" in the loins which you have palpated and mark a point on the horse's skin representing the level of the actual lumbosacral joint.

Now step back and look at your horse. If he's standing more or less square on level ground, you can proceed to connect the two points you've just marked. If the line connecting the two points is within 4" of level, your horse's

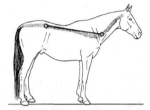

Fig. 38. Photo and analytical drawing showing a well-balanced horse. (See also Figs. 13 and 15). Stippled line shows the trace of the row of vertebral centra. Body balance is best measured from the widest point palpable at the base of the horse's neck (a point which approximately overlies the 5th-6th cervical vertebrae) to the centrum at the L-S joint (i.e., from open circle to open circle). The closer to horizontal is the line connecting these two points, the greater the natural balance of the horse, and the more easily loin coiling will produce lightening of the forehand. In movement, when the point at the base of the neck rises to the same level as the point at the L-S joint, the horse has achieved the essential prerequisite for collection.

balance is within a normal range. If he is well-conformed otherwise, you can safely expect him to be a perfectly trainable specimen possessed of at least average capabilities.

If the line connecting the two points angles down sharply toward the front, the horse is "front-weighted" and has a downhill overall balance. Lightness — which means the lifting of the whole forehand from the loins — is difficult for such horses to achieve. So is collection and the mobility in the forehand demanded by such activities as cutting, spins, pirouettes, or half-passes. "Downhill" horses only do really well as flat racers.

If the line connecting the two points angles uphill, the horse is "rear-weighted" and has an uphill overall balance. Such horses are naturally light but can suffer strains to rear joints.

Overall balance plus good conformation of the individual body parts produces the desirable picture called "harmony" in the lucky horse possessing it. Harmony cannot be produced by overfeeding the horse and covering his bumps and angles with fat; nor by wishful thinking, which seeks to excuse structural flaws by saying that a poorly structured horse is useful or even beautiful because its parts "flow together." The balanced horse with excellent conformation will also seem to "flow", a symphony for the eye both standing and in movement.

The most harmonious horse pictured in these volumes is mare #4, Lab Exercise 7 of this volume; other really good examples in this volume are mare #3, lab exercise 4; stallion #2, lab exercise 5; gelding #3 and mare #4, lab exercise 6. For additional study of well-balanced horses, take another look at horses #1 on pp. 16 and 65, #3 on p. 49, #1 on p. 56 and #3 on p. 90 of Volume II. I doubt I'll need to wait long to find out which animal you would like to buy.

The main purpose of this series of three booklets on equine conformation has been to enable the buyer, owner, rider, and trainer to think along correct lines. A correct and useful line of reasoning only becomes possible when the horseman has learned to observe and analyze anatomical structure by comparing many horses. A true understanding of how the epaxial, neck, back, and belly muscles work is a necessity in understanding movement and the process of collection. These organs work with greatest ease and efficiency when the horse is well-conformed; indeed, that is how "good" conformation is defined. The Bible says, "as a man thinketh, so also doth he do," and armed with the information presented in these three volumes, it is my hope that your actions as rider and trainer will come into closer alignment with the actual nature of the horse.

About The Author

Deb Bennett, PhD, is the author of EQUUS magazine's "Conformation Insights" series, as well as a contributing editor of the magazine. A graduate of the University of Kansas, she worked at the Smithsonian Institution until 1992 when she founded the Equine Studies Institute.

Dr. Bennett is also a major contributor to the Elsevier *World Animal Science Encyclopedia*. Her research interests include the history of domestication and world blood-lines and breeds.

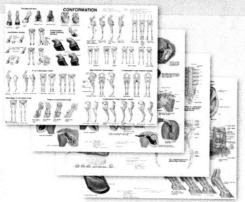

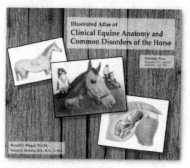

CPSIA information can be obtained
at www.ICGtesting.com
Printed in the USA
BVHW091927180719
553820BV00004B/89/P

9 781929 164608